Colección Támesis

SERIE A: MONOGRAFÍAS, 193

T0313628

A COMPANION TO
CATALAN LITERATURE

ARTHUR TERRY

A COMPANION TO
CATALAN LITERATURE

TAMESIS

First published 2003
by Tamesis, Woodbridge
Paperback edition 2010

Transferred to digital printing

ISBN 978-1-85566-089-2 hardback
ISBN 978-1-85566-206-3 paperback

Tamesis is an imprint of Boydell & Brewer Ltd
PO Box 9, Woodbridge, Suffolk IP12 3DF, UK
and of Boydell & Brewer Inc.
668 Mt Hope Avenue, Rochester, NY 14620, USA
website: www.boydellandbrewer.com

A CiP catalogue record for this book is available
from the British Library

This publication is printed on acid-free paper

CONTENTS

LIST OF ABBREVIATIONS

AC   *Antologia catalana*

BHS   *Bulletin of Hispanic Studies* (Liverpool)

ENC   *Els nostres clàssics*

ER   *Estudis Romànics* (Barcelona)

HR   *Hispanic Review*

MLR   *Modern Language Review*

SdO   *Serra d'Or* (Barcelona)

PREFACE

Essentially, this book is a revised and much enlarged version of a small volume on Catalan literature which I published in 1972 and which has long been out of print. Strictly speaking, it is neither a conventional history of literature nor exactly a work of literary criticism, though it has aspects of both. A 'Companion', as I understand it, should be a supplement to the texts themselves, and in no way a substitute. Above all, it should direct the reader to the most important works, placing them in their historical and social context, commenting on their most distinctive features and, where necessary, referring to the biography of their authors. In all this, I have tried to be as objective as I can; nevertheless, there is also a personal element involved, since I have not attempted to hide my own preferences, even when these run counter to received opinion.

In writing this book, I have tried to bear in mind the needs of the non-specialist reader (preferably with some knowledge of Spanish) who wishes to know more about an important but, on the whole, neglected, area of Peninsular culture. Where English readers are concerned, the task, unfortunately, is long overdue: in the *Penguin Companion to European Literature* (1969), the whole of Catalan literature is given the same space as Jean-Paul Sartre, and in John Sturrock's otherwise excellent *Oxford Guide to Contemporary World Literature* (1996) it is omitted altogether. This seems characteristic of a situation which few specialists have as yet tried to alter. The chief barrier, of course, is linguistic: yet, especially if one knows another Romance language, it is not difficult to acquire at least a reading knowledge of Catalan, and for reasons which are given in Chapter I, the older literature is relatively accessible to a modern reader compared, say, with that of France or Spain.

This accessibility gives an impression of coherence to the entire range of Catalan literature which is reinforced to a great extent by social and historical tendencies. Roughly speaking, this literature follows a recognizable European pattern, with one notable exception: the fact that its course is interrupted for something like three centuries by what is usually known as the period of 'Decadence' (see Chapter 2). To see why this should be so demands an awareness of certain historical facts, and these in turn point to the close interpenetration of literature and society which is evident in most phases of Catalan culture. Both the nineteenth-century revival and the more conscious programme of *noucentisme* in the twentieth are attempts to create a new national identity, a task which has lost none of its urgency since the Spanish Civil War. At various stages in Catalan history, this sense of identity has existed within the context of some larger political unit: Carolingian France, Aragon, Spain. This makes for many of the tensions and difficulties which still beset Catalan writers and which give the best contemporary literature its most characteristic flavour. At the same time, an impartial observer cannot fail to be struck by the very distinctive nature of Catalan society compared with the rest of the Peninsula, and by the obvious European quality which goes with the best features of its society and literature. In the last century, an impressive number of Catalan painters, architects and musicians – Miró, Dalí, Tàpies, Gaudí, Roberto Gerhard, Pau Casals, Montserrat Caballé, Raimon – have been acclaimed outside their own country. What is not generally realized is that all of these share a common cultural heritage and their achievement in the non-verbal arts is matched by a similar degree of excellence in literature. As I have tried to show, modern Catalan writers are just as much concerned with their earlier traditions as their contemporaries in other countries, and their reactions are often suggestive outside their own immediate literary context.

Needless, to say, a book like this makes no claims to exhaustiveness. Since information on Catalan writers is generally lacking in English, it seemed best to give as much space as possible to major authors and tendencies, and to exclude those minor writers whose interest is mainly documentary. At the same time, I hope that something of the general social background has emerged, and I have tried in the opening section to touch briefly on certain basic facts of language which directly affect the growth of literary expression. I have also added literal versions of the passages quoted in Catalan and a list of available English translations. In order to keep the bibliography within manageable limits, I have only listed basic editions of literary texts, though a good many works of criticism are referred to in the notes. In this, as in the rest of the book, my chief aim has been to provide the reader with a clear and, as far as possible, accurate introduction to a literature which I hope he will be encouraged to explore for himself.

In conclusion, I should like to thank my friend Professor Alan Yates for so carefully reading the typescript. But my greatest debt, as always, is to my wife, Molly, for her constant encouragement and cheerfulness.

Chapter 1

MEDIEVAL AND EARLY RENAISSANCE

I. Language and History

The origins of Catalan literature, like those of any other, depend very largely on the interplay of language and history. Of the Romance languages, Catalan is one of those, like Provençal and Portuguese, which have remained closest to their Latin roots. As might be expected from its geographical distribution, it forms a bridge language between the Ibero-Romance and Gallo-Romance groups, sharing in both, but never completely absorbed by either. Two facts stand out from pre-Roman times: the existence of an ethnic division, running south-south-east from the central Pyrenees, which affected the later dialect division between eastern and western Catalan; and, conversely, an early ethnic and cultural link between north-east Catalonia and the South of France which remained unbroken until the middle of the thirteenth century. Thus, when the Catalan language began to take on a separate identity in the course of the eleventh century, the old Roman division of Septimania, with its centre at Béziers, was still united with the Tarraconensis, the north-east province of Spain, while ecclesiastically the whole area was controlled by the Archbishop of Narbonne. From a linguistic point of view, this meant that Catalan, which might have become another language of the Ibero-Romance group, was pulled in the direction of Gallo-Romance at the most crucial period in its formation.

The political origins of Catalonia add another dimension. A little before AD 800, less than a century after the Moorish invasion, the country was conquered by the Franks and divided into counties; later, in 864, these were regrouped to form the *Marca Hispanica*, conceived as a Carolingian buffer-state between France and Moorish-occupied Spain. By 900, the Frankish influence was beginning to weaken, and a strong Catalan dynasty had established itself in the north-east of the Peninsula, with its focus in Barcelona. The effect of the Frankish connection, however, continued to make itself felt in other ways: as a result, Catalonia and the South of France developed a more comprehensive feudal system than the rest of Spain, and the links between the newly founded monasteries on either side of the Pyrenees helped to establish Ripoll, the traditional mausoleum of the counts of Barcelona, as an international centre of learning in the eleventh century. On the other hand, the early centuries of the Reconquest did little to strengthen relations between Catalonia and the rest of the Peninsula, and by the time Catalan interests moved beyond the Ebro, in the second half of the twelfth century, it was too late for the basic features of the language to be affected.

Between 900 and 1300, the Catalan language developed fairly quickly; any later changes were minor and more gradual.[1] This rapid evolution of the language coincided with a period of territorial expansion. In 1137, the Houses of Barcelona and Aragon were united by the marriage of Ramon Berenguer IV to the Aragonese heiress, Petronila, an event which had the effect of postponing the union of Aragon and Castile for several centuries. Early in the thirteenth century, relations with the South of France suffered a permanent setback when Pere I[2] was killed at the battle of Muret (1213), fighting in support of the Albigensians against the army of Simon de Montfort.[3] By this defeat, Catalan rights north of the Pyrenees were restricted to Roussillon and Montpellier, a situation which was confirmed by Pere's successor, Jaume I, in the Treaty of Corbeil (1258). In the same reign, however, Catalan ambitions turned in two new directions. It was at this stage that Catalan expansion in the Mediterranean began, with the conquest of Mallorca (1229), followed closely by that of the other Balearic Islands: the first phase of a movement which was eventually to spread to Corsica, Sardinia, Naples, and the Aegean. And almost simultaneously, with the conquest of Valencia (1238) and the settlement of the lands to the south, the modern limits of the Catalan-speaking area were practically filled out, with Valencian and *mallorquí* as its two most important dialects.

Literary Catalan remains extraordinarily unified throughout the Middle Ages. The main reason for this, apart from the relatively static nature of the language itself, is the standardizing influence of the Royal Chancellory of Aragon. Dialect usages, except for occasional Valencianisms, only appear to any extent after 1500, that is to say, in the period of literary decline which follows the break-up of the Catalan Court.

Compared with French or Spanish, Catalan is more faithful to Latin, and consequently more archaic in appearance, even at the present day. Anyone hearing the language for the first time will be struck by its consonantal

---

[1] One of the earliest non-literary texts, the *Homilies d'Organyà*, a collection of six short sermons dating from the first half of the twelfth century, bears a certain similarity to Provençal, but already shows some of the most characteristic features of standard Catalan.

[2] After 1137, the Counts of Barcelona are also Kings of Aragon. The joint nomenclature is sometimes confusing; thus Pere I is at the same time Pedro II of Aragon, and Alfons I is also Alfonso II in Aragonese terms. I have used the titles which are normally given them by modern Catalan historians.

[3] Catalan rights over territories in the South of France had greatly increased in the course of the twelfth century. In supporting the Albigensians, Pere I was defending his own vassals; as a result of his intervention, the Counts of Toulouse, Foix and Comminges swore allegiance to him, thus making him sovereign – for seven months – over the entire Midi.

quality; in W.J. Entwistle's phrase, 'Catalan is more abrupt than Spanish'.[4] There are two main reasons for this: the loss of post-tonic vowels other than *a* (*e* is occasionally found as a support-vowel, e.g. PATREM > *pare*), and the absence of the spontaneous diphthongization which is such a feature of Spanish (e.g. CAELUM > Sp. *cielo*, but Cat. *cel*).[5] The first of these tendencies means that Catalan has a much higher proportion of final consonants than Spanish or Portuguese.[6] This gives a distinctive rhythm to the language, which is particularly noticeable in verse. Thus, the opening lines of a famous poem (XXXIX) by Ausiàs March (see below, pp. 35–40):

> Qui no és trist, de mos dictats no cur,
> o en algun temps que sia trist estat, ...

(Let no one who is not sad, or who has never known sadness, heed my verses)

appear in the Spanish translation of Jorge de Montemayor (1560) as:

> No cure de mis versos, ni los lea
> quien no fuese muy triste, o lo haya sido.

It is such facts of language which give a piece of prose or verse its distinctive sound and weight, a source of energy which the best Catalan writers of any period exploit to the full.

II. The Catalan Troubadours

It may seem strange to begin a survey of Catalan literature with an account of poetry in Provençal. One needs to remember, however, that no other vernacular literature existed in Catalonia before the 1260s, and that the close similarity between Catalan and Provençal at this stage was accentuated by the deliberately restricted idiom of troubadour poetry. More important still, one can point to the continuity of a tradition which remained virtually unchallenged until the fifteenth century. Though later poets often wrote a very defective kind of Provençal, they clearly had no intention of using their own language; on the other hand, Ausiàs March (1397–1459), the first major poet to write in Catalan, cannot be fully understood without a knowledge of the earlier tradition, to which he bears a strong, if oblique, relationship.

---

[4]   W.J. Entwistle, *The Spanish Language* (London, 1936), p. 84.
[5]   As against this, Catalan evolved its own distinctive series of diphthongs formed by combining a stressed vowel with *u*, e.g. CLAVUM > *clau*, CADERE > *caure*, BREVEM > *breu*, VIDERE > *veure*, NIDUM > *niu*, OVUM > *ou*.
[6]   Compare the treatment of the Latin past participle: CANTATUM > Fr. *chanté* ; Sp., Port. *cantado*; Ital. *cantato*; Prov., Cat. *cantat.*

In terms of quantity, the Catalan contribution to the body of troubadour poetry is quite small: 197 poems, out of a total of more than 2,500. Yet, of the twenty-four poets whose names are known, several are highly gifted, and at least one, Cerverí de Girona, is among the major exponents of the tradition. Their work spans roughly a century and a quarter, from about 1160 to 1290, though the most active period comes in the reigns of Alfons I (1162–96) and Pere I (1196–1213). During these years, many of the most famous Provençal troubadours visited the Catalan Court; both kings were amateur poets themselves, and Alfons is known to have taken part in a poetic debate with Giraut de Bornelh. It is clear, moreover, that such relations were not merely literary: like other rulers of the time, the kings of Aragon realized the political advantages of encouraging the troubadours, whose repertoire included topical and satirical forms like the *sirventes*, useful both for political propaganda and for ridiculing one's enemies.

After 1213, the centre of gravity of the troubadour tradition shifts south of the Pyrenees. From now on, poets tend to move about less, and when they do, it is usually in the direction of the Court of Toledo. There is also a noticeable change in social status: where the earlier Catalan troubadours, like Guillem de Bergadà, were often feudal lords whose poetry carried the weight of political authority, in the thirteenth century there is a blurring of categories between the troubadours and the minstrels or *joglars*. The distinction, in fact, had never been a very firm one: in theory, the troubadour was an original poet and the *joglar* a performer or reciter of other people's verse, yet there are various instances of minstrels, like Ramon Vidal de Besalú, who were poets as well. As far as Catalonia is concerned, the activities of the *joglars* are on the whole poorly documented, though there are signs that here, as in other countries, they were reciters of epic and narrative poetry. What these poems were, or in which language they were performed, one can only guess, though it seems clear that the chief epic cycles, in one form or another, were known in Catalonia by the second half of the twelfth century, possibly in Provençal versions, and that a native Catalan epic poetry, now lost in its original form, must have survived long enough to serve as a source for the prose chronicles of Desclot and Muntaner (see below, pp. 21–24).[7] As for the thirteenth century, it appears that, while the number of poets of noble origin declined, the demand for *joglars* increased, and, though the latter were still regarded chiefly as entertainers, those who were also original poets, like Cerverí de Girona, occasionally achieved great fame at Court.

---

[7]   The *Ensenhamen* of Guerau de Cabrera (*c.* 1150), a verse inventory of the poetry which a *joglar* might be expected to know, lists four Provençal troubadours, including Jaufre Rudel and Marcabru, and a great many narrative poems of the Carolingian, Breton and classical cycles. Guerau also makes an interesting distinction between poems which were sung and others which were simply recited, though he says nothing of the language problem.

One general impression emerges from the poetry of the time: that the greatest successes of the Catalan troubadours almost invariably lie outside the sphere of the courtly love poem which is usually taken to be the central achievement of the tradition. Nearly all of them make use at times of the commonplaces of troubadour love poetry, and several, like Guillem de Cabestany (*c.* 1175–*post* 1212), achieve a certain distinction within their limited range. The most memorable poems of this period, however, are what Peter Dronke has called 'lyrics of realism',[8] meaning by this a kind of poem which, though not necessarily truthful in an autobiographical sense, either refers to real events or chooses to disregard conventional attitudes in favour of personal authenticity.

Three examples may help to make this clear. The first is Guillem de Bergadà (late twelfth century), probably the best instance of a poet who, though he writes in Provençal, has very little to do with the courtly love tradition. As a feudal lord continually at odds with other nobles, and at times with the king himself, it is hardly surprising that he should excel in satire and invective. Certainly, his poetry is full of unflattering allusions to his contemporaries, and he uses irony and ridicule with deadly effect. Or, as his early Provençal biographer puts it: 'he composed good *sirventes* in which he spoke ill of some and good of others, and used to boast that every lady was in love with him.'

Yet on the few occasions when he composes a serious love poem, he achieves a degree of refinement which can command the respect of Arnaut Daniel, perhaps the most fastidious of all his contemporaries. This ambivalence is characteristic of both the man and the poet. For a time in the 1180s, Guillem appears as the respected companion of Bertran de Born and Richard Coeur de Lion, then Duke of Aquitaine, and there are witnesses to his striking presence in the various Catalan Courts; nevertheless, there are signs that he was ill at ease among his own kind and that his real sympathies probably lay with the less reputable society of the *joglars*. This may account for one of the peculiar strengths of his poetry: its ability to draw on the melodies and rhythms of popular verse which has since disappeared, as in the refrain of the poem which begins 'Cantarey mentre m'estau' (I shall sing while I am at leisure):

> Puys van xantan liridumvau,
> balan, notan gent e suau ...
> puys van xantan liridumvar
> balan, notan autet e clar.

(For they sing *liridumvau*, dancing and playing prettily and lightly [...] for they sing *liridumvar*, dancing and playing high and clear.)

---

[8] Peter Dronke, *The Medieval Lyric* (London, 1968), p. 207.

This snatch of a children's song is all the more striking since it runs through a poem in which Guillem mercilessly attacks some of his worst enemies. Significantly, his one really moving poem, the *Planh*, or lament, for Ponç de Mataplana, comes from a similar clash of feeling. Sometime after 1180, Ponç de Mataplana, a man who is constantly vilified in his earlier poems, died fighting against the Moors. In the opening lines of the *Planh*, all the former hatred is retracted: the one-time enemy is praised for his bravery and generosity, and the poet wishes he could have fought beside him in his last battle. The sincerity of this is unquestionable, and the whole poem goes far beyond the range of the conventional lament. At the same time, there are moments when Guillem hints at the procedure laid down for such poems in the troubadour manuals of rhetoric, and particularly at certain religious *topoi*. Instead of the usual closing invocation to God or the Virgin, the poem ends with the vision of a curiously worldly paradise:

> E paradis el luoc melhor
> lai o.l bon rei de Fransa es,
> prop de Rolan, sai que l'arm'es
> de Mon Marques de Mataplana;
> e mon joglar de Ripoles,
> e mon Sabata eisamens,
> estan ab las domnas gensors
> sobre'u pali cobert de flors,
> josta N'Olivier de Lausana.

(I know that the soul of my Marquis of Mataplana is in the best part of Paradise, there where the good King of France is, near Roland; and there also are my minstrel from the Ripollès and my Sabata too, along with fair ladies, on a bed strewn with flowers, beside Oliver of Lausanne.)

The second example is a single poem, the verse dialogue by Ramon Vidal de Besalú which begins 'Abrils iss'e mays intrava' (April was departing and May was coming in). Ramon Vidal seems to stand at the point of transition between two distinct phases of troubadour poetry. In this poem, written possibly in 1212, the difference can be seen in the attitudes of the two speakers, the author himself and the young *joglar* with whom he discusses the aims and status of courtly poetry. The younger man complains of the decline in the quality of patronage which has taken place since the time of Alfons I; the more experienced poet accepts this, but appears to regard humiliation and lack of esteem as normal professional risks. There is no sense here, as there is later in Cerverí de Girona, that poetic skill is its own justification; everything still depends on the attitude of a discriminating audience, even if this has become harder to find.

It is perhaps significant that Ramon Vidal's best-known poem, the *Castia gilós*, or 'Warning to the jealous', looks back nostalgically to the Court of

Alfonso VIII of Castile (1170–1214). This fable of a jealous husband, set in a courtly framework and told with a sure sense of irony, suggests an easy kind of relationship between poet and audience which becomes much rarer as the century advances. Nevertheless, it would be wrong to regard Ramon Vidal as a backward-looking poet. If his main concern is to find the best way of pleasing his public, he has a sense of the universal appeal of poetry which goes beyond the courtly milieu. Like Guillem de Bergadà, he is aware of folk culture, and in his prose treatise on the art of poetry, *Las rasos de trobar*, he writes: 'There is scarcely a place, however remote or solitary [...] where you will not immediately hear singing [...] for the greatest pleasure men have – even the shepherds on the mountains – is to sing.'

Thirdly, there is Cerverí de Girona (also known as Guillem de Cervera), the last and greatest of the Catalan troubadours, whose poems were written between 1259 and 1285. Strictly speaking, Cerverí is not a troubadour, but a *joglar* who succeeded in establishing himself as a professional poet, first at the Court of Jaume I, and eventually in the service of the latter's son, the future Pere II (1276–85). The 119 poems of his which have survived show an astonishing variety of tones, from the popular lyric to the rhetorical inge-nuities of *trobar clus*. What impresses one in his best poems, apart from their strong moral overtones, is the combination of humour, commonsense and fluency. Once again, Cerverí is a poet who is able to draw on unsophis-ticated modes. One such lyric, the *viadeyra* which begins 'No.l prenatz lo fals marit, / Jana delgada' ('Do not take a false husband, delicate Jana'), is quite clearly a *chanson de mal mariée* of a type familiar in other literatures, though it is unlike any other Provençal poem of the period. The name *viadeyra* or *viandela* suggests a kind of poem which is improvised on a journey; it is referred to in the contemporary manuals of rhetoric as 'the lowest kind of song', a sure sign that it belongs to a popular tradition. The most surprising feature is the actual form of the verse: the use of parallelism and refrain reminiscent of the Galician-Portuguese lyric, a type of poetry which Cerverí must certainly have been aware of, since he is known to have visited the Court of Alfonso X of Castile in 1269. Beyond this, one can only speculate, though it is not unlikely, as Riquer suggests (I, 132), that the example of established poets who were not above making use of a different kind of popular tradition may have persuaded Cerverí to look more seriously at the possibilities of Catalan folk-song.

Though, of his 119 surviving poems, about 80 are addressed to the King, and some 50 have a political motive or topical reference, Cerverí is much more than a royal propagandist. Like many of the Provençal troubadors, he places love at the centre of his work, but, unlike most, he sees love as a means of refining knowledge, rather than of merely improving character. This is in keeping with the increasing stress on professionalism which char-acterizes the thirteenth century; Cerverí is aware that, for a man of no wealth, access to the Court can only be guaranteed by education. Hence the eclecticism of his sources: not only previous troubadour poetry, but also scholastic argument and certain preaching techniques, and his general equation of *trobar* with *saber*.

On the surface, the type of moral reflection which runs through much of Cerverí's verse sounds very like the observations one finds in the didactic poems of Ramon Vidal: a resigned pessimism in the face of a world which is not all that it should be. But if one compares these generalizations with the more detailed reflections on the status of the poet and his art, an important difference begins to emerge. Like Ramon Vidal, Cerverí is very conscious of his standing as a professional poet, but his general attitude is much less passive. In many of his poems, the use of the second person, *tu* and *vos*, is almost obsessive, as if he wished at all costs to establish a personal relationship with his audience. Few other poets of the time are as intimate as this, or as concerned to impress their moral independence on the hearer. Few, either, are so conscious of style or, as he himself puts it, of the need to achieve subtlety of expression without loss of clarity. What is really original in Cerverí, however, is the way in which all these considerations are woven into his conception of the artist. His complaints against the indignities which a professional poet is made to suffer by his masters are more specific than those of Ramon Vidal. As he says in a poem addressed to another *joglar*:

> Minten dizets als rics lauzengeria,
> minten prendetz qu'esters hom no.us daria,
> minten chantatz e comtatz ab falsia;
> mintetz per gaug e mintetz ab feunia ...
> qu'entratz manjar ses cost on que sia,
> e par siatz repentit d'eretgia
> que sols manjatz ses tota compaynia.

(By lying you flatter the rich, by lying you receive gifts which otherwise would not be given; you lie when you sing and tell tales, you lie by seeming to be happy when you are secretly angry [...] You eat free, but one would think you were a heretic, for you must eat alone.)

Sometimes he rejects the name of *joglar*; at other times he resigns himself to it, but reminds his audience that in the past the same profession has included kings and saints:

> Si motz laçan trobars es juglaria,
> eu e.l rey aut n'em juglar d'una guia.

(If by putting words together the making of poetry is *joglaria*, the great king and I are *joglars* in the same way.)

What sustains him, ultimately, is a sense of his own worth and a satisfaction in literary excellence for its own sake. And the sanction for this comes, not from any audience, but from nature itself:

> Dels lays dels auzelos
> c'ay auzits en la prada
> ay ma lengua afilada

(From the songs of the birds which I have heard in the fields I have refined my tongue.)

In one of his most memorable poems, Cerverí is asked why he is reluctant to recite his poems in public. His answer is that a beautiful lady keeps them under lock and key; in this way, she is made to say, 'pus jo esmer e aprim ton saber' (I adorn and refine your knowledge all the more). The allegory is finely conceived: the lady represents the desire for perfection, and the longer she keeps the poems concealed from the public the more subtle the poet's skill will become.

Such confidence in the poet's own powers, like the high conception of poetry it implies, is almost unique in medieval Catalan literature. Though courtly patronage continues to function, in one form or another, until the end of the Middle Ages, the whole poetic tradition declines sharply early in the fourteenth century, and already in the lifetime of Cerverí de Girona the literary scene is changing dramatically with the appearance of the first vernacular prose. Cerverí, the last major poet of the classical troubadour tradition, probably died in 1285. This is the point, one feels, at which Catalan might have replaced Provençal as the language of serious poetry. Nevertheless, Ramon Llull (1233–1316), the first great master of Catalan prose, continued to write his own poems in a form of Provençal, even though their content is very different from that of troubadour poetry. No doubt the linguistic situation seemed much less clear-cut at the time, yet there is one contemporary witness who, perhaps because he was writing at some distance from the centre of literary activity, shows signs of having grasped what was happening. This is Jofre de Foixà, a Benedictine monk and a minor troubadour at the Sicilian Court. His grammatical treatise, the *Regles de trobar* (1289–91), was written at the command of the King of Sicily, soon to become Jaume II of Aragon. Though it was intended as a complement to the *Rasos de trobar* of Ramon Vidal de Besalú (see above, p.6), the differences are very striking. For one thing, Jofre de Foixà is much more conscious of linguistic differences: not only does he define the territorial extension of Provençal with considerable accuracy, but he asserts that French and Catalan are distinct languages, which must not be confused with Provençal. Though basically he is arguing for the purity of poetic language, he does so in terms which could hardly have occurred to Ramon Vidal. In the intervening period, two things have taken place: the original cultural unity of Catalonia and the South of France has been weakened, and the

Catalan language has emerged as a serious prose medium. Much of his detailed discussion of grammatical usage depends on a clear awareness of the differences between Catalan and Provençal. At one point, however, he goes further and states an important general principle:

> I admit that, in terms of art, he [i.e. Ramon Vidal] spoke the truth, and that such words should be written as he says; but I do not agree that the troubadours were wrong, for usage overrules art, and an established custom is held lawful when it imposes itself through usage.

'Art' here means grammar and 'usage' the language of everyday speech. Comparing this distinction with the earlier one between Provençal, a simple but crucial idea emerges: if grammar is based on fixed rules, Provençal is also a 'fixed' poetic medium in the sense that it deliberately excludes all dialect variations; 'usage', on the other hand, constantly changes, just as it is Catalan which is the naturally developing language of speech and written prose.

III. Ramon Llull; Arnau de Vilanova

Ramon Llull (1233–1316) is not only the creator of Catalan literary prose, but also one of the most remarkable men of his time. The first thirty years of his life give no indication of what was to follow: he was born in Mallorca, of noble parents; in his twenties, he became tutor and steward to the future Jaume II and, while at Court, he married and had children. In his most remarkable poem, *Lo desconhort* (Comfortlessness), written in old age, he remembers his early years: his life as a courtier had, by his own account, been ostentatious and dissolute, and in the course of it he had written a certain amount of troubadour verse, none of which has survived. Some time between 1262 and 1265, all this changed: as the result of a repeated vision of Christ on the Cross, Llull underwent what is usually referred to as his 'conversion'. This was the beginning of a period of intense spiritual activity and copious writing which lasted until his death. After pilgrimages to Compostela, Rome and Jerusalem, he devoted himself to religious studies, and by 1275 is known to have written sixteen books, including one of his major works, the *Libre de contemplació*. By the end of his life, this number had increased to 243; in the meantime, he had founded the monastery of Miramar (Mallorca) as a centre for the teaching of oriental languages, had preached in North Africa and defended his ideas at the Sorbonne, and had crossed and recrossed the south of Europe many times, expounding his plans for the renewal of Christendom before kings, popes and councils of the Church. These plans entailed three simple but demanding aims: the conversion of non-Christians, the correction of theological errors (particularly those of the Averroists) through books and public controversy, and the training of missionaries for work in North Africa and the Middle East.

Though the energy which Llull devoted to these projects was unique, the directions they took clearly owed a great deal to contemporary circumstances. The crusading ideal which determined so many of his actions was still generally felt in Western Europe, and must have been all the more real for Llull by the fact of living in Mallorca, a recently conquered territory which still retained a large Muslim community. Moreover, his project for an *Ars magna* belongs to the revival of theology and legal theory which culminated in the *Summa* of his slightly older contemporary, St Thomas Aquinas (*c.* 1227–74), just as his strong bias towards teaching and writing in the vernacular seems to reflect the whole background of late thirteenth-century popular devotion. One must be careful, however, not to draw the links too close. Llull's independence of mind is present in almost everything he wrote: though his ideas are indebted to the teaching of several religious orders, he seems never to have identified himself completely with any one, and, unlike his contemporary Arnau de Vilanova (see below, pp. 19–20), he remained indifferent, if not actually hostile, to the popular movements of the time.

Catalan prose before Llull consisted entirely of translations: legal texts, chronicles and parts of the Bible. Llull's special distinction lies in having been not only the creator of philosophical and theological writing in Catalan, but also of imaginative prose. Though he also used Latin and Arabic on occasion, it is his presence as a philosopher-poet of genius at the beginning of the vernacular tradition which is of incalculable significance for the later history of literary Catalan. The normative value of his work is clear from the extent to which its diffusion helped to create the linguistic standards which were later to be maintained by the Royal Chancellory. Llull himself had no illusions about the difficulty of achieving such a norm. In the *Libre de contemplació* (*c.* 1272), he complains of the inadequacy of words to express the subtleties of the mind:

> Car moltes vegades s'esdevé que enteniment entén una cosa, e paraula ne significa altra contrària a la veritat que l'enteniment entén …

> (For it often happens that the understanding grasps one thing and the word signifies another which is contrary to the truth perceived by the understanding.)

His attempt to overcome this limitation through the use of similitudes (*semblances*) which speak to the imagination is central to his literary technique. A similitude for Llull can mean anything from an aphorism to a complete fable. The technique is basically that of the popular preacher, though Llull's use of it can be extremely subtle; as he himself recognized, obscurity itself can serve a useful purpose in stretching the mind of the reader: 'Car on pus escura és la semblança, pus altament entén l'enteniment qui aquella semblança entén' (The more obscure the similitude, the higher the understanding of the intellect which penetrates it).

Another part of Llull's rhetorical theory – his insistence that the aesthetic value of words depends entirely on the intrinsic value of the objects or creatures they signify – may seem strange to a modern reader. Yet if 'angel' and 'king', as he argues, are nobler words than 'knight' or 'peasant', this follows naturally from the medieval notion of a hierarchical universe which Llull takes as the basis of his own speculations. It is important to realize that there is no clear dividing-line between his more literary writing and the rest: his entire work is an attempt to relate the nature of the created universe to that of God Himself, and in basing his arguments on the accepted world picture he knew that he was working with elements common to the Christian, Jewish and Muslim traditions – a fact which was of enormous importance for his missionary aims.

No brief account can convey either the imaginative sweep or the mathematical coherence of Llull's vision of creation.[9] One of his many proverbs sets the tone for his whole endeavour: 'Puja ton entendre e pujaràs ton amor' (Raise your understanding and you will raise your love). The idea that man's ultimate justification lies in his love of God is common to many religious writers; what distinguishes Llull is the importance he attaches to the role of the understanding. This, in turn, accounts for the expository nature of so much of his work, the extent to which he feels bound to explain and illustrate every detail of his complex system of truths. Exposition, in Llull's sense, often goes beyond rational discourse: at times he needs to speak through metaphor and fable because words themselves are insufficient. In practice, his attempts to convince his readers take many forms; what varies most is his technique of persuasion, the types of strategy which determine the angle of approach in individual works. From a literary point of view, Llull's most memorable effects are achieved through allegory and symbol: the tree of life in *L'arbre de ciència*, the prison of love in the *Arbre de filosofia d'amor*, and the mysterious forest through which the hero of the *Blanquerna* moves on his spiritual quest. Allegory for Llull is not only a means of giving imaginative force to his ideas, but a way of drawing together an encyclopaedic mass of detail in a final overarching synthesis.

Llull's immense skill in controlling a complex pattern of events and reflections is demonstrated very clearly in his two prose narratives, the *Blanquerna*, or *Romanç d'Evast e Blanquerna*, and the *Libre de Fèlix*, also known as the *Libre de meravelles*. If one hesitates to describe these books as

---

[9]   The best short exposition of Llull's system is R. Pring-Mill's *El microcosmos lul.lià* (Palma de Mallorca, 1961), now included in *Estudis sobre Ramon Llull* (Barcelona, 1991), pp. 33–112. For Llull's *ars memoriae*, see Frances Yates, *The Art of Memory* (London, 1966), chapter VIII.

novels – a term which was only invented much later – it is only because they contain an unusually high proportion of expository and other non-fictional material. In view of Llull's actual intentions, however, this is scarcely a fault. Like the rest of his work, both these books are primarily didactic; the fact that for once Llull was willing to explore the resources of contemporary verse narrative (notably the *roman* and the *fabliau*) merely shows his wish to enlarge his audience by working in more popular genres.

Of the two works, the *Blanquerna* is the more perfectly achieved. Its structure is impressively simple. Each of its five books corresponds to a particular mode of existence: the first describes the married life of Blanquerna's parents, Evast and Aloma, together with his own birth and upbringing; subsequently, Blanquerna becomes in turn a monk, an abbot and a bishop, is elected pope, and finally achieves his original intention of living as a hermit. In this last state, he composes the *Libre d'Amic e Amat*, the finest of Llull's mystical writings, and the *Art de contemplació*, a short treatise on the art of meditation.

Technically, the *Blanquerna* shows a number of features which look forward to later and more celebrated works of fiction. The plot itself both advances through time and returns on itself in a cyclical pattern: in the central part of the action, we see how Blanquerna's sense of vocation is frustrated, though his experience is enriched as a result. More strikingly, Llull projects himself into the story at several points through the figure of 'Ramon lo foll', a former nobleman now deranged by the love of God, who has come to Rome in order to expose the vices of the Papal Court. Finally, in both the *Blanquerna* and the *Fèlix*, Llull uses the device of the 'book within a book': in the epilogue to his story, Blanquerna is reading the *Libre de contemplació* (one of Llull's earlier works) when he is interrupted by a minstrel who has repented of the evils of his profession; as a penance, Blanquerna orders him to spread good through the world by reading publicly from 'The Romance of Evast and Blanquerna'.

What makes the *Blanquerna* a masterpiece, however, is the depth and range of human experience which it conveys. The major decisions which the hero is compelled to make are hardly ever simple choices between right and wrong. Though we are convinced that it is spiritually necessary for Blanquerna to leave home, and, in doing so, to disappoint his parents' ambitions for him, we are made to feel the emotional force of his mother's distress. In this and other episodes, the dramatic tension comes from the sense of moral rectitude which is present in each of the protagonists. Similarly, even when the interests of one party are morally flawed, as in Aloma's plans for Blanquerna's marriage, we are allowed to sympathize with the purely human aspect of the situation. Llull's greatest psychological achievement, however, is in the presentation of his hero. Blanquerna's spiritual quest, as the structure of the book makes clear, is a highly tortuous one, in which chance plays almost as great a part as conscious decision. This pattern is repeated in many of the individual episodes: Blanquerna is made credible precisely because he is prone to make mistakes and to experience temptation, and in the end this gives him an authority which other characters are obliged to recognize. In Chapter LII, for example, Blanquerna is riding through a forest with a young girl whom he has just rescued from the knight who had kidnapped her. Both are tempted to sin: Blanquerna resists, but the girl, in her gratitude, offers herself to him. Neither the author nor his hero makes any attempt to condemn her: she has merely revealed a human failing which Blanquerna himself has had to overcome. Blanquerna speaks to her unpretentiously of God and the power of prayer, and she accepts his words without hesitation:

> La donzella conec que Blanquerna li deia aquelles paraules per ço car havia conegut ço de què era temptada, e loà e beneí Déu, qui tanta de virtut havia donada a Blanquerna contra temptació.

> (The girl realised that Blanquerna had spoken those words to her because he himself had known the same temptation; and she praised and blessed God who had given Blanquerna such power against temptation.)

Though Blanquerna's quest takes him through forests and wildernesses, several parts of the book are densely populated. The social spectrum which Llull presents is as comprehensive as anything in medieval fiction, ranging from popes and emperors to the thieves and prostitutes of Rome. In a sense, this is another aspect of the novel's credibility: if Blanquerna's spiritual progress is to carry conviction, it must be shown as humanly possible within the terms of contemporary society. Sooner or later, however, the question of realism arises, of how far Llull is concerned with accurate social observation. On this point, modern critics are noticeably divided. To take one example: Blanquerna's father is a merchant who has married a woman of noble birth. In the opening chapters, both parents are concerned to give Blanquerna the kind of education which will enable him eventually to administer the family fortunes. Some critics have seen this as a deliberate attempt on Llull's part to emphasize the role of the new middle classes, a fact which, if it were true, would support the view that the novel is an essentially bourgeois genre. It is possible to argue, however, that they are forcing the evidence: that, in fact, the particular humility which Llull ascribes to Evast only makes its full effect when his commercial activities are seen from an aristocratic point of view.

Here, and in other episodes, it is easy to exaggerate the 'social truth' of a situation by applying exclusively modern criteria. What is unquestionable is the degree of intimacy which Llull achieves in describing the married life of Evast and Aloma, and the extent to which he is prepared to suggest the quality and detail of everyday life. In Chapter XII, for instance, the pair of them, having sold their possessions in order to devote themselves to charity, are begging at the houses of two rich couples who have gone to Mass. It starts to rain, and, we are told:

> De cascún dels albergs eixí una serventa, qui portaven a l'esgleia capa de pluja e galotxes a son senyor e a sa dama.

> (A maidservant came out of each of the houses, carrying to the church a cloak and a pair of overshoes for her master and mistress.)

More impressively, in Chapter XIX, Natana, the girl whom Blanquerna has refused to marry, looks out of her window and sees in turn a bridal procession, a funeral and a criminal being led to execution. Such telling details help to create an effect of social depth; for the most part, though, this is achieved by suggestion rather than by the steady accumulation of realistic observation. What realism there is in the book tends to be limited and fragmentary. The main emphasis is on social concern, rather than on actual observation, a bias which is particularly evident in the Third Book, which describes Blanquerna's career as a bishop. The formation of Blanquerna's social conscience, in fact, is a fundamental part of the book's message: the vision of a Christian utopia which does not reject existing society, but shows how faith and good actions can transform the most common human situations.

Blanquerna's double vision of society is suggested in the actual title of Llull's other fictional narrative, the *Fèlix*, or *Libre de meravelles.* In the context, the word *meravelles* is clearly ambiguous: not only does the hero marvel at the wonders of creation, he is also amazed and horrified at the extent of man's corruption. Compared with the *Blanquerna*, the *Fèlix* is more loosely knit, and its total impact less forceful. The narrative interest is thinner, and a large part of the book is modelled on the type of encyclopaedic dialogue between master and disciple common in medieval didactic literature. The most remarkable section, the *Libre de les bèsties*, was written earlier than the rest of the book and forms a completely independent narrative. In it, Llull uses the technique of the beast fable to write a bitter satire against corrupt kings and their courts. Though there are obvious debts to the *Calila e Dimna* and the *Roman de Renart*, Llull's manipulation of his sources is extremely skilful. In contrast to other examples of the genre, the *Libre de les bèsties* reverses the technique by which men are made to tell stories about the moral behaviour of animals, so that it is the animals who take their examples from human actions. Nor is it a satire against feudal society: it is clear from other works, like the *Libre de l'Orde de cavalleria*, that Llull completely accepted the hierarchical system of his time, and in the *Libre de les bèsties* there is a strong implication that the sense of honour is confined to the upper levels of society.

If the *Libre de les bèsties*, for all its artistry, is related only obliquely to Llull's major concerns, the *Libre d'Amic e Amat*, which forms part of the final book of the *Blanquerna*, is the finest of all Llull's spiritual writings and one of the greatest mystical texts of the Middle Ages. Because of this, it is a work which cannot be discussed in purely literary terms. Though it contains passages of great beauty – in some ways it is a far greater achievement than Llull's actual poetry – the *Libre d'Amic e Amat* is not a text intended for continuous reading, but a series of 366 verses or aphorisms, each one of which is sufficient for a whole day's meditation along the lines set out in the *Art de contemplació*. In the preface, Llull explains that the book is composed in the manner of the *sufis*, or Arab mystics, which may account for the fact that the two personages of the dialogue – the lover, or soul in search of mystical union, and the beloved who is his ideal – are each represented by a masculine noun (*Amic, Amat*), in contrast to the bride-bridegroom relationship of other mystical works. As in Llull's fiction, the quest theme lies behind some of the most haunting images:

> Anava l'Amic per una ciutat com a foll cantant de son Amat, e demanaren-li les gents si havia perdut son seny. Respòs que son Amat havia pres son voler, e que ell li havia donat son enteniment; per açò era-li romàs tan solament lo remembrament ab què remembrava son Amat.

> (The lover was walking through the city like a madman, singing of his beloved, and people asked him if he had lost his reason. He replied that his beloved had deprived him of his will and that he had surrendered his understanding to him; and thus he was left only with the memory with which he recalled his beloved.)

What is characteristic here is the introduction of certain intellectual terms into the general lyrical pattern. A modern reader may be inclined to see the *Libre d'Amic e Amat* as a series of disconnected prose fragments interspersed with more abstract reflections. But if one relates what is being said to the system of ideas which Llull expounds in his other writings, the effect is very different. There are very few verses, in fact, which do not refer in one way or another to the operation of the three powers of the soul–memory, understanding and will – which appear in the passage just quoted;[10] if one reads the book in this way, one finds that every verse contributes, separately and in combination, to a single total pattern which conveys the essence of Llull's theological speculations. Because of this, the *Libre d'Amic e Amat* embodies with dazzling accuracy what is perhaps Llull's central insight, that in the search for God, love and understanding are equally necessary:

> Tant amava l'Amic son Amat, que de tot ço que li deia lo creia, e tant lo

[10] See R.Pring-Mill, 'Entorn de la unitat del *Libre d'Amic e Amat*', in *Estudis sobre Ramon Llull*, pp. 279–306 (see above, note 9).

desijava entendre, que tot ço que n'oïa dir volia entendre per raons necessàries. E per açò l'amor de l'Amic estava entre creença e intel.ligència.

(The lover so loved his beloved that he believed all that he had said to him, and so desired to understand it that he wished to understand all that was spoken of him by necessary reasons. And thus the love of the lover was between faith and intelligence.)

After the *Libre d'Amic e Amat,* Llull's metrical verse may seem disappointing. In his early years, he had written secular poems in the troubadour manner; later, he saw himself as a spiritual *joglar*:

L'art, Sènyer, de joglaria començà en vós a loar e en vós a beneir; e per açò foren atrobats estruments e voltes e lais e sons novells amb què home s'alegràs en vós.

(The art, Lord, of minstrelsy began as a means of praising and blessing Thee; to that end were invented instruments and dances, lays and new types of music, so that man should delight in Thee.)

The language of his poetry is closer to Catalan than that of the troubadours, though it preserves the link with Provençal, as well as the metrical variety of troubadour verse. Even his best poems, however, suffer from monotony of rhyme: it is clear that Llull valued metre and rhyme chiefly as aids to memory, and the greater part of his poetry, in fact, is purely didactic in intention. Yet even his most pedestrian verses contain passages which are memorable in a literary sense, and three or four of his poems rise to a far higher level of achievement. Several are original reworkings of established forms: thus, the *Concili*, addressed to the Council of Vienne (1311–12), is a lively combination of the *sirventes* and the crusading song, and the *Plant de Nostra Dona Santa Maria,* which contains some of his most powerful descriptive writing, belongs to the traditional genre of the *Planctus Mariae*.[11]

Llull's finest poems, the *Desconhort* and the *Cant de Ramon*, are both autobiographical. The *desconhortz* was a recognized troubadour genre, and Llull's poem is written in alexandrines, to be sung 'al so de Berard', i.e. to the tune of an epic poem of the Carolingian cycle. The poem, which runs to over 800 lines, takes the form of a debate between the author himself and a hermit whom he meets in a wood. The prevailing mood is one of depression and self-doubt: in the course of the dialogue, the hermit reproaches Llull for

---

[11] In particular, it bears a close resemblance to an anonymous Catalan poem of the mid-thirteenth century, 'Augats, seyós qui credets Déu lo payre' (Hearken, sirs, who believe in God the Father). See the critical edition of this poem by R. Aramon i Serra in *Hispanic Studies in Honour of I.González Llubera* (Oxford, 1959), pp. 11–40.

the failure of his missionary plans and accuses him of overambitiousness and pride. Both speakers are clearly aspects of Llull's own temperament, and the strength of the poem lies in the absolute honesty with which Llull puts his spiritual motives to the test. In the end, the hermit is convinced by the author's self-defence, and the two leave in separate directions, as friends engaged in the same spiritual enterprise.

This symbolic restoration of mental equilibrium is a genuine victory over the doubts which Llull must have experienced at many stages in his career. The *Cant de Ramon* (1299), though briefer and more economical, reflects another similar moment with complete frankness and humility:

> Som hom vell, paubre, menyspreat,
> no hai ajuda d'home nat
> e hai trop gran fait emparat.
> Gran res hai de lo mon cercat;
> mant bon eximpli hai donat:
> poc som conegut e amat.

(I am an old man, poor and despised. I have no living creature to help me and I have undertaken too great an enterprise. I have searched through a great part of the world and given many good examples: I am little known and loved.)

The next line, however, plunges abruptly into the world of mystical experience: 'Vull morir en pèlag d'amor' (I wish to die in a sea of love). This note recurs throughout the poem, especially in the lines which refer to the founding of the monastery of Miramar, the symbol of all Llull's missionary endeavours:

> Lo monestir de Miramar
> feu a Frares Menors dar,
> per sarraïns a predicar.
> Enfra la vinya e'l fenollar
> amor me pres, fe'm Déus amar
> enfre sospirs e plors estar.

(I had the monastery of Miramar given to the Friars Minor, so that they might preach among the Saracens. Between the vine and the fennel, love seized me and made me love God and remain torn between sighs and tears.)

The vine and the fennel, sighs and tears; elsewhere, love and the lack of love, faith and intelligence. Llull's mind seems to work most naturally in terms of such polarities; an argumentative mind which knows, nevertheless, that the greatest truths can only be communicated through the imagination and the spirit.

*

One contemporary figure is often linked with Llull: that of the Valencian, Arnau de Vilanova (*c.* 1237–1311), who achieved international fame as both a physician and religious visionary. As Professor of Medicine at Montpellier and personal doctor to a series of kings and popes, he enjoyed enormous prestige, and his appeal to reason and experience in medical treatment, based on a combination of Galen and Arabic teaching, retained its authority until the eighteenth century. His spiritual activities were much more controversial, and complicated, as in the case of Llull, by his direct knowledge of Muslim and Jewish practices. Beyond this, there is very little resemblance between the two men: where Llull is contemptuous of the less orthodox religious movements of the time, Arnau de Vilanova was strongly influenced both by the Franciscan Spirituals and by the wave of messianism which swept the Jewish communities of Europe in 1295. In the last fifteen years of his life, he seems to have devoted himself entirely to the propagation of his beliefs concerning the imminent coming of the Apocalypse and the urgency of religious reform. Having met with hostility in Paris and Rome, he pinned his hopes on the Royal House of Aragon and on the Court of Frederick III of Sicily, for whom he wrote the *Informació espiritual* (1310), a treatise on the qualities of the ideal Christian ruler, which was used as the basis for the *Constitutions* of Sicily.

Apart from the *Informació* and a pair of letters to royal patrons, only three of Arnau's works in Catalan have survived: the *Confessió de Barcelona* (1305), an exposition of his millennial beliefs, delivered in the presence of Jaume II and the Catalan Court; the *Lliçó de Narbona* (1305–08), a sermon on the evangelical idea of poverty preached to the Beguines of Narbonne; and the *Raonament d'Avinyó* (1310), a defence of the Beguines and the Spirituals which comes close at times to the missionary ideals of Llull. This small handful of texts in itself represents a considerable literary achievement: the lack of spiritual criteria which leads Arnau to accept all kinds of false prophecies and oracles is relatively unimportant, compared with the impact of a compelling personality who manipulates the language with superb oratorical skill. At its most serious, Arnau's style probably owes a great deal to his experience in writing Latin, and here, at least, there is a sense of grammatical strictness, of logical articulation, which looks forward to Eiximenis (see below, pp. 26–27). What is even more striking, however, is the extraordinary vigour and flexibility of a language which can turn from the exalted to the mundane in a single sentence, as when he describes the enforced humility of the Spirituals:

[A]ixí com perles en arena, e moxons en barça d'espines, e tortres en selva, per la multitud e.l poder dels adversaris.

(Like pearls in sand, or sparrows in a thorn bush, or doves in a forest, by reason of the multitude and power of their enemies.)

As with Llull, though on a much smaller scale, one is continually surprised by the maturity and variety of a literary language for which there are no surviving precedents.

IV. The Four Chronicles

If Llull is an isolated genius and Arnau de Vilanova an interesting eccentric, the more normal literary activity is represented by the four great chronicles which, in the absence of any major fiction or poetry, fill the gap between Llull and the humanistic movement of the fourteenth century. The strong dynastic sense which made the monastery of Ripoll an early centre of historiography in Latin could hardly have failed to affect vernacular literature.[12] What is particularly striking, however, is that two of the major Catalan chronicles, those of Jaume I and Pere III, are virtually royal autobiographies.

The *Libre dels feyts* of Jaume I (1213–76) is written entirely in the first person. Its textual history is complicated, though the directness and intimacy of many of its best passages leave no doubt as to the intervention of the king himself. As for the process of composition, it seems certain that the original materials were set down by Jaume and his collaborators shortly after the capture of Valencia in 1238. The early part, which consists largely of Jaume's memories of the Valencian campaign and the earlier conquest of Mallorca (1229), was completed in its original form by 1244. Much later, possibly in 1265, the chronicle was resumed and eventually brought up to the year 1274, a time-sequence which accounts for the relatively confused description of events between 1240 and 1265. This original text has not survived: in 1313, at the orders of Jaume II, it was translated into Latin by Petrus Marsilius, who added the final part and divided the whole work into chapters; the definitive Catalan version was then completed, probably in 1327, by imposing the structure of the Latin text on that of the original and by incorporating various stylistic revisions and amplifications introduced by the Latin translator.

The *Libre dels feyts* is a personal chronicle in more senses than one. The 'deeds' of the title are for the most part the military actions accomplished by the king and his armies; little space is given to diplomacy, and there are none of the outbursts of patriotism one finds in Desclot and Muntaner. As against this, there is a strong sense of the workings of Providence and of the

---

[12] For a vivid and well-documented account of Ripoll as a cultural centre, see R. d'Abadal, *L'abat Oliba, Bisbe de Vic, i la seva època* (Barcelona, 1948).

value which lies in recording individual feats of heroism. Both themes are handled with a notable lack of exaggeration: if God appears to favour the Catalans, there are no spectacular interventions of the supernatural, and the bravery of the Catalan troops is set firmly in a background of detailed strategies. This relative objectivity is remarkable in a chronicle which conveys so much epic feeling: what controls the description of events, of course, is the temperament of the narrator who is at the same time the chief protagonist. There is no doubt that Jaume I was familiar with the values of epic poetry, and passages like those which describe his pride in possessing a sword which had belonged to the Cid, or his courageous behaviour after being wounded in the siege of Valencia, show how closely he modelled his own attitudes on those of the epic heroes. The point is rather that such attitudes are made to seem only part of a much more complex vision of events which ranges from the trivial to the frankly confessional. At either level, the results can be extraordinarily direct:

> E fom a Borriana. E quan venc que'n volguem levar la host, una oreneta havia feit niu prop de l'escudella, en lo tendal; e manam que no'n levassen la tenda tro que ella se'n fos anada ab sos fills, pus en nostra fe era venguda.

> (And we left for Borriana. And when we came to strike camp, [we found that] a swallow had made its nest on the roof of our tent, and we gave orders not to take down the tent until it had gone away with its little ones, since it had placed its trust in us.)

Or, at a crucial point in the campaign against Valencia:

> Ab tant anam nos gitar, e no volguem descobrir les paraules a null hom que fos ab nos. E ja fos en temps de gener, que fa gran fret, contornam nos, la nuyt, més de cent vegades e'l lit, de la primera part de l'altra, e suavem també com si fossem en un bany.

> (At this we went to bed, and would not reveal the conversation to any of those who were with us. And though it was January, and bitter cold, we tossed and turned in bed more than a hundred times in the course of the night, and sweated as if we were in a bath.)

Almost every page of the *Libre dels feyts* is stamped by its author's powers of observation and by the psychological truth of his reactions. In comparison, the chronicle of Desclot, written between 1283 and 1288, is much less vivid, though its language is vigorous and supple, and its account of events highly detailed. The author himself remains a shadowy figure: his identity is still uncertain, though it is clear from the text that he was a well-educated member of the Catalan Court, with easy access to official documents. This relative anonymity, in fact, seems to have been deliberate:

what matters, for Desclot, are the facts themselves, not their interpretation, and this objectivity is translated into a literary formula: 'Ara lexa a parlar lo libre [de tal cosa] e torna a paralar [de tal altra].' (Now the book leaves off speaking [of this matter] and turns to speak [of another].)

His chronicle begins in the time of Ramon Berenguer IV (1131–1162), but, apart from the first fifty chapters, is entirely concerned with the reign of Pere II (1276–85). Like the *Libre dels feyts*, the early chapters make use of existing verse material, with a marked preference for the chivalresque and the fantastic, as in the legendary account of the birth of Jaume I, used also by Muntaner.[13] The real protagonist of the chronicle, however, is Pere II, and the principal events it records are the Catalan-Aragonese intervention in Southern Italy and the unsuccessful French invasion of Catalonia. It is clear that Desclot's patriotic feelings are directed towards the king himself, rather than towards his dynasty or his country. Perhaps the greatest triumph of the chronicle lies in the skill with which it dramatizes the growth of the king's authority from adolescence to maturity. Here, particularly, Desclot shows the impartiality and sense of moral justice which run through his entire work. Though his admiration for Pere II is very great, he makes no attempt to pass over his moral weaknesses or the atrocities he commits in the course of the war with the French. The same honesty appears in some of his minor portraits, notably in that of the great admiral, Roger de Llúria, whose laconic speeches are among the most memorable things in the book. Like Muntaner, Desclot has a strong antipathy towards the French, though this does not prevent him from praising the noble qualities of their leaders. Compared with the *Libre dels feyts*, Desclot shows more concern for the spirit of chivalry, and it is obvious that Pere II himself at times went out of his way to appear in a chivalresque light, as in the famous episode of the challenge of Bordeaux (1283). What pleases Desclot, however, is the contrast between the oversophistication of the French and the tough simplicity of the Catalans. When Pere returns from Bordeaux, having triumphed over the treachery of Charles d'Anjou, he is seen:

> tot sol en son cavall, ab les armes e'l dors; e fou tot suat e colrat del solell e del calor qui era molt gran.

> (riding alone, with his weapons slung behind him; and he was running with sweat and tanned by the sun and by the great heat.)

---

[13] The whole question of the use of verse sources in the chronicles is complex and controversial. See, for example, F. Soldevila, *Les prosificacions en els primers capítols de la Crònica de Desclot* (Barcelona, 1958), and 'Un poema joglaresc sobre l'engendrament de Jaume I', in *Estudios dedicados a Menéndez Pidal* VII (Madrid, 1957), pp. 71–80; M. Montoliu, *Les quatre grans cròniques* (Barcelona, 1959), pp. 141–9.

The same contrast appears in the chronicle of Ramon Muntaner (1265–1336), written between 1325 and 1328. At the time of the French invasion of Catalonia in 1285, Muntaner was twenty; he himself describes the sacking of his native town, Perelada:

> Que jo e d'altres que en aquella hora hi perderen, hi perdem gran res d'açò que havíem, e no hi som pus tornats per habitar, ans som anats per lo món cercant consell amb molt mal e molt treball e molts perills que n'havem passats, e dels quals la major part ne són morts en les guerres aquestes que la Casa d'Aragó ha haüdes.

> (For I and others who were vanquished at that time lost a great part of our possessions; and we never went back to live there, but rather have gone through the world seeking counsel and meeting with great ills, hardships and dangers, and the greater part of us have died in these wars of the House of Aragon.)

In the course of his wanderings, Muntaner became an important actor in the historical events he was later to record. In 1300 he went to Sicily, where he took part in the siege of Messina and became administrator to Roger de Flor, the ex-Templar who two years later commanded the Catalan military expedition to Constantinople. He himself took part in the campaigns in Greece and Asia Minor and for several years was commander of the garrison at Gallipoli. Though in his later years he was involved in a number of important acts of diplomacy, the chief historical interest of his chronicle is the unique account it gives of the expedition to the Near East. As far as objectivity goes, the contrast with Desclot could hardly be greater. Muntaner writes first and foremost as a military leader, whose literary culture is drawn mainly from the Bible, troubadour poetry and the romances of chivalry. Though his narrative runs from the birth of Jaume I to the coronation of Alfons III (1328), it concentrates chiefly on the French invasion of 1285 and his own experience of the Near Eastern campaign.

Of all the chronicles, this is the most personal; in the prologue, Muntaner relates how an old man appeared to him in a dream, saying 'Muntaner, leva sus, e pensa de fer un libre de les grans meravelles que has vistes' (Muntaner, rise up and try to write a book about the great marvels you have seen). His engaging lack of modesty comes from the sense of his own value as a unique observer of unparalleled events. It is perhaps symptomatic that he always refers to his work as a 'book' and never as a 'chronicle'; certainly, the effect is of a book of memoirs which at the same time is partly intended to serve as a 'mirror for princes'. This comes out both in his constant appeals to an audience (his favourite narrative formula is 'Què us diré?' – 'What can I say to you?') and in his enthusiastic praise of the Aragonese dynasty. Unlike Desclot, he sometimes omits or distorts important episodes, or describes in great detail events at which he was not present.

Such lapses from truth are often a condition of his brilliance as a narrator; at a deeper level, however, it is clear that Muntaner was attempting to give an impression of imperial unity at a time when the Catalan-Aragonese domains were in serious danger of disintegrating. And on top of this, there is another problem which must have caused him particular difficulty as a Christian: the fact that several of his masters, like Pere II, had been excommunicated and had fought against the Church. In practice, by skilful manipulation of the facts, Muntaner upholds the infallibility of Rome and at the same time gives an account of events which completely discredits the authority of a particular pope, Martin IV, whose unworthy conduct is shown to be largely responsible for Pere II's bad relations with the Curia. Like the *Libre dels feyts*, though in the face of increasing difficulties, the chronicle of Muntaner succeeds in giving a providential account of history in which the achievements of the House of Aragon are enveloped at times in an atmosphere of Old Testament grandeur.

I have already referred to some of the differences between these last two chronicles: Desclot's reticence as against Muntaner's controlling personality; Muntaner's tendency to suppress the tensions of the dynasty in order to show a country whose allegiance to its monarch is undivided. In contrast to this, Desclot is much more inclined to give us the whole of a situation, in other words, to justify the actions he is describing. And the endings of the two chronicles are characteristically different: Desclot's terminates sadly, with the death of his hero, Pere II, Muntaner's with the coronation of Alfons III, as if to underline his imperial vision of the future. For Muntaner, everything comes down to action, which for him needs no justification; he relies on his dramatic personality to carry the reader along without searching for explanations. Compared with this, as Josep Miquel Sobré argues, Desclot is the better historian and looks forward to more modern versions of history; Muntaner, on the other hand, personalizes his narrative – he has, after all, been a witness of most of the actions he relates – and, in so doing, creates an effect not unlike that of fiction, something of enormous consequences for the future of prose narrative and in particular for a novel like *Tirant lo blanc* (see below, pp. 46–50).[14]

The last of the four chronicles, that of Pere III (Peter the Ceremonious), is very different from the others. In the first place, its general conception is much more sophisticated: its author is not only an able politician, but also one of the outstanding cultural figures of his time, a superb orator and letter-writer, as well as a minor poet. Above all, Pere III is a king with a passion for history (the *Libre dels feyts* was one of his favourite books), and a clear sense of the value of historical writing as a means of justifying imperial policy. Secondly, though his chronicle resembles the *Libre dels feyts* in

---

[14] J.M. Sobré, *L'èpica de la realitat: l'escriptura de Ramon Muntaner i Bernat Desclot* (Barcelona, 1978), p. 126.

its autobiographical aspect, it owes much more to contemporary documents, so much so that whole sections of it are little more than diary entries based on the lists of events drawn up by the royal assistants. Its content is divided into seven chapters or books, beginning with the king's birth in 1319 and ending in 1382, five years before his death. Within each chapter, the distribution of material is more selective than in any of the other chronicles, and is generally focused on a single major episode. Thus the third and longest deals with the reincorporation of Mallorca in the kingdom of Aragon and the fourth with the War of the Union against the rebel nobles of Aragon and Valencia. In a letter written to his principal collaborator, Bernat Descoll, in 1375, Pere expresses the wish that 'all facts should be mentioned, though some may be to our discredit'. Clearly, he hoped that even his most violent actions would in the long term be seen as part of a providential design; in practice, the effect of such honesty provides the chronicle with scenes of breathtaking callousness. From a literary point of view, the same directness accounts for the brilliance of many of the individual portraits, notably those of Peter the Cruel and Bertrand du Guesclin, and also for the extraordinary sense of detail which runs through the whole chronicle:

> Apres poc temps venc allí [a Barcelona] l'infant En Jaume, fort mal aparellat de malaltia, en tant com nós li isquem a rebre'l, com entràvem en la ciutat, un hom faia jocs per alegria, que passava e anava de part a part del carrer per un fil prim. E nós li diguem: – Frare, veets aquests jocs? – E ell dix: – Senyor, no veig res –. E tantost com fo en la posada sua, gità's en son lit, e, a cap d'alguns jorns, reté la ànima a nostre senyor Déu.

> (A short time afterwards, Prince Jaume reached Barcelona, much troubled by sickness. When we went out to receive him, coming back into the city, a man was performing tricks for entertainment, crossing from one side of the street to the other on a thin rope. And we said to him: 'Brother, do you see this sport?' And he replied: 'My Lord, I see nothing'. And as soon as he arrived at his lodgings, he took to his bed and after a few days rendered up his soul to our Lord God.)

Each of the four major chronicles is unique in its way, despite certain common features of style. In the long run, however, what marks off the chronicle of Pere III so sharply from the others has nothing to do with literary qualities: it is quite simply that the nature of government is changing. Just as Catalan culture in the second half of the fourteenth century is beginning to feel the first effects of the Italian Renaissance, so the chronicle of Pere III reflects the way in which medieval political structures are reluctantly yielding to a newer and more absolutist conception of monarchy which comes to rely increasingly on the support of the middle classes in its struggle against the aristocracy.

V. Eiximenis, Metge, Canals and others

Inevitably, the shifts in the sources of power are reflected in the best writers of the late fourteenth century. One cannot help noticing how many prose works of the time are aimed at a middle-class audience. This explains, for instance, why the reign of Pere III is a great age of translation, and why so much fourteenth-century religious writing is concerned with everyday morals and the nature of the urban community. The most instructive example here is Francesc Eiximenis (*c*. 1340–1409), a Franciscan friar who achieved a position of great influence at Court and for many years played a leading part in the administration of Valencia.

Eiximenis's major work is *Lo Crestià*, an encyclopaedic treatise on Christian society. Apart from its vast scale (of the thirteen books originally planned, only four were written, though these in themselves comprise 2,587 chapters), what strikes one in *Lo Crestià* is its absolute faithfulness to the scholastic tradition. In his basic arguments, and in his occasional credulity, Eiximenis is medieval in the most conventional sense: he has none of the sophistication of Llull, and his guarded attitude to the classics sets him apart from a slightly later writer like Bernat Metge. For a modern reader (and, one imagines, for many of his contemporaries) the great attraction of his work lies in the vivid presentation of fourteenth-century society which fills out the scholastic framework. This rich social vision is a direct consequence of the author's intention to write not only for the highly educated, but also for 'the simple layman with no great learning' ('persones simples e legues e sens grans lletres'). His attempt to engage the interest of non-specialist readers accounts for the presence of so many details of public and private life, and also for the vigorous simplicity of the language, as in his description of corrupt princes:

> E fan de la llei tela d'aranya, que no pot retenir res que sia fort, més reté mosquits e coses sense força.
>
> (And they make the law into a spider's web, which can hold nothing strong, but only flies and other weak creatures.)[15]

Though basically his language is sophisticated rather than popular, Eiximenis's mastery of dialogue is equalled only by his contemporary Sant Vicenç Ferrer (see below, p. 27). What gives weight to such incidentals, however, is the way in which they are made to illustrate the general principles of a Christian state. Despite his constant references to Aristotle and St Augustine, there is no doubt that Eiximenis's political and social theories are based on observation: the city which he describes is a real one –

---

[15] Though the image is taken from Seneca, the vividness of the language is Eiximenis's own.

Valencia or Barcelona – and he sees the Crown of Aragon as part of a Christendom whose unity, at the time of writing, is flawed by the Papal Schism.

Recent historians have praised the insight with which he sees *pactisme* (rule by mutual agreement) as the distinguishing feature of the Catalan political tradition.[16] He is aware, moreover, that such a tradition can only be maintained with a good deal of effort and mutual trust, and that the royal council of his day is going through a crisis because of the conflicting interests of the city councillors and the king's officials. More often than not, Eiximenis appears to share the urban middle-class mentality of the readers whom he is addressing, as in his undisguised contempt for the peasants. Nevertheless, his position as a friar, and his personal experience as an administrator, enable him to range with confidence over the whole social spectrum. If all political power comes ultimately from God, he argues, the prince is the head of the Christian republic, whose strength lies partly in the integrity of his noble advisers, and partly in his willingness to respect the opinion of his lesser subjects through the machinery of pacts. One of the constant themes in his work is the need to encourage the usefulness of every member of the state, even the physically disabled. And at every point, whether he is speaking of the dignity of labour or of the education of the ideal prince, he is able to appeal to scholastic authority with a simplicity of religious belief which never seems to conflict with his strong sense of practical values.

Such confidence is becoming rarer by the end of the fourteenth century, though one finds it still in the sermons of the Dominican Sant Vicenç Ferrer (1350–1419), an extraordinary example of a sophisticated theologian who deliberately creates a popular idiom in order to communicate with an uneducated public. At the other extreme, there is the strange figure of Anselm Turmeda (*c.* 1352–*post* 1423), a Franciscan who, as the result of a spiritual crisis, became a Muslim, though he continued to write as a Christian, notably in the *Disputa de l'ase* (The Ass's Debate; 1418), a small masterpiece of irony now lost in its original form.[17] Though parts of the *Disputa* are in verse, it begins with the prose fable of the animals who wish to choose a new king – a common theme in medieval and earlier literature. This is followed by the real nucleus of the work: a debate between Turmeda and an ass in which the former finally proves that man is superior to the beasts. It has been shown that the nineteen points of this debate are based largely on a tenth-century Arabic encyclopaedia which Turmeda obviously knew. Nevertheless, this is more than a case of mere plagiarism: where the original

---

[16] See, for example, J. Vicens Vives, *Noticia de Catalunya* (Barcelona, 1954), pp. 114–16.

[17] The Catalan original was published in Barcelona in 1509, but no copy has survived. It is now only known from a French translation, which appeared in 1544 and was reprinted by R. Foulché-Delbosc in *Revue Hispanique* XXIV (1911). There is a modern Catalan version by M. Olivar in *ENC* (Barcelona, 1928).

is wholly serious, Turmeda's version is shot through with irony and burlesque, sometimes verging on blasphemy. Here and elsewhere, he is particularly scathing about the religious orders, and, though the book as a whole is ostensibly written from a Christian point of view, Christianity itself is regarded with a certain scepticism – hardly surprising, given Turmeda's Muslim faith. The result is a work of enormous vitality, though not one to be taken as a serious apology for the Christian religion.

One other minor work of this period deserves to be mentioned: the *Viatge al Purgatori* (Journey to Purgatory) of Ramon de Perellós, Viscount of Perellós and Roda (*c.* 1350–*post* 1405). This takes the form of a travel diary, though one whose motivation could hardly be more curious. In 1396, Joan I of Aragon had died in mysterious circumstances, and in the following year Perellós, who had been close to the king, set out on a journey to the so-called Purgatory of St Patrick at Lough Derg to discover how his former master had fared in the afterlife. Perellós's journey was accompanied by a good deal of publicity: in England, he was received by Richard II, who – of all things – issued him with a safeconduct for Purgatory. Various people tried to dissuade him from going, on grounds of danger, but Perellós, in true chivalresque spirit, persisted and survived the journey without mishap. The great merit of his account, written in 1397 or shortly afterwards, lies in its descriptions of the land and people of Ireland – a unique insight into four-teenth-century conditions in that country. As for his visit to the Purgatory, there is no reason to doubt that he actually went there, but his description of events disappointingly falls back on an earlier account by the twelfth-century monk Henry (or Hugh) of Saltrey, with one exception: a paragraph which he deliberately inserts and which is crucial to his whole account:

> E aqui jo vi bell colp de mos companyons, que jo conoisia, e de mos parents e parentes; e lo rei don Joan d'Aragó; [...] Enaprés parlí molt ab lo Rei, mon senyor, lo qual, per la gràcia de Déu, era en via de salvació. La raó per què sofria les penes no la volgué dir; ...

> (And here I saw a good number of my companions, whom I knew, and also of my relatives, male and female; and King Joan of Aragon; [...] Afterwards I spoke at length with the King, my Lord, who, through the grace of God, was on the road to salvation. The reason why he was suffering punishment he would not say ...)

With this single paragraph, Perellós's mission was accomplished: the spirit of Joan I was laid to rest, with details which would convince any contempo-rary reader. As for modern readers, the interest lies rather in the first-hand account of a civilization which was barely documented at the time and which continues to occupy the researches of more recent historians.

These last two works stand somewhat apart from the general tendencies of the time. By 1400, however, a new spirit is beginning to make itself felt in another sector of Catalan prose. Here again, the decisive period is the reign of Pere III. In the first half of the fourteenth century, the vernacular works of Llull continue to act as a criterion for later prose writers; in the second half of the century, precisely at a time when Llull's reputation is beginning to wane, linguistic uniformity is maintained by the increasing importance of the Royal Chancellory. The reform of the chancellory under Pere III had literary consequences which could hardly have been foreseen at the time. The formation of a group of royal notaries, skilled in writing Latin, Catalan and Aragonese, coincided with the growing demand for translations from classical Latin. At first, such classics were valued chiefly for their moral content; eventually, however, in the early 1380s, there comes a stage at which certain stylistic tendencies begin to emerge, notably the attempt to adapt Ciceronian prose to the vernacular. This aesthetic revaluation of prose on the part of a group of professional writers with a taste for classical culture led to a new type of humanism which is sometimes referred to as the Catalan Pre-Renaissance. The presiding figure in this movement is not Pere III but his successor, Joan I (1387–96) – already referred to in connection with Ramon de Perellós – whose marriage to Violant de Bar and relations with the Court of Avignon brought Catalonia for a time into the cultural orbit of France. And, significantly, it is Joan I who is the protagonist of the one masterpiece the movement produced, the *Somni* (The Dream) of Bernat Metge.

Bernat Metge (*ante* 1346–1413) was closely involved in the events of the time. His stepfather, Fernan Sayol, was chief notary to Eleanor of Sicily, the third wife of Pere III; his translation of the *De re rustica* of Palladius Rutilius and his early interest in Cicero established him as a respectable minor humanist, and it seems likely that his literary tastes had a strong influence on Metge himself. The latter joined the chancellory and continued to serve under his friend and patron Joan I. After the sudden death of the king in 1396, Metge was accused, along with a number of other officials, of administrative corruption, and probably imprisoned. Shortly afterwards, he was rehabilitated, and eventually became secretary to the new king, Martí I.

Most of Bernat Metge's literary work was composed between 1381 and 1399, and it shows very clearly the transition from medievalism to something distinctly more modern. His allegorical poem, the *Llibre de Fortuna e Prudència* (1381), poses the question of Providence in purely medieval terms, with obvious debts to Boethius and the *Roman de la rose*. The *Història de Valter e Griselda*, written seven years later, is very different: a translation of Petrarch's Latin version of a story from the *Decameron*. This may seem a perverse way of translating Boccaccio; its real significance, however, lies in the excellence and novelty of its prose and in the fact that its preface contains the first eulogy of Petrarch by a Peninsular writer.

Metge's praise, significantly, is for Petrarch the Latin humanist, not for the vernacular poet, and it is this aspect of the older author which comes to dominate his own literary work. In 1395, shortly before the death of Joan I, he spent some time at the Papal Court in Avignon, where he met the famous Aragonese humanist Juan Fernández de Heredia, and almost certainly read the *Secretum* of Petrarch, a powerful confessional dialogue composed at a time of intense spiritual crisis. Metge's own *Apologia*, written under the first impact of the *Secretum*, is an early, over-literary attempt to adapt the Ciceronian dialogue to his own language; in retrospect, however, it reads like a first sketch for his masterpiece, *Lo somni* (1399).

The *Somni* is divided into four books. In the first, the ghost of Joan I appears to Bernat Metge in prison, accompanied by Orpheus and Tiresias. The king's own situation (it emerges that he is in Purgatory for having over-indulged his taste for hunting, music and astrology) leads to a discussion concerning the immortality of the soul, and in the second book the dialogue hinges on the circumstances of the author's own political disgrace. In the third, Orpheus and Tiresias, who symbolize the king's love of music and astrology, tell their own stories, and the latter delivers an angry diatribe against women; in the final book, Metge replies with a defence of the famous women of antiquity and the present day, ending with a passage in praise of the new queen, Maria de Luna, and a satire against the vices of men.

The greater part of the *Somni* is based directly on passages from other authors, among them Cicero, Ovid, Valerius Maximus, Boccaccio and the Church Fathers. What saves it from being mere plagiarism is the author's own intellectual attitude. The humanistic note is struck early in the first book: 'hom són aixi com los altres, e cové que seguesca llurs petjades' (I am a man like other men, and I must follow in their footsteps). In practice, this amounts to a combination of generosity and scepticism: generosity in the sense of friendship which colours the relationship between the author and his dead master, scepticism in his reluctance to go beyond the evidence of his senses. The liveliness of the opening dialogue depends to a great extent on the constant questioning of the king's present state and, though in the end Metge allows himself to be won over by the Christian arguments for the immortality of the soul, it is his scepticism which really convinces:

> Bé saps tu [says the king] que moltes coses creu hom, que no pot veure. – Ver és – diguí jo – mas no els tenc per savis aquells que n'usen. Ço que veig crec, e del pus no cur.

> (You know very well that men believe many things which they cannot see. – Indeed, said I, but I think them not wise who indulge in such things. I believe what I see, and pay no attention to the rest.)[18]

---

[18] It is difficult to gauge the extent of Metge's scepticism. That he was known as a

If this sceptical *persona* raises the *Somni* above the level of a literary exercise, much of its urgency comes from the immediate circumstances of its composition. It is clear that, in writing it, Metge was not so much concerned with the immortality of the soul or the denunciation of vices, as with justifying his own actions. One of his motives for writing in Catalan, one suspects, was the desire to make his self-defence available to any educated reader, and to one reader in particular, Martí I. One can only admire the strategy by which he enlists the support of the dead king, and, judged by its practical results, his defence appears to have been completely successful. From a literary point of view, an immense distance separates Bernat Metge from a writer like Eiximenis. The polish and restraint of *Lo somni* are quite new in Catalan prose and, if its tone reminds one at times of Montaigne, this is merely one way of observing the real, though limited, extent to which it anticipates the Renaissance.

Though Bernat Metge is the most talented of the Catalan humanists, his scepticism reflects a more general tendency to rationalism of which other writers of the time were aware. One finds a very different reaction, for example, in the work of Antoni Canals (*c.* 1352–1419), the eminent Dominican and translator of Valerius Maximus, Seneca and Petrarch. Intellectually, Canals is closer to Eiximenis than to Bernat Metge, but, unlike Eiximenis, he deliberately sets out to fight the sceptics with their own weapons. His strictly religious works, the *Escala de contemplació* (Ladder of Contemplation) and the *Tractat de confessió* (Treatise on Confession), show a nostalgia for the contemplative life, conceived in terms of the Dominican mystical tradition. In the prefaces to the classical translations, however, he clearly hopes that those readers who no longer acknowledge the authority of the Bible will be attracted to the Christian virtues by the example of the classical moralists. Thus, he dedicates his version of the *De providentia* of Seneca to the Governor of Valencia, Ramon Boyl, with the words:

> [N]o em direu que lo dit Sèneca sia profeta ni patriarca, qui parlen figurativement, ans lo trobarets tot filòsof, qui funda son fet en juy e raó natural.
>
> (You will not tell me that the said Seneca is a prophet or one of the patriarchs, who speak in figures; rather will you find him in every part a philosopher, who bases his matter on judgement and natural reason.)

Canals, in fact, never allows his sense of classical values to conflict with his religious faith. If he is a less original author than Bernat Metge, this is

---

sceptic in the lifetime of Martí I is evident from the King's reproaches in *Lo somni*. Despite his apparent 'conversion', one might suspect that he was merely suppressing his scepticism so as not to prejudice his chances of rehabilitation by Martí's successor.

partly because he never sees himself as a literary writer. His aim is quite simply 'to create the perfect and finished man' ('fer l'hom perfecte e acabat'); not Renaissance Man, but a Christian humanist who will embody the best values of medieval orthodoxy and classical antiquity. In this, of course, he is close to Petrarch himself, and it is the example of Petrarch's Latin writings which, more than anything, gives an appearance of unity to the series of minor humanists who follow one another almost until the end of the fifteenth century.

VI. Poetry from Llull to Roiç de Corella

Compared with the achievement of fourteenth-century prose, the poetry of the same period is on the whole dull and repetitive. The main reason for this lies in the tyranny of the Provençal tradition. Llull, as we saw, continues to use the language of troubadour poetry, though his aims are quite different. After him, the same tradition was maintained, with none of Llull's originality, as a consciously artificial kind of writing, increasingly divorced from the vital centres of Catalan culture. This process is paralleled in the South of France. Just as the first organization of troubadour poets, the *Sobregaia companhia dels set trobadors*, was set up at Toulouse in 1323, with a complicated apparatus of rules and prizes, so, seventy years later, the *Consistori de la gaia ciència* was founded in Barcelona, with very similar intentions. The effect of this was to confirm the general stagnation of serious poetry in Catalonia which had come about earlier in the fourteenth century. There is nothing to compare here with the way in which Italian poetry was able to develop through the *stil nuovo* to Dante and Petrarch, nor with the innovations of French poets like Machaut and Alain Chartier. Even so, there are some interesting exceptions. The only fourteenth-century collection of poems to have survived, the *Cançoneret de Ripoll* (The Ripoll Songbook), contains a number of more popular pieces, notably by the Capellà de Bolquera (first half of the fourteenth century), and the anonymous lament which begins:

> Lassa, mays m'agra valgut
> que fos maridada
> o cortes amich agut
> que can suy mongada.

(Alas! It would have been better for me to be married or to have had a gentle lover than to have been a nun.)

These poems are mostly written in a hybrid of Catalan and Provençal, sometimes tending one way, sometimes the other, the one exception being a number of satirical poems which have survived from the later part of the century, like the anonymous *Disputació d'En Buc e son cavall* (Dispute between Master Buc and his Horse), the *Sermó* of Bernat Metge and the *Elogi dels diners* (Praise of Money) of Anselm Turmeda.[19]

This, then, is the situation in Catalan poetry around 1400: Provençal is still being maintained, with increasing difficulty, as an artificial language, but against this one has to set the sporadic beginnings of a satirical poetry in Catalan. And, curiously enough, the courtly love tradition, after remaining sterile for over a century, is going through a successful minor revival, partly through Italian influence, in the work of poets like Gilabert de Pròixita, Melcior Gualbes and Andreu Febrer (*c.* 1375–*c.* 1444), one of the earliest translators of the *Divine Comedy*.

The finest representative of this moment is Jordi de Sant Jordi, a Valencian aristocrat who died in 1425, still in his twenties. Unlike the more conventional poets of his time, Jordi de Sant Jordi wrote love poems which are both moving and elegantly phrased – so much so, that it is tempting to say that all the tradition needed, even at this late stage, was a poet of sufficient talent and personality. How he might have developed had he lived longer, one can only guess. The poems he managed to write show him still using a slightly Catalanized form of Provençal, still moving very consciously within the orbit of troubadour poetry, though with occasional touches which suggest that he had read Petrarch. More important, the courtly attitudes of his poems seem to reflect his own circumstances, so much so that one might wonder whether it is possible to speak of an 'ethics of chivalry' which runs through his entire work. Like Andreu Febrer and his Castilian contemporary the future Marqués de Santillana, Jordi de Sant Jordi was a member of the Court of Alfons IV (Alfonso the Magnanimous), and, along with Febrer and Ausiàs March, took part in the expedition to Corsica and Sardinia of 1420. In 1423, he was captured and imprisoned for a short time in Naples, an event which is recorded in one of his most successful poems, the *Presoner*. Here, the early part of the poem describes the poet's loss, which goes from his physical circumstances to the final atrophy of his thought and will. But, as the poem develops, a different attitude begins to emerge: the poet and his companions are now morally superior to adversity, since they have done their duty. This feeling is elaborated in what follows: the poet has been taken prisoner serving his king in the face of unequal forces, to the utmost of his ability, and therefore has no reason to reproach himself, or as he puts it more strongly, 'no per defaut gens de cavalleria' (not through lack of chivalry). And from his high moral position, Jordi de Sant Jordi can both thank the king for past favours and reproach him for

---

[19] In reality, the *Elogi dels diners* forms part (stanzas 60–69) of a much longer poem, the *Libre de bons amonestaments* (Book of Good Advice), but is often printed as a separate anthology piece.

having got them into this mess; all this without the slightest loss of dignity on his part:

> Per que noi say ni vey res al presen
> que.m puixe dar en valor d'una scorça,
> mas Deu tot sol, de qui prench fundamen
> de qui fiu, hi.b qui mon cor s'esforça;
> e d'altra part del bon rey liberal,
> qui.m socorrech per gentilesa granda,
> lo qui.ns ha mes del tot en aquest mal,
> qu'ell me.n traura, car soy jus sa comanda.

(So at present I neither know nor see anything which might favour me one whit, apart from God, on whom I base myself, in whom I trust and in whom I am strengthened, and on the other hand the good, generous King, who helped me through his great courtesy, he who has landed me completely in this bad situation, who will get me out of it, since I am under his command.)

And in the *tornada*, he addresses the King directly: the only petition that he and his companions make is that the King should remember his royal blood, which has never abandoned his faithful servants. Put like this, it is a modest request, but one that implies a high concept of chivalry, one that runs through the whole poem and to some extent determines its actual structure.

Even in those poems which are not related to particular occasions, one is struck by the same sense of individual experience which breaks free from the topics of courtly poetry. His love poems are surprisingly free from abstractions: in the best of them, the *Stramps* (or unrhymed verses), the opening lines pick up a conceit used by earlier troubadour poets and turn it into a statement of great force and dignity:

> Jus lo front port vostra bella semblança
> de que mon cors nit e jorn fa gran festa,
> que remiran la molt bella figura
> de vostra ffaç m'es romassa l'empremta
> que ja per mort no se.n partra la forma;
> ans quan seray del tot fores d'est segle,
> çels qui lo cors portaran al sepulcre
> sobre ma faç veuran lo vostre signe.

(Beneath my brow I bear your fair countenance, because of which I make a great feast by day and night, for, contemplating your fine features, the imprint of your face has remained with me, so that not even death will take away its form; rather when I shall be completely out of this world, those who carry my body to the grave will see your sign on my face.)

Such a poem is a fine achievement in itself, and confirms the later judgement of the Marqués de Santillana: 'Compuso asaz fermosas cosas, las cuales él mismo asonava, ca fue músico excelente.' One can only regret the loss of the musical settings, though the texts alone bear witness to a talent which, even if it does not seriously question the earlier tradition, seems to point the way to more original possibilities. And in more general terms, it seems fair to say that this was possibly the last point in Catalan history at which such a poetry could have been written, a time when it still seemed possible to revive the classical troubadour tradition within the atmosphere of one of the last small medieval Courts.

The first major poet to write entirely in Catalan is Ausiàs March (1397–1459), and it is no coincidence that he is the greatest poet in the language. The relation of Ausiàs March to the courtly tradition is complex and fundamental: roughly speaking, what he offers is not so much an alternative tradition as a way out of the existing one, above all in the direction of introspection and self-awareness. And seen in this light, the reason for his choice of Catalan seems obvious: the independence of mind which shows through all his best writing positively demands a language which will remove his poetry at one stroke from the conventional associations of Provençal.

It is curious that both the father and uncle of Ausiàs March were talented, if relatively conventional, minor poets, and that his father, Pere March, was one of the people entrusted with drawing up the statutes of the *Consistori de la gaia ciència* in 1393. His family belonged to the minor Valencian nobility, though in fact it had only been raised to noble status in 1360, and there are moments in his poems when one detects a lack of confidence in his social status which contrasts very noticeably with a hereditary aristocrat like Jordi de Sant Jordi. Like Jordi de Sant Jordi, however, Ausiàs March took part in the wars in Naples, Sicily and North Africa in the early 1420s, but in 1425 he seems to have abandoned his military career, and not long afterwards he probably wrote his first poems. In his later years, one finds him engaged in the typical activities of a fifteenth-century squire: fighting lawsuits with rich neighbours, administering justice and raising falcons for the king. In 1437, when he was about forty, he married the sister of Joanot Martorell, the author of *Tirant lo blanc* (see below, pp. 46–50). Two years later, she died, and in 1443 he married a second time. This new marriage lasted eleven years, in the course of which Ausiàs March took up residence in the city of Valencia. Then, in 1454, his second wife died, five years before the poet himself, and it is possible that her death is related to some of his most moving verses.

The blurred impression which comes from the biographical facts contrasts strangely with the very strong sense of personality one finds in the poetry. The poet who can write at the climax of one of his most powerful poems 'Jo só aquest que.m dich Ausiàs March' (I am this man who is called

Ausiàs March) needs no biographer to bring out his individuality, and even at their most abstract, his poems give the impression of a living person who is anxiously debating matters which deeply concern him.

Out of a total of 128 poems, about three-quarters are love poems, most of which are related, directly or indirectly, to the courtly tradition. But taking his work as a whole, there is a good case for calling it 'moral poetry', rather than simply 'love poetry'. A few poems, in fact, are quite clearly moral poems, which meditate philosophically, and a little predictably, on questions like the nature of virtue and goodness. Much more important than these are the half-dozen poems which centre on death: these poems, which represent Ausiàs March's supreme achievement, are concerned not merely with death in a general way, but with the death of a particular person, a woman whom the poet has loved in the fullest sense, and inevitably they lead him to thoughts about his own death.

Ausiàs March's love poems form a number of cycles, each of which is addressed to a single woman, who is identified in the *envoi* by a pseudonym or *senhal*: 'llir entre cards' (lily among thorns) or 'plena de seny' (full of intelligence), to name the two most important. Each cycle has its own distinctive features: thus, the 'plena de seny' poems insist on the woman's ungratefulness, sometimes in derogatory terms; also, though both cycles introduce the subject of death, this is a much more central theme in the 'llir entre cards' sequence, which also refers to the poet's timidity, to his shame at his previous love affairs, and to the divine nature of the woman concerned.

One of the 'llir entre cards' poems (XXIII) begins:

> Lleixant apart l'estil dels trobadors,
> qui, per escalf, traspassen veritat …

> (Leaving aside the style of the troubadours, who, carried away by passion, exceed the truth …)

It would be wrong to take this as a general denunciation of troubadour poetry: in the context of the whole poem, which is concerned with praising a particular woman, it is as if the poet were saying 'We all know that the troubadours are inclined to exaggerate; what I am about to say is the plain truth'. Yet one should not underestimate this opening gesture: there can be no question that, taking the poems as a whole, the kind of introspection they contain goes much deeper than anything one finds in the troubadours, and that this depth depends to a great extent on not idealizing their subject. In this particular poem, we are reminded at various moments that, although the woman is a model of perfection, she is still a human being, and never more so than when she is told: 'verge no sou perquè Déu ne volc casta' (you are no virgin, since God wished you to bear offspring).

Death, for Ausiàs March, is bound up with the destructive power of love and the extreme difficulty of avoiding this. When he theorizes about love, he adopts the threefold division of spiritual love, animal passion and *amor mixtus* which runs through the whole courtly love tradition. Where he goes further than other poets is in exploring the frontier between body and spirit. If love is a torture, as it so clearly is in many of his poems, this is not simply a matter of the opposing natures of body and spirit, but of the way in which these two natures continually act on one another, so that the flesh tries to rise into the orbit of the spirit, whereas the spirit is always inclined to demean itself and sink to the level of the flesh. On this view, the kind of compromise implied in *amor mixtus* is bound to fail: the body will always win. In fact, he goes further than this: not only can the body and the spirit never be reconciled, but, he argues, there is a conflict within the spirit itself. Just as the body and the spirit tend to usurp one another's domains, so the spirit is torn apart when love degenerates into the selfish passion of the instincts.

This is the central source of tension in Ausiàs March, and however he tries to argue himself out of it – and he does this at times with great subtlety – it is something to which he is always forced to return. Because of his tendency to indulge in extended philosophical argument, some critics are inclined to speak of him as a philosophical poet, a writer with a basically intellectual cast of mind. This seems an exaggeration: his knowledge of scholastic theory is surprising in a fifteenth-century Valencian aristocrat, though it hardly goes beyond what one would expect to find in any reason-ably educated scholar of the time, and of course it tells us nothing about the quality of the poetry. The main thing is that it gives him a consistent frame of reference within which to analyse his feelings. In his less successful poems, there are disconcerting shifts from concrete, personal passages to abstract, moralizing ones, but in his finest work, the combination succeeds magnificently, just because, through the use of allegory and simile, he is able to present his abstractions in concrete terms.

On the one hand, then, his poetry is continually testing personal experi-ence by submitting it to rational analysis. On the other, it is a kind of poetry which often tries to extend that experience by comparing it with other human situations. Here, Ausiàs March's mind tends to work by analogy: time after time he begins a poem by saying 'I am like the man who ...', or, 'Like one who ... so it is with me'. And it is in this type of poem that we are made most aware of the kind of images which seem to have haunted his mind. These, almost without exception, are sombre and disturbing: compari-sons drawn from the sickbed, the prison cell and the dangers of the elements, particularly of his great symbol of turbulence, the sea:

> Bullirà el mar com la cassola en forn,
> mudant color e l'estat natural,
> e mostrarà voler tota res mal

> que sobre sí atur un punt al jorn;
> grans e pocs peixs a recors correran
> e cercaran amagatalls secrets:
> fugint al mar, on són nodrits e fets,
> per gran remei en terra eixiran.   (XLVI)

(The sea will boil like a pot in the oven, changing its colour and natural state, and it will appear to hate anything which rests for a moment on its surface; fish great and small will rush to save themselves and will seek secret hiding places: fleeing from the sea where they were born and bred, they will leap on to dry land as a last resort.)

The six poems usually known as the *Cants de mort* (XCII–XCVII) refer to the death of a woman who is quite distinct from those addressed in the other cycles. The most dramatic of all is the fifth: here, the poet's grief comes from the fact that he does not know whether, as he puts it, 'God has taken her to Himself', or whether He has 'buried her in Hell', and because of this uncertainty, he does not know how to address her. If she is in Hell, he reflects that he himself may have been the cause of her damnation:

> Si és així, anul.la'm l'esperit,
> sia tornat mon ésser en no res,
> e majorment si'n lloc tal per mi és;
> no sia jo de tant adolorit.   (XCVI)

(If it is so, cancel my spirit, let my being return to nothingness, the more so if she be in such a place for my sake; let me not suffer so great an anguish.)

This is perhaps the most terrible problem of conscience in his whole work: the idea that he may have brought about another person's damnation. To whom could these poems possibly be addressed? In the third of them, he turns to the reader, saying that those who know that he has previously described sinful passion will perhaps fail to recognize that he is now writing about an honest love. In the cycle as a whole, there is no sense that this was an unattainable love, and in the final poem there is a moving reference to the woman's dying moments:

> Enquer està que vida no finí,
> com prop la mort jo la viu acostar,
> dient plorant: – No vullau mi leixar
> hajau dolor de la dolor de mi.   (XCVII)

(Her life had not yet ended, when I saw her lie near to death, saying amid tears: 'Please do not leave me, have pity on my pain.')

If one tries to imagine these poems as referring to any of the women of the other cycles, the differences stand out immediately; quite simply, it is difficult to conceive this situation as one which involves another man's wife. Addressing the reader at another point, Ausiàs March writes:

> Als que la Mort toll la muller aimia
> sabran jutjar part de la dolor mia.   (XCII)

(Those from whom Death has taken *la muller aimia* will be able to judge part of my grief.)

The crucial phrase is 'muller aimia': 'loved woman'?, 'beloved wife'? One cannot be sure, though it is tempting to relate the poems to the death of the poet's second wife, Joana Scorna, in 1454. If this were true, it would mean that here, in some of the most moving poetry he ever wrote, Ausiàs March has left behind the courtly tradition in a quite unprecedented way.

The *Cants de mort* are poems which attempt to deal with the possibilities of salvation and damnation, that is to say, with matters which lie at the centre of Christian belief. In these particular poems, Ausiàs March does not try to generalize beyond the context of the individual relationship. It would be surprising, however, if a poet who questions so much in his own experience were not equally introspective about his relations with Christianity, and there is one poem, the *Cant espiritual* (CV), which sums up a great deal of what we find scattered through the rest of his work. The whole poem, which runs to over two hundred lines, is cast in the form of a prayer, and the general sense is quite clear: the speaker wishes to achieve salvation, but feels that he is too weak to do so without the help of God. Of all the poems, this is the one which goes furthest along the line of self-reproach. This is not just a question of confessing to various sins; it is also a recognition of the poet's failure in his relations with God. At one point he says 'Jo tem a Tu més que no't só amable' (I fear You more than I love You), and this inability to feel genuine love for God is at the heart of the poem and its tensions. For one thing, he is caught between his fear of death and the wish to die before he commits any further sins, and for another, he recognizes that there can be no possible salvation without love. One critic, Joan Fuster, has claimed that God, for Ausiàs March, is no more than the basic piece in a moral system, at most a judge, but in no sense the active, personal God of Christianity.[20] One sees what he means, though he is surely oversimplifying. What is clear, here and elsewhere, is Ausiàs March's total inability to delude himself. Because of the energy of his verse and the intensity of his self-enquiry, the results are never merely negative. One phrase in particular stays in the mind as a superb expression of the state from which so much of his poetry derives: 'en tot lleig fet hagué lo cor salvatge' (in all base actions, mine was a savage heart), an appropriate note on which to leave a poet

---

[20] Ausiàs March, *Antologia poètica*, ed. Joan Fuster (Barcelona, 1959), p. 35.

whose sheer intelligence and energy enabled him to use the existing tradition to produce great poetry.

Like Ausiàs March, the two other important poets of the fifteenth
century, Jaume Roig and Roiç de Corella, are both Valencians. This points
to a striking feature of the literary scene after about 1450: the tendency, in
poetry at least, to divide into separate schools. Thus, the Barcelona poets
tend to maintain the courtly love tradition, and at the same time to produce a
fairly conventional kind of religious verse, whereas the Valencians concentrate more on satire and what, for want of a better term, one may call the
'humanistic lyric'. Of the two major schools, the Valencian is the more original, and the vitality of its satirical writing continues well into the next
century. Its most remarkable exponent is Jaume Roig (c. 1400–78), an
eminent physician and city councillor, whose long poem *Lo spill* (The
Mirror) or *Llibre de les dones* (Book of Women), was written between 1456
and 1461. What immediately strikes one about the *Spill* is its unusual metre:
over 16,000 lines of four or five syllables each, rhyming in couplets:

> Una en penjaren,
> viva escorxaren,
> gran fetillera
> e metzinera.
> De nit venia
> sens companyia,
> sola pujava
> e arrancava
> dents e queixals
> dels qui, en pals
> ben alta muntats,
> eren penjats.

(They hanged one of them and flayed her alive, a great witch and
poisoner. She used to come at night, unaccompanied, and would climb up
alone and tear out the teeth and molars of hanged men on their tall
gallows.)

Though the poem is narrated in the first person, it is not autobiographical.
The plot is complex and episodic: the protagonist is compelled to live by his
wits, and his chief aim in life is to settle down as a respectable married
citizen of Valencia. This intention is frustrated by a series of disastrous
marriages; the whole book, in fact, consists of a virulent and exhaustive
denunciation of women, interspersed with an enormous variety of anec-
dotes. The many touches of humour are really only incidental: in the long
run, few medieval works are so unremittingly pessimistic, and one can only
wonder at the gulf which separates the fiction from the known facts of the
author's life. The *Spill*, nevertheless, is a remarkable work, and precisely for

its fictional qualities: a strange combination of anger and ingenuity which, cast in a different form, might have been the ancestor of the picaresque novel.

The work of Joan Roiç de Corella (1435–97) could hardly be more different, in itself a sign of the extraordinary variety of Valencian culture in the second half of the fifteenth century. The greater part of his writings is in prose, and his reworkings of Ovidian fables show a marked pleasure in the aesthetic possibilities of myth. In his prose, the delight in craftsmanship often produces an intricate and convoluted style – 'valenciana prosa', as it was called at the time – quite unlike the relative austerity of earlier Catalan writers. The same is true of his love poetry: apart from Ausiàs March, he is the only fifteenth-century poet of importance who succeeds in escaping from the tyranny of the courtly tradition. Occasionally, as in the *Balada de la garsa i l'esmerla* (Ballad of the Magpie and the Blackbird), he achieves a simplicity and a delicacy which can compare with the best poetry of the Spanish *cancioneros*. This, however, is rare: more often than not, his love poetry moves in an atmosphere of solemn ritual and syntactical elaboration, with occasional echoes of Petrarch and other Renaissance poets.

As a Master of Theology, Roiç de Corella wrote a number of fairly undistinguished religious works in prose, as well as translating the Psalms and the *Vita Christi* of Ludolphus of Saxony. His religious poems, on the other hand, are impressive whenever their lapidary style is able to combine with the richly sensuous imagery he had learned to use in his paraphrases of Ovid. Thus, in his fine poem on the Descent from the Cross, the *Oració a la Santíssima Verge Maria tenint son fill, Déu Jesús, en la falda* (Prayer to the the Most Holy Virgin Mary, Holding her Son, Lord Jesus, in her Lap), he describes the mourning universe in almost surrealistic terms:

> crida lo sol plorant ab cabells negres,
> e tots los cels vestits de negra sarga
> porten acords al plant de vostra lengua.

(The sun cries out weeping with black hair and all the heavens clothed in dark sackcloth accompany the lament of your tongue.)

Though it is clear that he was a careful reader of Ausiàs March, there are ways in which his love poetry is quite different from March's, not only because he avoids any kind of philosophical discussion, but also because his whole ethical stance is very much his own. Two of the keywords in Corella's vocabulary are 'honestat' (honesty) and its opposite, 'dishonesty', a polarity which occurs time and again in his secular verse. At the root of this concept of love is the sense that in love, as against mere lust, body and soul must complement one another. 'És impossible', he says, 'delit gran en aquest món sentir, si l'ànima i el cos abdus no el senten' (it is impossible to feel great delight in this world, unless soul and body feel it together). In practice, however, love is always dangerous, since it can so easily involve dishonesty. Thus, in the long run, true honesty is possible only in a love which is not returned in a physical sense, or which is held at a distance.

This is the meaning behind one of his finest poems, *La sepultura* (The Tomb), in which he describes how his own effigy is sculpted on the tomb of the woman he has loved. The whole poem is immensely subtle, fluctuating as it does between the poet himself, the dead woman and the people who will come to see her tomb. And it ends:

> Mudarà el gest la mia forma en pedra,
> quan llegiran aquest mot en la tomba:
> 'Pensant per mi, haveu après de plànyer'.
> E no em doldrà la mia vida trista,
> que sol per vós la poguí bé despendre.

(My form in stone will change its gesture when they read this sentence on the tomb: 'Thinking of me, you have learned to lament.' And my sad life will not grieve me, for only for you could I spend it well.)

This brings us back to the tomb as spectacle. What the visitors will read on the tomb amounts to a second epitaph, this time placed there by the woman. Though on the surface it is laconic enough, by this stage in the poem it is full of implications. When she says 'Pensant per mi' (Thinking of me), she is really taking up the speaker's thoughts in the rest of the poem, in other words, she means 'thinking of me as you do', in terms of her salvation. It is by thinking of her like this that the speaker has 'après de plànyer' (learned to lament), or suffer, and she, in her turn, now recognizes the virtuous quality of his love. But there is one final twist. Why will the speaker '[mudar] el [seu] gest' (change [his] gesture)? This is explained, surely, by the last two lines: it is now the public reading of the epitaph, and the general recognition of its truth, that lead the speaker to a final consolation; though his life is sad, because his love can never be completely fulfilled, it will no longer be a source of suffering, since he will have spent it in the service of an exceptional woman.

One remarkable piece, the *Tragèdia de Caldesa*, stands somewhat apart from the rest of Corella's work. This brief text – it takes up five pages in most modern editions – is a mixture of prose and verse; it concerns an event supposed to have taken place in contemporary Valencia, one which involves (or appears to involve) the poet himself. On the surface, it is the simple anecdote of a woman who betrays the poet by taking another lover. In practice, however, this is complicated by a persistent lack of definition: is this, as some critics have argued, a sentimental romance, or do the prose passages, as I am inclined to believe, serve merely as an introduction to the two poems which form its climax? And there is surely a discrepancy between the high rhetoric of the first poem and what is, after all, a fairly banal happening:

> E, si és ver vos diguí mai 'Senyora',
> no es trobe en l'any lo jorn de ma naixença,
> mas lo meu nom, a tots abominable,
> no sia al món persona que l'esmente;

(And if it is true that I ever said 'Lady' to you, let the day of my birth never be found in the year, but let no one in the world mention my name, abhorrent to all.)

In a way, this is a return to the equally apocalyptic denunciation of the opening prose passage, but, coming where it does, the self-condemnation, though it is only a hypothesis, is much more powerful than the renunciation of the individual woman. And this seems appropriate, since, rather than building on the anecdote, Corella appears to be renouncing love in general. At the same time, there is a sense in which the woman may be open to compassion and pity. And it is this latter sense which comes to dominate in the second poem now spoken by the woman in reply to the first:

> Déu no farà que el passat fet no sia;
> mas, si espereu esmena de mon viure,
> jo la faré, seguint a Magdalena,
> los vostres peus llavant amb semblant aigua.

(God will not cancel my past deed, but, if you hope I shall correct my life, I will do it, following Mary Magdalene, washing your feet with water like hers.)

We must not forget, of course, that it is Corella himself who is writing these lines, and the fact that he offers the woman the choice of behaving like Mary Magdalene seems to point to the same possibility of compassion which is hinted at earlier in the text. In one of the manuscripts, the piece stops here, which bears out what is surely true: that it is the poems, and not the anecdote, that form the climax of the *Tragèdia*, that they comprise, as it were, the lyrical centre of a work which loses its consistency if we persist in reading it as a sentimental romance. However, in the text as it is usually printed, there are two more paragraphs of prose. The last of these hardly affects the body of the text; the first, however, is different, and takes us back to the original distinction between honesty and dishonesty:

> E fóra més alegre, aquesta bella senyora en parts de singular partida, la sua gentil persona ab tan subtil enteniment fos la part mia, e la sua falla e moble voluntat, de falsa estima guiada, cercàs un cos lleig e diforme, en part d'aquell qui indignament l'havia tractada.

(And it would be happier if this beautiful lady could be divided in two, and that her gracious person with its subtle understanding could be my part, and that her frail, changeable will, guided by false affection, could seek an ugly, crooked body on the part of him who had treated her unworthily.)

It is easy to imagine that at this point Corella was remembering some lines from Ausiàs March:

> Llir entre cards, ma voluntat se gira
> tant que jo us vull honesta i deshonesta.
> Lo sant aïr – aquell del qual tinc festa –
> e plau me ço de què vinc tost en ira.   (LIII)

(Lily among thorns, my desires shift so wildly that I want you to be both honest and dishonest. I hate that saint whose feast day I keep, and I take pleasure in what soon makes me angry.)

However, Corella's emphasis differs from March's. March wants his women to be honest and dishonest – virtuous and unchaste – at the same time; Corella can only imagine them as honest or dishonest, and his wish to split the same woman in two, as he knows, is an impossibility. Caldesa, therefore, has no choice, she must be one or the other, and thus she becomes a pretext for Corella's attack on love in general.

Corella, in the past, has often been described as a writer with one foot in the Renaissance, as if this in some sense made him better. This, I think, is doubtful: his treatment of Ovid, for instance, seems to fall entirely within the medieval tradition, and his secular poetry follows naturally from Ausiàs March and Jordi de Sant Jordi – with certain differences, of course, but not enough to indicate a new sensibility. In my view, then, he is the last important Catalan poet of the Middle Ages, one whose incomparable, though difficult, prose and whose beautifully written verse entitle him to a firmer place in the canon than he has so far achieved.

VII. Fifteenth-Century Fiction: Curial e Güelfa and Tirant lo blanc

Two major works of fiction date from the fifteenth century: the anonymous *Curial e Güelfa* and the *Tirant lo blanc* of Joanot Martorell and Martí de Galba. Both are usually referred to as novels of chivalry, though compared with Castilian examples of the genre such as *Amadís de Gaula* they contain very little fantasy, and the actions of their protagonists, however remarkable, tend to remain within the bounds of credibility. Reading the documents of the time, one is struck by the extent to which chivalresque behaviour dominates the lives of the fifteenth-century aristocracy: the personal feuds and private wars of the Catalan and Valencian nobility are conducted with precisely the kind of ritual described in the novels, in a way which seems to imply a steady interaction of life and literature.[21]

Both novels are concerned with the education of a single knight, a process which is conceived for the most part in practical terms. *Curial e Güelfa*, the less ambitious of the two, survives in a single anonymous manuscript, written sometime between 1435 and 1462 by an author who is familiar with Italian topography, possibly a member of the Neapolitan Court. (In its general lines, and some of its details, it bears a certain resemblance to Antoine de Sale's *Le petit Jehan de Saintré* (1456), notably in the humble background of its hero and in the way he is adopted by a young widow of noble birth.) The preface makes it clear that Curial is to become an exceptional lover, as well as an excellent knight, and the strategy employed by Güelfa, his young patroness, allows for both possibilities:

Ma intenció és fer-lo home, emperò no li entenc donar la mia amor, sinó treballar en fer-lo prous e valerós donant-lo entendre que l'am.

(My intention is to make a man of him, though I do not mean to give him my love, but to strive to make him noble and valiant by having him believe I love him.)

In personal terms, the purpose of Curial's education is to make him worthy of Güelfa, whom he eventually marries. Like Tirant, Curial is emotionally timid and easily tempted by the symbolically named Laquesis, the daughter of the Duke of Bavaria. The erotic atmosphere which surrounds Laquesis is one of the triumphs of the book, as is (for similar reasons) the episode in which Curial is entertained for the night in a French convent. Though the manners which the novel records are strictly contemporary, it is also in a sense a historical narrative, since the action is set in the second half of the thirteenth century, and the most vivid character of all is Pere II (1276–89), whose portrait is clearly based on the chronicle of Desclot (see above, pp. 21–22).

The basic values of the novel are medieval, though there are times when it approaches the world of fifteenth-century humanism, as in the episode of the visit to Mount Parnassus, a curious digression which seems at odds with the rest of the book. This is not the only false note in the novel: Curial's adventures in North Africa, though vividly described, are neither chivalresque nor humanistic, and they seem to foreshadow the sentimental novel without realizing its full implications. Taken as a whole, however, *Curial e Güelfa* is remarkable both for the skill of the writing and for the way it suggests a code of manners which is beginning to disintegrate. This is

---

[21] See Martí de Riquer, ed., *Lletres de batalla*, *ENC* (Barcelona, 1963), 2 vols.

partly a question of verisimilitude: Curial's family is poor and undistinguished, and he depends on Güelfa, a rich young widow, for economic support; yet, as the King of France recognizes, these things do not exclude a man from the order of chivalry. This more liberal view, which is opposed by some of the more snobbish characters, is hardly the traditional one, and it is combined with more practical considerations: like Tirant, Curial kills no monsters, and for most of the novel is simply a brilliant military commander. But the most telling criticism of chivalry takes a different form. Sangler, a French knight whom Curial has defeated, reappears later as a monk on Mount Sinai, where he urges Curial to change his way of life:

> E tu, qui has batallat per les vanitats mundanes, batalla ara contra el diable en defensió de la tua ànima [...] Oh catiu! ¿e no et penits de les batalles que has fetes per la vanaglòria del món? Has morts hòmens, has trameses ànimes als inferns.

> (And you, who have done battle for worldly vanities, fight now against the devil in defence of your soul [...] Oh, wretched one! Do you not repent of the battles you have waged for the vanity of the world? You have killed men and sent their souls to Hell.)

The voice is almost that of Llull and, though Curial ignores the advice, it points unmistakably to a basic flaw in the chivalresque ideal.

Tirant lo blanc is even less of a novel of chivalry in the conventional sense. Its author, Joanot Martorell (*c.* 1410–68), seems to have been a typical member of the Valencian nobility, quarrelsome, aggressive, and continually involved in personal feuds which took him at different stages in his career to both England and Portugal. His only other known work, *Guillem de Varoic* (William of Warwick), is partly incorporated in the early chapters of *Tirant lo blanc*; the *Tirant* itself was begun around 1460 and completed after the author's death by Martí Joan de Galba, whose contribution is still undecided.[22] Cervantes's opinion of the novel is well-known:

---

[22] María Jesús Rubiera, in her article '*Tirant lo blanc* and the Muslim World in the Fifteenth Century', included in Arthur Terry, ed., *Tirant lo blanc: New Approaches* (London, 1999), provides the most conclusive evidence so far of the book's dual authorship by showing how in chapters 301–49 – presumably the work of Galba – Martorell's relative familiarity with the Muslim world, based on his knowledge of the *mudéjares* of Valencia, suddenly lapses, only to be resumed at a later stage. Recently, the possibility of a third author – Joan Roiç de Corella – has emerged. As Josep Guia and Curt Wittlin have shown ('Nine Problem Areas Concerning *Tirant lo blanc*', in the same volume, pp. 109–26), the *Tirant* contains many phrases and passages which seem to be taken directly from Corella, so much so that it seems reasonable to believe that Corella himself put them there in the first place. This, on the face of it, seems extremely likely, though for the moment the extent of Corella's possible participation remains a matter for speculation.

[P]or su estilo es éste el mejor libro del mundo; aquí comen los caballeros y duermen, y mueren en sus camas, y hacen testamento antes de su muerte, con otras cosas de que todos los demás libros de este género carecen. (*Don Quixote* I, vi)

The realism which struck Cervantes is one of the most consistent features of the novel. Roughly speaking, the *Tirant* is the story of an imaginary knight, whose greatest achievement is to deliver Constantinople from the threat of the Turks. After the early scenes, which take place at the English Court, the action centres on the Mediterranean. Tirant, by now a famous general, takes part in the French expedition to Rhodes and becomes commander-in-chief of the Byzantine armies; later, after a series of adventures in North Africa, he returns to Constantinople, marries the Emperor's daughter, Carmesina, and dies of an illness shortly afterwards.

To summarize the book in this way, however, leaves out a great deal of what is really interesting: Tirant's protracted wooing of Carmesina and the setbacks this entails, the surprising juxtaposition of the erotic and the spiritual, and the way burlesque is continually used to defeat the reader's expectations. Moreover, it is clear that the manners and customs of the Byzantine Court are an accurate reflection of those of Valencia, though Martorell's realism is so convincing that it is often difficult to say where his social observation gives way to invention. One of the most striking features of this society is its love of ritual, which affects everything from personal relationships to the elaborate protocol that surrounds the most brutal behaviour. The common factor in all this is language: the characters of the *Tirant* take as much pleasure in drawing up an elegantly worded challenge as in postponing their sexual pleasures with fine talk. And in both areas of experience, ritual is linked with strategy: not only detailed schemes for defeating one's enemy in war, but also the deliberate manipulation of potential sexual partners.

So much would be obvious, one imagines, to a sensitive modern reader. However, there is one further dimension of the book which would appeal to a fifteenth-century audience, but which we may possibly underestimate. This is its encyclopaedic nature, the way it can be made to serve as a compendium of knowledge on all manner of things, from social behaviour and the kind of speech this entails, to the qualities of a good knight and the detailed conduct of war. And this affects the actual structure of the book, the way much of this comprises a mosaic of previous writers from Homer to Boccaccio, including a number of Catalan sources. This is where modern ideas of 'originality' and 'plagiarism' are merely distracting. For Martorell, who comes near the beginning of a vernacular tradition of fiction, this recourse to previous authors is not so much a matter of plagiarism as of establishing authority, of bringing to bear the wisdom of the past on a strictly contemporary enterprise. And this is where the idea of a compendium is most effective: in providing his readers with a mass of authorities, many of whom have a bearing on actual conduct, he is deliberately stretching his fiction to achieve the encyclopaedic dimension for which it must originally have been valued.

More than 500 years after its publication, *Tirant lo blanc* remains deeply enigmatical: a major work of art, certainly, but one which defies classification and whose ambiguities – deliberate or unintentional – are far from being resolved. These ambiguities operate at both an external and an internal level. Externally, there is the question of its relation to known fact: Martorell began his book around 1460, seven years after the actual fall of Constantinople to the Turks; since he makes no mention of this, is he attempting to rewrite history by putting real events into reverse? And what is his stance towards chivalry itself? Does he regard it as still valid, or, despite his admiration for its values, does he recognize that it is becoming a thing of the past? More specifically, is he re-creating this world in fictional terms in order to demonstrate the imaginative truth of chivalry to a society whose values are becoming progressively less aristocratic? (This would perhaps explain why he admits certain non-ideal elements, not with the intention of undermining the ideal, but as a way of making it more meaningful.)

Much of the internal ambiguity of the *Tirant* has to do with the objectivity of the narrative. It is hard to think of another work before the sixteenth century in which the author's guiding hand is so conspicuously absent, or which is so free from moral comment. For all the gaiety with which he treats sexual relationships Martorell never allows his humour to soften the impact of what he is describing. His only concern seems to be to persuade the reader that this is how things must have happened, and it is for the reader himself to allocate praise and blame – hence, for example, one's difficulty in knowing how seriously to take the ending. Is the apparent solemnity of Tirant's death undermined by our awareness of his earlier sham deaths? And how does the final burlesque of Hipòlit's marriage to the Empress reflect on the earlier episode?

As Frank Pierce has observed, sex in the *Tirant* has more to do with courtly life than with courtly love.[23] Many episodes in the book would be merely pornographic, were it not for the humour and naturalness with which they are presented. What is surprising, as I remarked earlier, is the frequent juxtaposition of the erotic and the spiritual, as when Tirant conceives eternal love for Carmesina after an accidental glimpse of her breasts:

> E per la gran calor que feia [...] les finestres tancades, estava mig descordada mostrant en los pits dues pomes de paradís [...] les quals donaren entrada als ulls de Tirant, que d'allí avant no trobaren per on

---

[23] See Frank Pierce, 'The Role of Sex in *Tirant lo blanc*', *ER,* X (1962), 291–300.

eixir, e totstemps foren apresonats en poder de persona lliberta, fins que la mort dels dos féu separació.

(And on account of the great heat, for she had had the windows closed, she was half unlaced, revealing her breasts, like two apples of Paradise [...] which allowed Tirant's eyes to enter in such a way that from that moment onwards they could find no means of leaving, and they remained forever imprisoned in the power of one who was free, until the two of them were parted by death.)

At a moment like this, Martorell still preserves a measure of courtly elegance; sometimes, however, this kind of situation becomes sheer farce, as in the scene where Plaerdemavida, the lady-in-waiting, smuggles Tirant into Carmesina's bed and proceeds to warn him whenever her mistress shows signs of waking. Plaerdemavida, in fact, is memorable largely because she combines the greatest freedom in sexual matters with the highest degree of personal chastity. The most corrupt person in the book is the ageing Empress of Constantinople, who at one point conceals the young squire Hipòlit in her bedroom for fifteen days; later, after the Emperor's death, she marries him, though significantly referring to him as 'mon fill' (my son). In this and other episodes, the *Tirant* comes close to suggesting the existence of the subconscious, particularly in the importance it attaches to dreams, both real and pretended. One especially striking example of this also brings out the author's subtlety as a narrator. In chapters 162–63, we are told how Carmesina and Estefania arrange to spend the night in the palace with their lovers, Tirant and Diafebus, while Plaerdemavida spies on them through a keyhole. At first, the actions of the lovers are not described: all we know is that they spend the night together and separate at dawn. Only later does Plaerdemavida reveal to the two other women that she has been an eyewitness, and this she does indirectly, by claiming that she has seen everything in a dream. Thus, throughout the whole episode, Martorell keeps the reader in suspense with masterly skill, not the least by his inversion of the natural order of events.

This pleasure in narrative technique is one of the great strengths of the novel, and is more sophisticated than anything in earlier Peninsular fiction.[24] Yet one should resist attempts to make the *Tirant* more 'modern' than it is. Though some of the techniques which Martorell uses in rendering certain complex situations are more frequently to be found in nineteenth- and twentieth-century fiction, what is really impressive, one could argue, is that his most original effects are obtained largely by exploiting the existing possibilities of medieval narrative, both the romance and the chronicle. Though any

---

[24] For a brilliant discussion of Martorell's narrative technique, see Mario Vargas Llosa's introduction to the Spanish translation of *Tirant lo blanc* by J.F. Vidal Jové (Madrid, 1969).

attempt at an overall interpretation must remain open-ended, the narrative itself serves as an endless source of fascination, not the least because it comes from a mentality very different from our own. Because it makes so few concessions to conventional morality, the *Tirant* is a disconcerting book, and this in itself is a sign of its vitality. In the end, however, it is the scope and depth of the vision which make it a masterpiece, a vivid and densely populated fictional world which still retains its power to convince and to draw its readers into an endlessly ramifying process of discrimination.

VIII. Medieval Drama

Compared with the achievement in prose and poetry, the few surviving examples of medieval Catalan drama are slight and fragmentary, though here again there are interesting differences between Catalonia and the rest of the Peninsula. With very few exceptions, most Catalan plays before the nineteenth century are religious. There is evidence to show that some kind of liturgical drama in the vernacular existed at least from the fourteenth century onwards, centering, as one might expect, on the festivals of Christmas, Easter and Corpus Christi. Moreover, it now seems clear that the early Latin liturgical drama entered Spain by way of Catalonia, and that it was basically a Catalan rather than a Castilian form. As R.B. Donovan has pointed out, this was partly the result of the liturgical situation itself: the fact that the Gallo-Roman rite established by Charlemagne spread to the newly founded Catalan monasteries, which for several centuries maintained their connection with the other side of the Pyrenees.[25] (The most striking example of this is the close relationship which existed between Ripoll and Saint-Martial de Limoges, an association which is of unique importance in the early history of liturgical music and trope singing.)

The French influence can also be detected in matters of staging. Though it is almost impossible to decide the exact point at which mere pageant or recitation gave rise to genuine dramatic representation, it appears that the multiple stage characteristic of the French mysteries had a greater effect in Catalonia, and particularly in Mallorca, than elsewhere in the Peninsula. To judge from the body of plays which has survived from the early fifteenth century, there seems reason to believe in the existence of a separate Mallorcan dramatic tradition which is only reflected sporadically on the mainland. In both Barcelona and Valencia, however, there is enough evidence to show that the Corpus pageants had developed into genuine

---

[25] R.B. Donovan, *The Liturgical Drama in Spain* (Toronto, 1958), pp. 25–9. See also N.D. Shergold, *A History of the Spanish Stage from Medieval Times until the End of the Seventeenth Century* (Oxford, 1967), chapters I–III.

mystery plays at least by the early sixteenth century, and that these continued to be performed until much later alongside the more recent *autos sacramentales*.[26] In the sixteenth, seventeenth and eighteenth centuries, such plays of medieval origin did a great deal to maintain popular traditions in a period of decadence; moreover, though the texts which have been preserved are often simple to the point of crudity, modern productions have shown that, given an adequate setting and a talent for mime, the results can be surprisingly impressive.

Some of the simpler forms of dramatic representation, like the *Cant de la sibil.la* (Song of the Sybil; mid-thirteenth century?) and the Mallorcan *consuetes*, are still performed in connection with particular church festivals.[27] Occasionally a text has survived in something like its original form, like the fragments of a fourteenth-century Passion or the fourteenth-century *Visitatio sepulcri* from Vic. The language of this last play, though still noticeably influenced by Provençal, is simple and vigorous, as at the point where the Jews address the Roman soldiers who have witnessed the Resurrection:

> Com stats vos, cavallers?
> Marrits e tristz, com vos pres?
> Par que bataya haiats haüda,
> Mas que no la haiats vensuda.
> Tots vos vahem spauorditz:
> Are ges no paretz ardits.
> Vosaltres tots tremolats.
> Dietz que'us ha 'nderroquats.
> Sabetz si es al monument Jesus?
> Dietz ho, e leuats sus.

(How is it with you, sirs, downcast and sad? What has happened to you? It seems that you have been in battle, but that you have not won. We see you all filled with terror: you seem to have no courage left. You are all trembling. Tell us, what has cast you down? Do you know if Jesus is in the tomb? Tell us, rise up.)

This is an unusually authentic example from an area in which ambitious vernacular productions seem to have been performed at a relatively early

---

[26] See A.A. Parker, 'Notes on the Religious Drama in Medieval Spain and the Origins of the "Auto sacramental" ', *MLR*, XXX (1935), 170–82. Recent scholarship confirms Parker's view that the *auto sacramental* is a Castilian form, whereas the mysteries are Catalan, Valencian or Mallorcan.

[27] Modern theories concerning the song of the Sybil who prophesies the birth of Christ and its later development, the dialogue between the Sybil and the Emperor, are summarized by Donovan, pp. 165–71. The term *consueta* originally referred to the *ordinarium* or manuscript which recorded the order and content of the various church ceremonies, though later it became identified with the plays themselves.

date. More often than not, however, the surviving texts have been greatly modified in the course of time. Thus the most famous of all these plays, the *Misteri d'Elx* (Elche), still performed each year on 12 and 13 August, dates only from the early seventeenth century in its present form. Like other surviving texts from Valencia and Castellón, this play is intended for performance on the Feast of the Assumption, and makes use of two pieces of stage machinery, the *mangrana*, or gilded cloud, which opens to reveal the angel of the Assumption, and the *araceli,* an aerial platform by which actors may be lowered from Heaven to Earth and raised again in the course of the performance. The use of such devices in itself suggests the strong element of pageantry which is inseparable from these productions. Clearly, it would be wrong to judge the texts of such pieces from a strictly literary point of view: none of them pretends to be more than a libretto, and the test of their value lies in their ability to survive as examples of a genuine popular culture which is no less real at the present day than at the time they were first written down.

Chapter 2

DECADENCE AND ENLIGHTENMENT

Questions of survival and loss are quite crucial to the next major phase of Catalan literature, which runs from about 1500 to the beginning of the nineteenth century. This period is usually known as the 'Decadence', and, however much one may want to qualify the term, one can hardly reject it altogether. From the death of Roiç de Corella to the second half of the nineteenth century, there are no major writers in Catalan and until about a hundred years before this, the literary scene is one of almost unrelieved mediocrity. The reasons for this are complex, but there are several important points to bear in mind: (i) the decline in literature is one of standards, not of quantity; (ii) this decline is specifically literary: other kinds of art, for example, painting and architecture, did not suffer to nearly the same extent, and the eighteenth century in particular produced a number of outstanding intellectuals who wrote in Castilian; (iii) the literary situation does not correspond in any precise way to the pattern of economic prosperity and decline; (iv) nor does it reflect a change in the status of the Catalan language: Catalan remains the official language of the country until 1714, and the teaching of Catalan in schools is not prohibited until 1768.

It is only when one considers the apparent abruptness of the literary decline that a different kind of factor begins to emerge. The fifteenth century, clearly, is a period of considerable achievement, but even here there are signs that the situation is changing for the worse. After 1412, the country is ruled by the Castilian dynasty of the Trastámaras: Castilian becomes the familiar language of the Court, and one sign of this is the number of writers in the second half of the fifteenth century who use both Castilian and Catalan. This situation is confirmed by the union of Castile and Aragon in 1474, and in the sixteenth century, the Court withdraws still further from the Aragonese territories. As a result, the Catalan aristocracy is attracted more and more to the Castilian-speaking Court, while the mercantile classes fail to create a genuine culture of their own. When one reflects that practically any writer of importance before 1500 was connected in some way with the Court, one sees how serious the consequences were for literature. With the disappearance of the chancellory, the chief source of literary criteria was also removed; the desertion of the nobility and a succession of Castilian viceroys helped to complete the process.

Yet this picture is not altogether accurate. For one thing, Valencia, where bilingualism has deeper roots, tended to pull away from the influence of Barcelona: apart from the satirical poets, who continue to flourish until the seventeenth century, Valencian writers after 1500 go over almost entirely to Castilian, often with notable results.[1] And this coincides with a certain disintegration of the Catalan language itself, so that the weakening of linguistic norms leads to an increasing fragmentation of dialects. Many sixteenth-century writers continue to defend the use of Catalan for literary purposes, though never very forcefully, and their efforts merely emphasize the lack of any major talent.

The second qualification is even more important: it should be clear that, in speaking of 'decadence', one is thinking of sophisticated writing. Popular poetry, by contrast, remained the one source of genuine vitality throughout the whole period, even though its full importance was not realized until the nineteenth century. Compared with popular poetry in Castilian, the records are fairly sparse: the splendid examples incorporated in the Catalan translation of the *Decameron* (1429) are exceptionally early survivals; the first serious transcriptions date from the sixteenth century, and several important collections of the time, such as the *Cancionero de Uppsala* (1556) and the *Flor de enamorados* (1562), contain versions of Catalan songs. As in other countries, popular songs were often glossed or imitated by well-known poets: at least one of the pieces in the *Flor de enamorados* is by the dramatist Juan de Timoneda, and this and several others appear in different versions by the Catalan poet Pere Serafi (*c.* 1505–67). Many of these poems are religious: several of the best Catalan Christmas carols, like 'Oh, oh, oh, gran meravella' (Oh, oh, oh, Great Marvel), date from the fifteenth and sixteenth centuries;[2] some of the *goigs*, or poems in praise of the Virgin, are at least as old as this, though their very individual rhythms have continued to attract serious poets up to the present day.[3]

---

[1] In the sixteenth and early seventeenth centuries there is a whole school of Valencian dramatists which includes Juan de Timoneda (*d.* 1583), Rey de Artieda (1549?–1613?), Cristóbal de Virués (1550–1609) and Guillén de Castro (1569–1631). The only Barcelona writer of any consequence in this period is the poet Juan Boscán (1474?–1542).

[2] This and a number of other carols were collected in the *Cançoneret Rovirosa* of 1507. See Josep Romeu, *Cançons nadalenques del segle XV, ENC* (Barcelona, 1949) and the same author's study, *Les nadales tradicionals, estudi i crestomatia* (Barcelona, 1952).

[3] The traditional *goig* is composed in hexasyllabic quatrains, with alternate masculine and feminine rhymes, e.g.:

> Al goig e ab alegria,
> Senyor, del naixement,
> lausem Santa Maria
> et Déus omnipotent.

(With joy and happiness, Lord, at Your birth, we praise the Virgin Mary and Almighty God.)

The other great source of popular poetry is the ballad: unlike their Spanish counterparts, Catalan ballads were not seriously collected until the nineteenth century, though it is clear that many of those which survive were composed as early as the sixteenth. Though their history is often difficult to reconstruct, two things seem certain: they make little or no use of episodes from medieval Catalan history, and the majority show a strong French or Castilian influence. Nevertheless, some of the finest Catalan ballads, like the *Comte Arnau* (Count Arnau) and *La dama d'Aragó* (The Lady from Aragon), are almost certainly of native origin, and from the seventeenth century to the nineteenth ballad-making appears as a natural response to historical events, from the anti-Castilian revolt of 1640 to the Napoleonic Wars.

The only kind of literature which continues to flourish after 1500, therefore, is precisely the one which does not depend on the existence of a Court or of a cultured middle class. When one turns to sophisticated writing, the situation is very different. To put it briefly, Catalan literature, which seems on the point of adapting itself to the Renaissance in the fifteenth century, fails to keep pace with the full expansion of vernacular literatures in the sixteenth. What happens in poetry is symptomatic of the whole situation. In the sixteenth century minor poets like Pere Serafí and Joan Pujol continue to write in the style of Ausiàs March, though with none of his power or subtlety. The influence of Petrarch and later Italian poets, on the other hand, fails to dominate the older Provençal tradition, and when it finally does so, in the next century, this is mainly through the conscious imitation of Castilian models. The better poets of the period, in fact, seem curiously divided: Pujol is also the author of an epic poem on the battle of Lepanto (1571); Serafí is not only an imitator of Ausiàs March, but also a composer of emblems and one of the more successful popularizing poets of the time. The best example here is Vicenç Garcia, Rector of Vallfogona (1579/82 –1623), the most skilful sonnet writer of his day, but also the author of a quantity of burlesque and obscene verse which has tended to overshadow his more serious achievement. Within his limits, Vicenç Garcia is a talented satirist, with occasional undertones of melancholy. Nor can one blame him for imitating Góngora and Quevedo: far better models, certainly, than the tired conventions of the troubadours. His basic failure lies deeper than questions of derivativeness; what is so conspicuously lacking in his work is any sense of the real seriousness of poetry. And with this goes an inevitable coarsening of language: however much one sympathizes with his attempt to enlarge the poetic vocabulary of his time, the fact is that his works are full of unassimilated Castilianisms and unnatural twists of syntax.[4]

---

[4] The opening quatrain of one of his best-known sonnets shows some of the difficulties:
           Ab una pinta de marfil polia
           sos cabells de finíssima atzabeja,

The only seventeenth-century poet who seems aware of the need to restore the dignity of the Catalan language is Francesc Fontanella (1615–*c*. 1680/85), a more skilful imitator of Garcilaso and Góngora, and the author of a pastoral *comedia, Amor, firmesa i porfia* (Love, Firmness and Persistence), in the manner of Calderón, which represents a serious, though unsuccessful, attempt to create a new type of Catalan theatre. As for prose, it is curious that one of the few books of any merit – Riquer calls it 'the most important prose work of the decadence' – should be a forgery: the *Libre dels feyts d'armes de Catalunya* (Book of Feats of Arms of Catalonia) published under the name of Bernat Boades, an early fifteenth-century rector of Blanes, but actually composed by a later historian from the same town, Fra Joan Gaspar Roig i Jalpí (1624–91). This work, which continued to deceive scholars until half a century ago, is written in a pastiche of fifteenth-century Catalan and presented with a background of circumstantial evidence which must have seemed very convincing at the time. The following, for example, is part of a description of Jaume I:

> Mas empero ell fo bon Rey qui regi lo seu Reyalme el comtat de Barcelona e tota la demes terra, e nauem molt bones ordonances que ell fae en Catalunya per lo bon regiment dels catalans, e fo molt bellicoros e guerrejador, e de la sua persona molt alt e molt dispost, e molt bell de cara e de cors, e de molt bona paraula, e casi be tostemps parlaua ab la nostra lengua catalana, car lauors aquesta era la mes polida en Spanya. E axi mateix fo molt saui e molt letrat, car ell per la sua gran virtut hauia depres en la sua puericia no tan solament saber manejar les armes, e tirar la ballesta, e jugar la lança, e be servirsen de la scona o de la spasa, e de les altres armes, mas encara bones letres, e de la sagrada Scriptura, e daltres moltes coses bones, axi com sen pertanyia a un Rey Darago e comte de Barcelona …

> (But he was a good King, who ruled his kingdom well – the county of Barcelona and the rest of his lands – and we have inherited from him excellent decrees which he made in Catalonia for the good government of the Catalans, and he was very bellicose and warlike, and very tall and well disposed in his person, and very fair in face and body, and of excellent speech, and he spoke almost all the time in our Catalan tongue, for in those days it was the most elegant in the whole of Spain.

> a qui los d'or més fi tenen enveja,
> en un terrat la bella Flora un dia.

(Literally: One day, on a flat roof, Flora was polishing with a comb her hair of finest jet, of which that of finest gold is envious.) Both situation and diction suggest a weak imitation of Góngora. Apart from an obvious Castilianism like 'atzabeja' (= azabache) and the clumsy repetition of 'finíssima … més fi', the third line is rhythmically very lame, and the hyperbaton of the fourth sounds much more forced in Catalan than it would in Spanish.

And in the same way he was very wise and learned, for through his great virtue he had in his youth not only learned to manage weapons and to shoot the crossbow and fight with a lance, and to use the javelin or the sword and other arms, but had studied good books and the Holy Scriptures and other excellent things, as was fitting for a King of Aragon and Count of Barcelona ...)

The actual literary merits of the *Libre dels feyts* are modest but genuine: the whole point of the forgery, however, was to provide evidence of the past greatness of Catalonia at a time when the future of the country was in the balance after the War of Separation of 1640–51. And, seen in this light, it takes its place in a debate which gathers momentum in the course of the eighteenth century and is eventually carried into the Romantic period.

With the eighteenth century, the whole tone of Catalan culture changes once the intellectual life of the country moves into the orbit of the Enlightenment. At first, the signs are unpromising: the reprisals taken against Catalonia after the War of the Spanish Succession (1700–14) threatened to abolish its national identity altogether; the suppression of the autonomous government and the existing Catalan universities, together with the restrictions on the use of the Catalan language imposed by the *Decreto de Nueva Planta* (1716), were severe blows to what cultural life remained. Yet, even before 1700, there are signs of a revival of interest in civic and political questions among the professional classes and, despite the very real obstacles of the early eighteenth century, the continuity of the movement is never really broken.

The beginnings of the Catalan Enlightenment are tentative and unspectacular: one can point, however, to the growing importance of the University of Valencia and its connections with the newly established University of Cervera, or to the work of individuals like the Valencian historiographer Jacint Segura (1668–1749?) and the scholar and lawyer Gregori Mayans i Siscar (1699–1782). Nor should one overestimate the fact that most of the ideological writing of the time is in Castilian: for the most part, the language seems to have been regarded merely as an instrument of communication, without any real political implications. It is more to the point to notice the way in which the general current of ideas seems to lead naturally to the kind of defence of the Catalan language one finds in the second half of the century, culminating in the first modern Catalan grammar, the *Gramàtica i apologia de la llengua catalana* of Josep Pau Ballot (1815). After 1750, the growing concern with Catalan tradition is backed by the founding of new institutions: the *Real Academia de Buenas Letras* (1752), the *Junta de Comercio de Barcelona* (1758) and the *Academia de Ciencias* (1764). And above all, perhaps, one senses a new feeling of confidence in the commer-

cial society of Barcelona, especially after the opening-up of trade with the
South American colonies in 1778.

The impact of all this on the literature of the time is fairly oblique. As
in the rest of the Peninsula, there is a strong contrast between the vitality
of ideas and the relative mediocrity of imaginative writing. What is argu-
ably the best prose of the time, the *Calaix de sastre* (Box of Oddments)
of Rafael d'Amat i Cortada, Baron of Maldà (1746–1818), remained
unpublished for the best part of a century, and there is still no complete
edition. These memoirs, which run to sixty volumes, covering the period
1769–1816, contain vivid and detailed descriptions of contemporary
events and are a mine of information concerning the social life of the
time. There is nothing very personal or introspective about them: the fact
that they were written in Catalan merely suggests that their author was
following an established tradition of humorous writing, and they appear
to have been conceived mainly as a record of popular tastes and happen-
ings. Whatever their aims, they show gifts of observation and narrative
skill which, in a different age, might have been the makings of an excellent social novelist, but which, under the circumstances, probably
reached only a very small circle of readers.

For the most part, imaginative writing in the eighteenth century means
poetry. Apart from the mass of popular verse on political and historical
themes, most serious poetry of the time follows the prevailing Spanish
modes. In the second half of the century, the last traces of the Baroque
disappear in a wave of neo-classicism. Most of this poetry is tedious and
badly written, though occasionally, as in the verse tragedies of the
Menorcan writer Joan Ramis (1746–1819), one finds something which can
compare with the best European models of the time.[5] This neo-classical
phase, however, is interrupted by the French Revolution and the Napoleonic
Wars, and the serious literary revival of the 1820s and 30s takes place under
the influence of Romanticism.

The transition from three centuries of decadence to the nineeenth-
century revival was anything but abrupt, and it is now quite clear that,
without the modest achievements of the eighteenth century, there would

---

[5] The appearance of a figure like Ramis is a sign of the distinctive cultural situation
which existed in Menorca during the eighteenth century. From 1713 to 1781, apart from a
brief French occupation in the course of the Seven Years War (1756–63), the island was
under British rule, and enjoyed a period of commercial prosperity in marked contrast to
conditions on the mainland. One result of this was the rise of an enlightened and cosmopolitan middle class, interested in maintaining economic and cultural connections with
England, France and Italy. Ramis himself was one of the founders of the *Societat de Cultura
de Maó* (1778–85), whose discussions ranged from archaeology and the natural sciences to
the works of Addison, Voltaire and Young. Once Menorca reverted to the Crown of Castile
in 1783, this movement came to an end, and Ramis himself virtually ceased to write in
Catalan.

have been very little to follow on later. There are at least two ways of misconstruing the history of Catalan literature between 1500 and 1800: one is to ignore the existence of popular traditions altogether; the other is to suppose that the vitality of such traditions was sufficient in itself to ensure the renewal of literary values. What was needed, of course, was a serious awareness of these cultural resources, the grounds for which were prepared in the eighteenth century by a whole series of minor writers and scholars who could scarcely have realized how important their work was to be for the future of Catalan literature.

Chapter 3

THE NINETEENTH CENTURY

I. The Early Romantics

In terms of actual achievement, the revival of Catalan literature in the early nineteenth century owes almost everything to the Romantic Movement. As early as the 1790s, in the pages of the newly founded *Diario de Barcelona*, one finds a growing interest in the remote and the exotic, and a little later, the traditionalist reaction provoked by the Napoleonic Wars brings with it a heightened sense of the national past which is easily assimilated into the ideology of the time. None of this is very consciously formulated before the 1820s: the first landmark is the publication of a magazine, *El Europeo* (1823–24), whose contributors describe themselves as an 'escuela romántico-espiritualista'. Two of the editors of *El Europeo*, Bonaventura Carles Aribau and Ramón López Soler, were eventually to become leading figures in the *Renaixença*, as the literary movement came to be known, the first as the writer of the first important Romantic poem in Catalan, and the second as the author of *Los bandos de Castilla* (1830), a historical novel in the manner of Scott, whose preface is one of the earliest manifestos of Catalan Romanticism. In spite of its short life, *El Europeo* reflects very accurately the major preoccupations of the moment: the aesthetics of Friedrich Schlegel, the vogue of Mme de Staël and Chateaubriand, the revaluation of Shakespeare, and, above all, the achievement of Goethe, Schiller, Scott and Manzoni. What was lacking at this stage was any serious attempt to write in the Catalan language, the whole status of which was to remain in doubt for the next few decades. Because of this, the work of those Catalan authors who continue to use Spanish is an important index to the sensibility of the time, and occasionally, as in the poetry of Manuel de Cabanyes (1808–33) and Pau Piferrer (1818–48) or the historical novels of Cosca Vayo (1804?–?) and Juan Cortada (1805–68), it contains some of the most original writing of the period.[1]

The language problem is partly a matter of audience: it is significant that the first successful plays in Catalan were not staged until the 1860s and that

---

[1]   See R.F. Brown, 'The Romantic Novel in Catalonia', *HR*, XIII (1945), 294–323. For Cabanyes and Piferrer, see E.Allison Peers, *A History of the Romantic Movement in Spain* (Cambridge, 1940), 2 vols., I, pp. 312–14 and II, pp. 228–9 respectively.

the first nineteenth-century novels of any serious literary merit came even later. In the early years of the *Renaixença*, the only new works to achieve any kind of public success were the bilingual *sainetes* of Josep Robrenyo (*c.* 1780–1838), an actor-dramatist who, despite his lack of literary pretensions, deserves the credit for having created a genuinely popular theatre in touch with the events of the time.[2]

With this one exception, the literary revival is exclusively concerned with poetry, and with poetry of a fairly conservative kind. The iconoclastic, anti-bourgeois note which appears in the Romantic literature of other countries is almost entirely missing from the *Renaixença*. In the 1830s, there was at least the possibility of a more radical, socially orientated type of writing which for various reasons – lack of cohesion, loss of nerve, the exile or death of some of its leading advocates – failed to materialize. Both before and after this, the movement is dominated by middle-class ideals and by the nostalgic evocation of a partly legendary past. It is symptomatic, for instance, that so many Catalan poets and critics of the Romantic period should refer to their language as 'lemosí', with all the troubadour overtones that the word conveys, and that the symbol of their group spirit should be the restoration of the interrupted tradition of the *Jocs florals* in 1859.[3]

The first nineteenth-century Catalan poem of any importance, Aribau's ode *La pàtria* (1833), owed its effect not only to its genuine literary merits, but also to the quite remarkable way in which it condensed the feelings of nostalgia towards the country and the language which run through a number of slightly earlier poems. Curiously enough, the motive behind the poem was purely circumstantial. Aribau was one of a number of writers who were invited to compose poems in various languages as a birthday tribute to the Madrid banker Gaspar de Remisa; the task of writing a poem in Catalan fell to Aribau, and the whole tone of his ode comes from his anxious attempt to compete with more securely established languages. There is no denying his success: the degree of linguistic refinement which he achieved is enough to make the poem a landmark, and its publication in the Barcelona literary magazine *El vapor* must have persuaded many readers that it was still possible to express a common mood with dignity and restraint.[4]

---

[2] See Josep Robenyo, *Teatre revolucionari*, ed. J.-Ll. Marfany, *AC* (Barcelona, 1965) and also J.M. Poblet, *Les arrels del teatre català* (Barcelona, 1965), pp. 41–71.

[3] 'Lemosí' or 'llemosí' = French 'limousin', the name given to one of the areas most closely associated with medieval Provençal poetry, and for a long time wrongly regarded as synonymous with 'Catalan'. *Jocs florals* (literally 'Floral games') was the title originally given to the literary contests organized in the fourteenth century by the *Sobregaia companhia dels set trobadors* (see above, p. 32), in which the winners were awarded jewels in the form of flowers. The *Jocs* are still celebrated regularly at the present day, though for a long time after the Civil War it was not possible to hold them in Catalonia itself.

[4] See Carles Riba, 'Entorn de les trobes d'Aribau', *Obres completes*, II, pp. 433–54.

Aribau's example was followed a few years later by Joaquim Rubió i Ors (1818–99), one of the outstanding scholars of the time. The poems published by Rubió under the pseudonym 'Lo Gaiter del Llobregat' represent a much more conscious attempt to re-establish the tradition of Catalan verse. The first nineteen of the poems were originally published in the *Diario de Barcelona* between 1839 and 1840 and later collected in two volumes (1841 and 1858), which contain a total of sixty poems. Though one misses the energy of Aribau, one can still admire the tact and skill with which Rubió adapts the gentler type of Romantic theme to his own language while avoiding the kind of linguistic purity which would have made his poems inaccessible to a popular audience. Their initial success was exactly what Catalan poetry needed at this stage, and the prefaces to the two volumes of *Lo Gaiter* are an accurate measure of their effect at the time. In the first, Rubió proclaims the need to create a new literature which will reflect the spiritual independence of the Catalan people. At this point, he admits that he is an almost solitary figure; seventeen years later, in the second preface, he is able to refer to a whole series of new poets who are following his example.

Characteristically, a number of these poets, like Víctor Balaguer (1824–1901) and Manuel Milà i Fontanals (1818–84), are also scholars, whose serious interest in history and popular traditions makes itself felt in a great deal of the patriotic poetry of the period. The turning point comes with the restoration of the *Jocs florals* in 1859: before this, it is difficult to speak of a school of Catalan poetry, but from now on, there is a much greater sense of collective enterprise, as well as an assured audience and easier means of communication. For all this, the *Jocs florals* had their drawbacks: the motto which summarized their aims – 'Pàtria, Fe, Amor' – encouraged countless untalented poets to express themselves in naïve and conventional terms and, at their worst, they merely confirmed and exaggerated the basic conservatism of the *Renaixença*. Yet their historical importance is beyond question; without them, it would probably have taken much longer for the new poetry to find an audience and, above all, they provided a starting point for those writers of the next generation – Verdaguer, Oller and Guimerà – whose work was to render their further existence superfluous.

II. Verdaguer

At the *Jocs florals* of 1877, the first prize was awarded to an epic poem in ten cantos, the *Atlàntida* of Jacint Verdaguer (1845–1901). Nothing could have prepared the audience for a poem of such scope and originality, and its reception immediately established its author as the first major Catalan poet of the nineteenth century. Verdaguer at the time was a young priest with country roots who, because of ill health, had spent several years as chaplain to a transatlantic shipping company, an experience which had encouraged him to complete a long poem on the destruction of Atlantis begun some years earlier and set aside. After this initial success, he wrote a second epic, *Canigó* (1885), as well as a number of other long poems and collections of lyrics. His later years were clouded by scandal: an over-zealous interest in exorcism and extravagant acts of charity which involved him in serious debt brought him into conflict with the ecclesiastical authorities, and for a time he was suspended from his duties as a priest. None of this, however, affects the achievement of his poetry or the esteem in which he was held by his contemporaries, and the whole episode points more to the basic simplicity of Verdaguer's temperament than to any lack of religious vocation.

Seen at this distance, the attempt to write epic poetry in the second half of the nineteeth century may seem naive and anachronistic. Certainly it suggests Verdaguer's isolation as a poet, though paradoxically it was this isolation which enabled him to rise above the existing poetic tradition. At the same time, neither the *Atlàntida* nor *Canigó* is in any sense an academic poem, and what saves them is the sheer energy of their vision and the language which matches it. This is not to deny their debts to other writers: the sources of the *Atlàntida*, for example, include Plato, Nieremberg, the early chroniclers of America and several nineteeth-century naturalists and explorers. What is surprising is the assurance with which Verdaguer knits his materials into an intensely personal rendering of the basic myth. In the final version of the poem, the story of Hercules and the destruction of Atlantis is told to the young Columbus, so that the discovery of the New World appears to restore the cosmic unity which was broken by the legendary disaster. Read purely as a narrative, the poem has its faults: its protagonists – Hercules, Hesperis and Columbus – are insufficiently charac-terized, and the Columbus episode is joined awkwardly to the central myth. But the real unity of the poem, one can argue, lies deeper: in a sense, its underlying theme is power, and Verdaguer's Romantic affinities are nowhere clearer than in his attempt to fuse the pagan and Christian worlds in a pattern of cosmic retribution and renewal. The most memorable passages of the *Atlàntida* are those which describe the fate of the corrupt yet beautiful civilization of Atlantis:

> Mes ja, pels llamps i onades arrabassats, sortien
> de Calpe els esgardissos i arrels a l'ample espai
> en daus cairuts i pannes que sa buidor omplien,
> l'hermosa llum a veure que no vegeren mai.
>
> I esgarrifats del caos, s'engorguen altra volta
> damunt carreus que els feien ahir de fonament,
> i els antres tenebrosos d'aquella mar revolta
> retronen i s'escruixen al gran capgirament.

De les gentils Hespèrides lo tàlem s'aclofava,
llurs cims, desarrelant-se, s'asseuen en les valls,
i en aücs horrorosos i gemegô esclatava,
com dona que en mal part llança els darrers badalls.

(But now, torn from their bed by waves and lightning, the sharp rocks and
foundations of Calpe [i.e. of Gibraltar, one of the two Pillars of Hercules]
emerge into the vast space, filling its void with their sheer blocks and
slabs, to see the beautiful light they had never seen before. And terrified
by the chaos, they plunge down again on stones which yesterday served
them as base, and among the dark caverns of the raging sea they thunder
and grind in the great upheaval. The marriage bed of the Hesperides sinks
down, their summits, breaking free from their roots, settle into the valleys,
and Atlantis bursts into terrible shrieks, like a woman in childbirth who
utters her dying groans.)

Such a passage conveys very powerfully the ugliness and terror which are
part of the spectacle of human weakness. This is to some extent a matter of
language: images like 'el sol caduc, a palpes buscant sos cabells rossos' (the
ageing sun, groping for his fair hair), or 'cremant com teranyines els núvols
de l'hivern' (burning the winter clouds like spiders' webs), have a visionary
sweep which at the same time is rooted in direct observation. The driving
force behind them comes from a clear-cut sense of good and evil in which
there is no place for ironies or ambiguities; again, the kind of effect which
would hardly be possible in a more sophisticated writer, yet is one of the
surest signs of Verdaguer's integrity as a poet.

Canigó, his second epic, is closer to the preoccupations of earlier
Romantic writers in that it deals with the legendary origins of Catalonia.
Again, there is a direct confrontation of pagan and Christian themes: the folk
tale atmosphere which surrounds the enchantment of a young Christian
knight by the mountain spirits of the Pyrenees is set against the Moorish
invasion of Roussillon, and the final defeat of the pagan spirits is symbolized by the founding of the Benedictine monastery of Sant Martí del Canigó.
Part of Verdaguer's intention, clearly, was to convey the workings of Providence in the formation of the Catalan national consciousness. The epic
dimension of the poem comes from his deliberate attempt to re-create the
spirit of the *chansons de geste*; compared with the *Atlàntida*, however, much
more importance is given to the lyrical episodes and to the reworking of
popular poems and legends. This makes for a degree of intimacy which is
unusual in a poem of this scope. Verdaguer's heroes are continually seen in
the act of contemplating a landscape which, despite its almost mystical
significance, bears a dense weight of local associations and specific detail:

A l'arribar al caire de la serra,
de Guifre i sos guerrers ell se recorda.
Gira ab recança la mirada enrera;

lo Rosselló a sos ulls que bell se mostra
voltat d'una filera d'alimares
que d'una a una en cada cim se posen!
En cada cap de puig dels que rodegen
la plana de Ruscino, hi ha una torre,
una torre gentil que al cel arriba
per abastar l'estrella ab què s'enjoia.

(When he comes to the ridge of the mountains, he remembers Guifre and
his troops. Regretfully he looks back; how beautiful Roussillon seems to
his eyes, encircled by a line of beacons, set one by one on every peak. On
each hilltop which surrounds the plain of Ruscino, there is a tower, a fair
tower which reaches to the sky, bearing aloft the star which crowns it like
a jewel.)

Because of this, *Canigó* is a more immediate poem than the *Atlàntida*,
and the actions of the human characters are interwoven with the processes of
an intensely animated landscape. In a sense, the Pyrenees themselves are the
real protagonists of the poem, and it is they who embody the conflict
between the symbolic world of Christianity and the densely populated
nature of pagan myth. Artistically, the richness of the poem depends on its
being able to make the most of both worlds: the sense of national purpose
and epic severity which come with the triumph of Christianity impose themselves on the disordered beauty of the pagan supernatural, but only after this
has provided the poem with its most luxuriant descriptions.

Between them, *Canigó* and the *Atlàntida* represent the height of
Verdaguer's achievement in the long poem. The range of their language and
vocabulary are unequalled in later Catalan poetry, and their appearance in
the last quarter of the nineteenth century established beyond any doubt the
possibilities of Catalan as a modern literary language. Verdaguer's shorter
poems, which run into several hundreds, are more closely linked to his religious vocation. A great many of them fall into the category of unpretentious
and undemanding devotional verse, yet even at his most conventional,
Verdaguer writes out of a sure sense of the values and language of popular
poetry, as in these lines from 'La Rosa de Jericó' (The Rose of Jericho):

En sa cambreta humil
pregant està Maria,
Maria està pregant
mentres lo món dormia.
Lo sol a l'Orient
per veure-la sortia.
Ella no el mira, no,
sol més bonic somnia;
lo sol que està esperant
mai més se li pondria.

(Mary is praying in her humble room, Mary is praying while the world
was sleeping. The sun in the East came out to see her. She does not look at
it, no, she dreams of a lovelier sun; the sun she is waiting for will never
set for her.)

His best collections of lyrics, like *Flors del Calvari* (1896) and *Aires del
Montseny* (1901), are more original. The first of these contains the poems
written in the course of his difficulties with the Church; in the second, which
seems to look back elegiacally over the whole of his past experience, he
achieves a conversational tone which is unlike anything in his earlier verse.
It is difficult to generalize about such a large and varied body of work. A
great deal has been written about Verdaguer's mysticism, though this hardly
seems the right word to describe a poetry which dwells so consistently on
the beauty of the natural world. What binds together both the popular and
religious strains in his verse is the kind of Franciscan simplicity, verging at
times on gaiety, which one find in these verses from *Aires del Montseny*:

> M'estic a l'hostal
> de la Providència,
> servit com un rei
> per mà de la reina.
> Ella em dóna el vi
> de la vinya seva:
> ella em dóna el pa,
> me'l dóna i me'l llesca

(I am at the inn of Providence, served like a king by the queen's own
hand. She gives me wine from her own vine; she gives me bread, gives
and cuts it for me.)

The final image could hardly be simpler, yet, as Carles Riba has noted,[5]
the verb 'llesca' brings with it a sense of the whole context of daily living.
This, one may feel, is traditional writing in the best sense, in that it draws on
a range of experience which inheres in the words themselves, and Verdaguer
is the first poet in modern times to be fully aware of the communal resources
of the Catalan language.

III. Narcís Oller

The successes of the *Renaixença* were almost entirely confined to poetry.
In their early years, the *Jocs florals* did a certain amount to encourage prose
writing, but it is doubtful whether on their own they could have created the
novel-reading public which is so clearly lacking before the 1870s. Predict-

---

5   See Carles Riba, 'Pròleg a una antologia de Verdaguer', *OC*, p. 272.

ably, the majority of mid-nineteenth-century fiction belongs to the *costumbrista* school, whose most talented representative in Catalonia is Emili Vilanova (1840–1905).[6] What was badly needed at this stage was a writer capable of making the transition from the small-scale *quadre de costums* to the full-length novel of society. In Spain, this transition had already been achieved by Galdós and other novelists; in Catalonia, the crucial moment came with the emergence of a complex and distinctive Restoration society which felt itself, however superficially, to be part of the European scene.

It is this European quality which strikes one in the work of Narcís Oller (1845–1930), the one really gifted Catalan novelist of the late nineteenth century. Like other writers of his generation, he began to write in Castilian, and it was only after attending the *Jocs florals* of 1877 – the occasion on which Verdaguer first read his *Atlàntida* – that he seems to have been convinced of the value of Catalan as a literary medium. Two years later, he published his first collection of stories, *Croquis del natural* (Sketches from Nature), and in 1882, the first of his four long novels, *La papallona* (The Butterfly), established him as the leading prose writer of the day.

Despite this success, Oller never regarded himself as a professional man of letters. His early years were spent in Valls (Tarragona), a provincial background which he used to great effect in his second novel, *Vilaniu* (1885). His closest friend at this stage was his cousin, Josep Yxart (1852–95), eventually to become one of the best critics of his generation, and one of the people whom Oller introduced into Barcelona literary society after he had permanently settled there in the early 1870s.[7] The later part of Oller's career was uneventful. Except for occasional visits to Paris, he continued to work as a lawyer until almost the end of his life: his last novel, *Pilar Prim*, was published in 1906; his literary memoirs, *Memòries literàries: història dels meus llibres*, break off at this same year and, apart from a few fragments, were only published for the first time in 1962.

Behind Oller's final silence there lies an awareness of a changing artistic climate in which there no longer seemed a place for his own kind of fiction. As he writes in *Memòries literàries*: 'L'alba del segle XX m'atrapà en un

---

[6]   Vilanova is the first real humorist of the *Renaixença*. His sketches of city life are finely observed, and contain passages of excellent dialogue. For the most part, however, they are lacking in depth, and one misses the sense of form which is the mark of the genuine short story writer. See Antoni Vilanova's preface to the *Obres completes* (Barcelona, 1949).

[7]   On Yxart, see the interesting essay by Joan Triadú, 'Josep Yxart en el seu temps', included in *La literatura catalana i el poble* (Barcelona, 1961). Oller's friendship with Yxart and Joan Sardà (1851–98), the two outstanding professional critics of the time, had a lasting effect on his own work, and the loss which he felt at their early deaths certainly contributed to the decline in his literary production after 1900.

estat de depressió moral terrible' (The dawn of the twentieth century found me in a terrible state of moral depression), and, after referring to the deaths of Yxart and Sardà, the other notable literary critic of the time, he goes on:

> [S]entint-me absolutament refractari a les temes i tendències que anaven dibuixant-se en el nou art batejat llavors de modernisme, m'entrà un descoratjament i tot ensems un fàstic tan gran per a seguir conreuant les lletres.

> (Feeling myself in complete opposition to the themes and tendencies which were taking shape in the new art then called *modernisme*, I was filled with discouragement and at the same time with a great revulsion towards the idea of continuing to write.)

As we shall see, it was not only *Modernisme* which ran counter to Oller's concept of the novel; the movement known as *Noucentisme* which succeeded it virtually ignored Oller's achievement in favour of a narrowly aesthetic approach to fiction.

Though his production is relatively small, there is an air of inevitability about Oller's novels which corresponds to the major phases of his own career. Thus, *La papallona* reflects his life as a student, *Vilaniu* the early background of Valls, *La febre d'or* (Gold Fever) his professional life in Barcelona, and *Pilar Prim* the complex vision of the experienced writer. It was to be expected that some of Oller's early critics should refer to him as a Naturalist, though Zola's preface to the French translation of *La papallona* was more perceptive. Speaking of Oller's gift for seeing things 'à travers un talent attendri', he observes that 'Barcelone s'agite dans les descriptions avec une réalité intense, tandis que les personnages marchent un peu au-dessus de la terre'. Oller's own comment on first reading Zola is also significant: it revealed to him, he says, 'el gran contingut de poesia que conté a voltes el natural per qui sap observar-lo' (the great amount of poetry which the natural at times contains for anyone capable of observing it).

Taken together, these remarks point to the strong current of Romantic idealism which runs through all Oller's work. Compared with Zola himself, he is more interested in individuals and much less in generalizations about society. Nothing could be further from Oller than Zola's peculiar kind of determinism: his marvellous sense of detail is never allowed to obscure the development of the plot. With the exception of *Pilar Prim*, all Oller's novels are *romans à thèse*, in which the triumph of moral justice tends to be achieved against the grain of events. This is particularly true of an early work like *La papallona*; in *Vilaniu*, the problem is more complex, in so far as the social milieu is more finely observed. Even so, it comes as no surprise to find that the more personal parts of the novel are based on an earlier story, *Isabel de Galceran*, which in turn reflects a sentimental episode from the author's own youth. Because of this, the accurate presentation of provincial society is at odds with the romantically idealized intrigue, and this conflict tends to undermine the realistic intentions of the whole. Oller, always his own best critic, seems to have realized at the time that he was attempting the impossible, and in his third novel, *La febre d'or* (1890–93), confined himself strictly to the observation of contemporary life. In many ways, this is his most ambitious work: as a picture of a society obsessed by financial speculation it could hardly be surpassed, and its documentary accuracy is completely convincing. Yet even here, there is a central flaw, in that the basic plot – the story of the financial rise and fall of a single family – is hardly strong enough to convey the full dimensions of the social drama. The final twist in the fortunes of the protagonist, Gil Foix, is touching and pathetic at a personal level, but takes place at several removes from the society which is so brilliantly analysed in the rest of the novel. What is lacking, ultimately, is a strength of characterization which would focus and dominate the realistic observation of a whole community.

No such criticisms affect the best of his shorter fiction, which shows an astonishing maturity from quite early in his career. Both *El transplantat* (The Man who was Transplanted; 1879) and *L'escanyapobres* (The Skinflint; 1884) achieve a perfect balance between description and plot, as if the need for economy had brought Oller's art to its finest pitch, something which he found it much harder to realize in his longer novels. Though the latter have tended to overshadow the shorter pieces, these clearly form an integral part of his work, and the fact that they include several masterpieces is not to be ignored.

In his last important works of fiction, the long story *La bogeria* (Madness; 1899) and the novel *Pilar Prim* (1906), Oller seems consciously to depart from the realistic formula of his earlier novels. Looking back on this period in his memoirs, he is aware that a new generation of novelists with more literary intentions is beginning to compete with his own, less reflective, kind of realism. Touchingly, and without the least sense of irony, he compares himself, not to the professionals like Daudet and Zola, but to another amateur novelist – Stendhal. Yet, just before his final silence, Oller seems to be on the verge of creating a distinctly more modern type of fiction. *La bogeria* traces the mental development of a psychopath through the intermittent memories of a first-person narrator, and in *Pilar Prim*, the most subtle of his novels, the entire plot is centred on the reactions of the characters themselves, to the almost total exclusion of naturalistic observation. The young widow of the title is the victim both of her husband's will and of a hostile society which condemns her emotional involvement with a younger man. Unlike Oller's other novels, *Pilar Prim* contains no moral: instead, he implies that, however much the heroine is dishonoured socially, she will be saved from moral degradation by the integrity of her own feelings. The conclusion of *La bogeria* had been pessimistic: in the asylum, as in life itself, 'L'ordre, el reglament, una habitud ordinària, el lucre, hi ofegaran el sentiment' (Order, rules, ordinary habit, financial profit, will always stifle feeling). In his last novel, Oller seems to qualify this and to suggest, what the more romantic side of his nature appears always to have believed, that the true measure of an individual lies in his feelings, and that these will always be the ultimate guarantee of his authenticity.

IV. Guimerà

The late 1870s are also crucial years in the history of the Catalan theatre. In the first half of the century, full-length plays in Catalan are non-existent: the typical productions of the time, both amateur and professional, continue the eighteenth-century tradition of the *sainete*, though occasionally, as in the work of Josep Robrenyo (see above, p. 61), there is a genuine attempt at a popular political theatre. Many of these short plays are bilingual: following the tradition, the most popular dramatist of the 1860s, Frederic Soler ('Serafí Pitarra'; 1839–95), defended the use of 'el català que ara es parla' (Catalan as it is now spoken), meaning by this the language of the lower classes of Barcelona. The limitations of such a criterion were severe, and, though many of the plays of this type are of great documentary interest, their literary value is negligible. At the very least, however, they kept the theatre alive through a difficult period, and the tradition of acting and production which grew up around them remained one of the great strengths of the late nineteenth-century drama.

Whatever its actual quality, the Catalan theatre of the time reflects very accurately the growing affluence of the urban middle classes. In 1865, the first full-length play in Catalan – *Tal faràs, tal trobaràs* (What You Do, So You Shall Find), by Eduard Vidal i Valenciano – was produced in Barcelona, and from that point onwards, the middle-class social drama tends to overshadow the more popular *sainete*. This cleavage appears very simply in the career of Soler, who, after establishing himself as the most popular dramatist of the time, followed the example of Vidal and turned over completely to the conventional thesis play.

The first attempts to raise the literary status of the theatre came from a very different direction: the Romantic historical drama. The pioneer here is the poet and historian Víctor Balaguer (see above, p. 62), whose tragedies, particularly those on Catalan themes, are a serious effort to bridge the gap between the theatre and the world of the *Jocs florals*. As plays, they are hardly more than sequences of dramatic monologues spread over a minimal plot; historically, however, they are the only precedents in Catalan for the infinitely more ambitious drama of Guimerà.

Àngel Guimerà (1845–1924) is the one nineteenth-century Catalan dramatist of European stature. His early poems, like *L'any mil* (The Year 1000), already show a Romantic sense of history and an objective vision which seem made for the stage. His first plays, *Gala Placídia* (1879) and *Judit de Welp* (1883), are historical verse dramas in the grand manner – the manner of Victor Hugo and the Spanish Romantics. Even granting a certain derivativeness, their importance in the theatrical context of the time is enormous, and their blank verse has a spaciousness and thrust which leave one in no doubt that a new dramatic language is being created. As for their subjects, perhaps only a writer with Guimerà's unqualified faith in Romantic values would have been capable of working effectively within such terms. The best of his verse plays, *Mar i cel* (Sea and Sky; 1888), has most of the ingredients of a Verdi opera: a young girl destined for a convent, captured on the high seas by a corsair of Othello-like nobility with whom she reluctantly falls in love, and with whom she finally dies at the hands of her sternly repressive father. An absurdly melodramatic plot: yet what gives the play its authority is Guimerà's superb sense of timing, the way in which the verse never fails to rise to a dramatic climax, and the use of creative metaphors which makes the language worth dwelling on for its own sake, as when Blanca, the heroine, reflects on her sheltered childhood:

> I al mur hi vaig pujar des d'una soca.
> Quin goig, mon Déu! … a l'altra part tot eren
> carrers i gent; a sota meu jugaven
> dos nens rossos com l'or; quanta ventura
> en son riure i saltar! Mes, d'una porta
> una dona sortí: fills meus, que arriba
> vostre pare, els va dir, quan ja els alçava
> en sos braços un home … tan ferèstec
> com aquestos ho son, i jo sentia
> ses paraules i besos amorosos …
> i plorava com ell; perquè ell plorava!
> Tot això va passar; coses de nena!
> Ja gran, després, tan sols en la clausura
> he desitjat lo goig d'aquí a la Terra.
> Mes, jo em pregunto avui: què has fet, oh dona,
> per ton Déu i Senyor? …

(And standing on a tree trunk, I looked over the wall. Oh God, what joy! … on the other side there were streets and people; below me, two children fair as gold were playing; what happiness in their laughter and jumping! But then a woman came out of a door: children, your father's coming, she said, as a man already lifted them in his arms … wild, as all men are, and I heard his words and loving kisses … and I wept as he did; for he was weeping! That all passed; childish things! Later, grown up, I have wished for the joy of Earth only in the cloister. But today I ask myself: what have you done for your God and Master? …)

Mar i cel is the last of the verse dramas, and already there are moments when the pressure of the dialogue seems to be forcing it towards prose. Guimerà's next play, *La boja* (The Madwoman; 1890), marked the beginning of a new phase in his work, one which was to include his two masterpieces, *Maria Rosa* (1894) and *Terra baixa* (Lowland; 1897). This phase has often been called 'naturalistic', and, on the surface at least, the contrast with the earlier plays is very striking. If *Mar i cel* suggests Verdi, the theme of *Maria Rosa* – the consequences of a vulgar crime among a group of roadworkers – might have appealed to Hauptmann or Brecht. These rural dramas clearly owe a great deal to direct observation, and the language of the characters is based on an accurate knowledge of provincial speech. If the question of Naturalism arises, it is precisely because of this absolute authenticity of setting and dialogue. Yet, in a sense, these are the most poetic of all Guimerà's plays, and the reason lies partly in their intention. The real power of both *Maria Rosa* and *Terra baixa* comes, not from their realism, but from a simple mythical pattern which is embodied in the lives of their chief protagonists. Both Maria Rosa and Manelic, the shepherd who is the hero of *Terra baixa*, are simple and passionate individuals who are made to suffer cruelly by a cynical piece of deception. Maria Rosa's husband dies in prison after being sentenced for a murder he did not commit, and the real criminal attempts to take his place in her life; Manelic is deceived into marrying Marta, the mistress of the local *cacique*, so that the latter's own marriage may take place without scandal. In each instance, the potential victim escapes from the net in a violent and magnificent gesture of self-assertion, though in *Terra baixa* the break is made much more cleanly than in the earlier play. Cleanly, that is to say, in an idealistic sense: as the play ends, Manelic, having killed the villainous *cacique*, makes for the mountains with Marta in his arms. On the stage, the intensity of this final moment is so great that one hardly pauses to think what the solution in real life might be. A simple and satisfying pattern is completed, and Guimerà's skill is such that he makes it appear to rise quite naturally from the realistic circumstances of the play. Because of this, *Terra baixa* is hardly the genuine tragedy it is sometimes made out to be; Manelic is potentially tragic in that he is an innocent and simple-hearted person who is compelled to recognize the existence of corruption, but it would take a more consistently realistic play, one feels, in order to sustain the tragedy. This is not so much a criticism of the play as an indication that its real interest lies elsewhere: in the pathos of a genuinely good individual who is made to realize that his marriage is based on a lie, yet is able to win his wife's affections by his simple authority.

Guimerà's later plays are more consciously symbolic and generally less convincing than the rural dramas. His most memorable effects are invariably linked to his mastery of the common language, and a play like *La reina jove* (The Young Queen; 1911), despite some powerful moments, really demands a sophisticated, Shavian type of dialogue which is outside his range. This play and others of his final period also tend to suffer from sentimentality, from a kind of social naiveness which is probably central to Guimerà, but which only becomes obtrusive in an urbane setting. These later plays are more openly didactic than the others, and usually in a social sense. And, though the genuineness of Guimerà's social conscience is never in doubt, the evangelical good faith which gave strength to his earlier work often makes his handling of political themes seem merely utopian. Even his weaker plays, however, show a kind of large-scale craftsmanship which was unknown in the Catalan theatre before his time and which has seldom been equalled since. Perhaps this was inevitable: Guimerà's great gifts were basically those of a Romantic artist, and it says a great deal for the integrity of his talent that he was able to translate the power of his original vision into an impressive variety of plays until well after the turn of the century.

V. Modernisme; Rusiñol; Maragall

With Verdaguer, Oller and Guimerà, the *Renaixença* as a serious movement came to an end: each of these writers, by the sheer force of his talent, had extended the range of literary Catalan beyond anything which could have been conceived in the 1860s. From this moment onwards, one can detect a new sense of urgency in the literary situation and, by the closing years of the nineteenth century, the European qualities which already appear in the novels of Oller have spread to other sectors of literature and the arts. This new sensibility of the 1890s came quickly to be known as *Modernisme* or, alternatively, *Decadentisme*, though neither term was very clearly defined. The poet Joan Maragall (1860–1911), in many ways the most clear-sighted critic of the process, saw it as a re-emergence of the Romantic spirit after the interlude of Naturalism. Other statements of the time, like those of Soler i Miquel, confirm what was probably the greatest strength of *Modernisme*, its renewed confidence in the value of artistic intuition.[8] Though their Romantic affinities are clear enough, one can gauge the novelty of the *modernistes* simply by listing the foreign writers who interested them: Carlyle, Ruskin, Nietzsche, Ibsen and Maeterlinck. As might be expected, these influences affected not only literature: the vogue of Maeterlinck, in particular, was used to justify the association of poetry and drama with other arts, and both the painting and the architecture of the time reflect the peculiar medievalism of the Pre-Raphaelites.[9]

---

[8] Josep Soler i Miquel, a close friend of Maragall, committed suicide in 1897 at the age of 36. His short essay, 'Decadentismo', included in his posthumous *Escritos* (1898), concludes: 'De la vulgaridad naturalista, de la verbosidad convencional y hueca, formada y fría, ya reniega el alma, que desea la invención *imaginaria* viviente, la palabra que enuncia sincera'.

[9] *Modernisme* produced one great architect, Antoni Gaudí (1852–1926). It should also

Because of the stress on intuition, the writer or painter is now thought of as someone who conveys his own vision of things, as someone who *intervenes* in reality in order to go beyond mere surface appearances. Yet none of this, of course, can take place in a vacuum. If these are ideal solutions, they need to be worked out in terms of a particular society, and it is here that the whole enterprise of *Modernisme* runs into difficulties. We can put this in the form of a paradox: if society is to be rejected for artistic reasons, how can this same society be regenerated without some kind of social intervention? It is this paradox which accounts for the two competing strands one finds in the early stages of *Modernisme*: what one can roughly call the 'Ivory Tower' attitude which comes to be known as *Decadentisme*, and the 'regenerationist' tendency which eventually becomes bound up with the politics of the turn of the century. And what keeps the paradox alive is the fact that *Modernisme*, far from wanting to impose a superficial cosmopolitanism on a culturally backward country, is out to produce a genuinely *Catalan* culture: one which will be 'modern' in a European sense, but which will also take into account the traditions and pressures of its own society.

One possible landmark is 1898, the year of the Spanish colonial disaster, the year which gave its name to a whole generation of Spanish writers. Yet here the parallel with the rest of Spain is misleading; though there is no doubt that the loss of the last Spanish colonies severely affected the Catalan economy and greatly increased the sense of alienation from the central government, it is equally clear that what I have been calling the 'regenerationist' aspect of *Modernisme* was already firmly established some years before, so that the events of 1898 did not call for any particular readjustment. What *does* seem to happen at this point is that the more positive side of *Modernisme* – the 'vitalist' side, we might say, as against the 'decadent' – begins to find common ground with the more political aspirations of *Catalanisme*. This in itself is a major shift: in the early 1890s, *Catalanisme*, though rather differently conceived, had been the main enemy of *Modernisme*; now, however, the artistic and political fronts start to converge in the general swing towards Catalan autonomy – a movement which will eventually bring about the eclipse of *Modernisme* itself. So, from this point on – roughly the years 1899 to 1906 – *Modernisme* begins to lose its identity as it dissolves into the more general tendencies of *Catalanisme*. One symptom of this is that the cosmopolitan aspect of *Modernisme* gives way to specifically Catalan themes, as in the poems of Maragall's 1900 collection, *Visions i cants* (Visions and Songs). This does not, however, mean the end of *modernista* writing: as we shall see, the first decade of the new century is the great period of the *modernista* novel, just as it continues to see new

be remembered that Picasso spent several years in Barcelona in the late 1890s and was influenced by some of the painters of the time, notably Isidre Nonell (1873–1911).

experiments in *modernista* theatre. Outside literature, nevertheless, there is a different kind of fading away, one which has much more to do with aesthetic taste. Where the other arts are concerned, as Marfany puts it, '*Modernisme* dissolves into modernity pure and simple'.[10] This means that, by the turn of the century, the affluent middle classes of Barcelona – though not, one gathers, great readers – are prepared to invest their wealth in the kind of 'modern' artefacts – buildings, paintings, the decorative arts – which only a few years before they had condemned or ridiculed. And so *Modernisme* threatens to become what it was never intended to be: a 'style', a pretext for conspicuous consumption, something to be assimilated by the very class to whose ideology it was opposed.

The crucial year for *Modernisme* was 1893, or rather the year which runs from September 1892 to September 1893: it is then that the leading journal of the time, *L'Avenç,* intensifies its campaign for modernizing the Catalan language; it is also the year when the poet Joan Maragall begins to write for the *Diario de Barcelona* and when Raimon Casellas, later to write the first *modernista* novel (see below, p. 99), contributes his first piece of art criticism to *La Vanguardia.* And the year ends with the first *Festa modernista*, held at Sitges under the patronage of the writer and painter Santiago Rusiñol (1861–1931), which included a production of Maeterlinck's play *L'Intruse* in a Catalan translation by Pompeu Fabra, later to become the great grammarian of his generation, and a performance of César Franck's Piano Quintet.

As organizer of the *Festes modernistes de Sitges* and as the dominating personality in the group of *Els quatre gats*, the famous *modernista* café, Rusiñol for a time provided the essential focal points of the whole movement. Much of his own literary work, as Maragall clearly saw (see below, p. 77), is characterized by pessimism and *fin-de-siècle* melancholy, the perfect embodiment of so-called *Decadentisme.* His early plays are variations on a theme which is also central to *Modernisme*: the conflict between the artist and society. Thus, in *L'alegria que passa* (Happiness which Passes; 1898), a group of circus artists (representing Freedom and Poetry) is banned by the inhabitants of a small and mediocre town, which thereafter is condemned to live in the realm of prose. By 1902, however, Rusiñol's attitude is beginning to change. In *El pati blau* (The Blue Courtyard), he leaves behind the allegorical dimension of his earlier plays in favour of the strictly realistic treatment of a contemporary situation: the love of a young painter for a girl who eventually dies, leaving him powerless in the face of the rich philistine who finally comes to dominate. Thus art, and the idealism it implies, are in the

---

[10] J.-Ll. Marfany, 'El Modernisme', in *Història de la literatura catalana,* VIII (Barcelona, 1986), p. 123.

end defeated, and there is no final condemnation, as there is in *L'alegria que passa*.

After this, Rusiñol tends to leave behind the question of the artist's relation to society in favour of more popular themes, as in the anti-militaristic satire of *L'Hèroe* (The Hero), produced in the following year – so much so that Marfany is able to describe the Rusiñol of 1903 as an 'ex-*modernista*'.[11]

There is, however, one exception to this: *L'auca del Senyor Esteve* (1907), a minor comic masterpiece which, in its way, is a serious, though unrepeatable, solution to the problems of the *modernista* novel which I shall discuss in the next chapter. The *auca* of the title is the Catalan equivalent of the *aleluya* or popular broadsheet tale, told in cartoon frames, each of which is accompanied by a humorous couplet. The couplets, in Rusiñol's novel, form the chapter headings, and the tale itself describes the rise to prosperity of a family of Barcelona haberdashers. As in other novels of the period, the technique is episodic and fragmentary, yet the deliberate echo of a popular art form creates a distancing effect which allows the author to move easily between satire and nostalgia. And woven into the basic plot for one last time is the theme which relates the whole book to one of the central preoccupations of *Modernisme*, the position of the artist in a society which one side of his nature rejects. Ramonet, Esteve's son, attempts to escape from his family by becoming a *modernista*; at the end of the novel, he is about to embark on his career as a sculptor, yet, ironically, he can only do this with the aid of his uncomprehending father: 'En faré perquè *ell* paga el marbre' (I shall make sculptures because *he*'s paying for the marble). This final compromise between artist and bourgeoisie – something unthinkable to a true *modernista* – means that Ramonet's liberation through art is strictly relative, and the final paradox is both an assertion and a criticism of *modernista* values. (In 1917, Rusiñol produced a stage version, more compact than the novel, which has remained popular to the present day.)

It is Maragall's relations with *Modernisme* which show most clearly the strengths and weaknesses of the movement. As a young man, Maragall had grown up into the Restoration society described in the novels of Oller. In his *Notes autobiogràfiques* of 1885–6, he discusses his misgivings at having embarked on a still uncertain literary career. By 1891, he had begun to make a name as a poet: the tenacity of purpose one senses in the *Notes* had been strengthened by a happy marriage and by friendships with several important writers, among them Yxart and Oller. Also, in one decisive aspect, his literary tastes were already formed: his translation of Goethe's *Römische Elegien* (1888), which seems to have had a liberating effect on the tone and rhythms of his own verse, had been one of the first results of his lifelong

---

[11]   J.-Ll. Marfany, *Aspectes del Modernisme* (Barcelona, 1975), p. 227.

devotion to the German writer, an influence which, at least in his early years, was as much moral as literary.

This sense of affinity with an older writer is one sign of the independence of mind which was to make Maragall the best critic of his generation. In 1890, he joined the staff of the *Diario de Barcelona* as private secretary to the editor, Mañé i Flaquer, a post which he held until 1903. As a journalist, Maragall not only wrote extensively on political and social questions but also reviewed many of the most characteristic productions of the *modernistes*. Much of the interest of his criticism comes from the sympathy he feels for the movement as a whole: his enthusiasm for Ibsen and Maeterlinck is unmistakable, and his reading of Nietzsche marked the beginning of a debate which profoundly influenced some of his later poems. Yet, with a few minor exceptions, the poetry which Maragall wrote at the time is scarcely affected by the prevailing mood, and before long he begins to criticize contemporary literary fashions. In Ibsen and Maeterlinck, for example, he finds on the one hand a rigidity of theme and on the other an excess of sensibility which in both instances lead to a fragmentary vision of life. But it is above all in his criticisms of the plays and stories of Rusiñol that he is able to point to the basic weakness of the whole movement:

> La tristeza [he wrote in 1900] parece ser el resorte estético de nuestro poeta-pintor; el humorismo, la *blague*, tan característico de su personalidad en muchas de sus obras, se nos figura como simple distensión de unos nervios que han vibrado demasiado en la belleza de las cosas tristes ...[12]

These critical pieces of the 1890s are an important stage in Maragall's education as a poet: in diagnosing the lack of vitality in a movement which nevertheless attracted him, he is feeling his way towards the conception of artistic wholeness which underlies the far greater achievement of his own later poems.

Maragall's poems are contained in five volumes: *Poesies* (1895), *Visions i cants* (1900), *Les disperses* (Scatterings; 1903), *Enllà* (Beyond; 1906) and *Seqüències* (Sequences; 1911). His early verse is mainly personal, though in some of the poems on natural themes (*Goigs a la Verge de Núria, La vaca cega* [The Blind Cow]), the balance between inwardness and objectivity already conveys the sense of nature as a source of energy and spiritual renewal which runs through his later work. And in one poem in particular, *Paternal* (1893), written after an anarchist bomb outrage, the idealistic anarchism which he had admired in Nietzsche is confronted with its practical implications in a synthesis which affects both public and private life. The anecdote on which the poem is based is strikingly simple; the poet, shocked

---

[12] 'La obra de Santiago Rusiñol', *Obres completes*, II, p. 130.

by the event he has just witnessed, returns home to find his wife feeding
their young child:

> A cada esclat mortal – la gent trèmula es gira:
> la crudeltat que avança – la por que s'enretira,
>   se van partint el món ...
> mirant el fill que mama, – la mare que sospira,
>   el pare arruga el front

> (At each mortal outburst people turn trembling: advancing cruelty,
> retreating fear divide the world between them ... watching the child
> which sucks the breast of its sighing mother, the father frowns.)

The obvious contrast between public violence and domestic peace is
deceptive. In the last line of the poem, the satisfied child 'laughs barba-
rously' ('riu bàrbarament'), and the phrase echoes the words which
Maragall had used a few years before to express his enthusiasm for the ideas
of Nietzsche: 'una refrescadora vuelta a las grandes sinceridades de la
barbarie'.[13] In the poem, as in his letters of the time, Maragall is clearly
horrified by the practical consequences of an attitude he had once approved.
As he presents it, the collective tragedy is 'barbarous' only in a negative
sense. Yet against its futile destructiveness there is only Nietzsche's own
vision of the child as the supreme creator of new values: 'The child is innocence and forgetfulness, a new beginning, a sport, a self-propelling wheel, a
first motion, a sacred affirmation' (*Also sprach Zarathustra*, 'Of the Three
Metamorphoses'). Maragall himself had translated this passage, and it
seems likely that he remembered it at what was a crucial moment for his
own beliefs. So in his poem, he strikes a precarious balance between the two
kinds of barbarism by suggesting the unconscious optimism of the child,
while condemning the sterility of the public act.

By 1900, Maragall had rejected Nietzsche, though one part of his imagination continued to dwell on themes of violence and heroism. As he wrote in
1902 to Pere Coromines:

> La lluita repugna a la meva naturalesa que en tot cerca un centre
> d'harmonia i serenitat, però els lluitadors m'interessen fortament perquè
> frueixen de la vida un aspecte que m'és desconegut.

> (Conflict is repellent to my nature, which seeks in everything a centre of
> harmony and serenity; but those who take part in it interest me greatly,
> since they enjoy an aspect of life which I have never experienced.)

Two years before this, he had published *Visions*, a group of poems on
Catalan legends and folk heroes, 'figuras de personajes legendarios

---

[13] 'Las leyes' (1893), *Obres completes*, II, p. 399.

catalanes tales cuales puede verlos un poeta de hoy' (letter to Felip Pedrell, 9 January 1900). The last phrase is revealing: Maragall was aware that he was dealing with figures – Joan Garí, the seventeenth-century bandit Serrallonga – who had already attracted earlier poets, including Verdaguer; at the same time, he sees them as a means of exploring the ambivalent feelings about the nature of power which occur in some of his poems and essays of the 1890s.

One of the poems of *Visions, El comte Arnau* (Count Arnau), continued to engage his imagination for the next ten years: encouraged by the composer Pedrell, who set the early sections of the poem to music, Maragall went on to write two further parts, the last of which was published in 1911, a few months before his death.[14] His apparently casual method of composition – he himself admitted that the full sense of the *Comte Arnau* sequence did not come to him until after it was completed – is based on the faith in the power of intuition which he discusses in *Elogi de la paraula* (In Praise of the Word; 1903), his Presidential address to the *Ateneu Barcelonès*, and, more subtly, in the *Elogi de la poesia* (1907). In these and other prose pieces of the same period, Maragall is concerned, not so much with criticism, as with redefining certain key terms – 'word', 'song', 'inspiration', 'people' – which he feels are in danger of becoming clichés. This attempt, which places him in the tradition of Carlyle, Emerson, Matthew Arnold and other nineteenth-century poet-thinkers, is a more conscious application of the organic principle which appears behind his longer poems. Maragall's whole view of poetry emphasized the fragmentary nature of poetic inspiration and the idea that the content of a poem should be dictated by what he calls 'rhythm':

> La força del ritme li duu paraules i sols després veu vostè el pensament que li porten: és la revelacio per la forma.

> (The power of rhythm brings you words, and only later do you see the thought which these convey: this is revelation through form.)

Such ideas explain Maragall's reluctance to *construct* a long poem, and also the fact that his most ambitious poems – the three parts of the *Comte Arnau* and the *Haidé* sequence – are really accumulations of shorter poems, held together by a number of recurring concepts. In Maragall's later work, these concepts come to centre around the twin themes of renunciation and redemption. So, in the final part of *El comte Arnau*, it is quite literally the power of poetry which redeems the legendary protagonist from the damnation he is made to suffer in the folk ballad, and in the *Haidé* poems, human love becomes a metaphor for divine grace.

---

[14] On the genesis of *El comte Arnau*, see Arthur Terry, *La poesia de Joan Maragall* (Barcelona, 1963 and 2000), chapter VI.

These, of course, are Romantic solutions: the striking thing is the way in which their basic assumptions seem rooted in the whole of Maragall's later experience. In 1911, after completing *El comte Arnau*, he wrote:

> Jo no puc concebre l'altra vida deslligada d'aquesta ... El fer de la vida humana, terrena i ultraterrena, una sola cosa, ve-li aquí el sentit més personal meu del poema, que no és sinó la preocupació fonamental de la meva vida.

> (I cannot conceive the next life as separate from this one ... To make human life, both earthly and supernatural, into a single whole, that is my own most personal interpretation of the poem, which is nothing less than the basic preoccupation of my life.)

This is the basic meaning, not only of the *Cant espiritual* (1910), Maragall's most searching meditation on death, but also of one of his finest articles on a civic theme, *La iglésia cremada* (The Burnt-out Church), in which he attempts to come to terms with the anarchist rising of the *Semana trágica* (1909).[15] In all these writings, and in his last major work, the verse play *Nausica* (1908–10), Maragall's thoughts seem to centre on the redeeming power of suffering. And in *Nausica*, based on Goethe's abandoned project for a tragedy on the episode from the *Odyssey*, it is the heroine herself who is made to suffer from the strength of her feelings, but who, through her renunciation of Ulysses, achieves a nobler conception of love in which memory becomes a permanent source of enrichment. This is the sense of the words spoken by her mentor Daimó, at the most moving point of the play:

> Resteu, resteu en vostra llar, donzella,
> enc que ara us sembli trista i desolada.
> Serveu la visió gran del pas de l'hèroe
> davant dels vostres ulls: tota la vostra
> vida en serà il.luminada; i sia
> vostra sort quina sia, sempre, sempre,
> en pau reclosa, o bé pel món enduta,
> en calma, en tempestat, en la vellesa,
> en dolors, en salut, en malaltia,
> sempre tindreu a dintre el cor la dolça

---

[15]   The immediate cause of the rising was the call-up of the Catalan reserves to fight in the war in Morocco. The protest which followed led to five days of rioting which was brutally suppressed by the Home Secretary of the time, La Cierva. Among those executed afterwards was Francisco Ferrer, a theoretical anarchist who had taken no part in the rising, and on whose behalf Maragall tried unsuccessfully to intervene. On the complex relationship between Maragall's writings of the time, which include the poem *Oda nova a Barcelona* and the essays *Ah! Barcelona...*, *La iglésia cremada* and *La ciutat del perdó* (The City of Forgiveness), see Josep Benet, *Maragall i la Setmana Tràgica* (Barcelona, 1963) and also Arthur Terry, 'The *Cant espiritual* of Joan Maragall', *BHS*, XXXVIII (1961), 265–73.

memòria gran d'aquest moment i hora
en què heu aimat a un hèroe en puresa,
i la seva presència fugitiva
haurà signat per sempre més, des d'ara,
vostre cor jovenil, bla com la cera,
amb segell immortal.

(Stay, stay here, girl, where you were born, though now the place may seem sad and desolate. Serve the great vision of the hero who passed before your eyes: it will illuminate your whole life; and whatever your fate may be, always, always, withdrawn in peace or driven through the world, in calm, in tempest, in old age, in grief, in health or sickness, always you will have within your heart the great, dear memory of the hour and moment when you loved a hero in absolute purity, and his fleeting presence will have stamped forever more, from this time on, your young heart, soft as wax, with an immortal seal.)

This is Maragall's last variation on a theme which had haunted him for years. In his relatively short lifetime, he achieved a quite remarkable authority, both through his unremitting honesty as a journalist and a public figure, and through his correspondence and friendships with Castilian writers like Giner de los Rios, Unamuno and Azorín. The best of his poetry has a similar authority, however much one misses the scope and richness of Verdaguer. In his complexities and hesitations, however, one is very aware of the difference in generations: in his relationship with *Modernisme*, Maragall succeeds, as no previous Catalan poet had done, in turning the potential weaknesses of his temperament into strengths, and in his Germanic affinities (Goethe, Nietzsche, and later, Novalis), he anticipates an important strain in more recent Catalan poetry.

VI. Poetry in Valencia and Mallorca

Modernisme is clearly centered on Barcelona, and Maragall, despite his very real feeling for landscape, is essentially an urban poet. Valencia and Mallorca, on the other hand, create their own verse traditions in the second half of the nineteenth century, and these continue to reflect the social and linguistic fragmentation which had taken place in the early stages of the Decadence. With few exceptions, nineteenth-century Valencian poetry hardly rises above respectable mediocrity. It is significant, for instance, that the Valencian *Jocs florals*, established in 1879, were bilingual, and were dominated somewhat tyrannically by one of the few genuine poets of the time, Teodor Llorente (1836–1911), who, despite some excellent songs and descriptive poems, too often falls back on the commonplaces of the *Renaixença* tradition.

In Mallorca, the situation is much more promising: here one can speak of a genuine school of poetry, with certain distinctive features lacking in other Catalan poetry of the time. Some of these can already be seen in one of the earliest Mallorcan poets, Josep Lluís Pons i Gallarza (1823–94): a purity of diction and a neo-classical restraint in the handling of patriotic themes, as in his fine poem *L'olivera mallorquina* (The Mallorcan Olive Tree). The best of the Mallorcan poets, Joan Alcover (1854–1926) and Miquel Costa i Llobera (1854–1922), were exact contemporaries, though Alcover, who began as a poet in Spanish, only turned to Catalan under the stress of personal bereavement. His own explanation of the change – 'llavors tota parla que no fos la materna va rebutjar-la el llavi febrosenc, com el contacte de quelcom inexpressiu, fred i metàl.lic' (then my feverish lips rejected every form of speech but their own, like the contact of something inexpressive, cold and metallic) – suggests the urgency, if not the measured dignity, of the elegies contained in his first collection, *Cap al tard* (Towards Evening), and his instinctive sense of poetic structure is still more evident in his second book, *Poemes bíblics* (1918), a series of biblical narratives in which the personal note of the earlier poems gives way to an almost Parnassian objectivity.

It is the same kind of clarity, seen in terms of classical, Mediterranean values, which one finds in the poems of Costa i Llobera, a priest whose Romantic feeling for landscape and sense of Christian vocation was controlled by a deep preoccupation with classical forms. His best volume, *Horacianes* (1906), not only shows great skill in the use of classical metres, but also a belief in the objectifying power of art which is very different from the *modernista* criterion of intuition. In Costa, as in other Mallorcan poets, there is a sense of belonging to a Mediterranean world which embraces both the pagan and the Christian traditions. And in Costa particularly, the serenity of the vision is matched by a purity of language which still seems surprisingly modern.

The independence of both Costa and Alcover was clearly recognized by the next generation of Catalan poets. The conscious artistry of their best work, and above all its civilized, 'Mediterranean' quality, came to be seen as a desirable alternative to the undisciplined introspectiveness of *Modernisme*. The chief agent in this process was Josep Carner (see below, pp. 89–91), the most active and versatile of the younger poets, for whom the influence of Costa came at a crucial stage in his early career. In the words of Miquel Ferrà:

> La influencia de Miquel Costa en Cataluña se hizo sentir principalmente con sus luminosas *Horacianes* [...] Quien señaló en esta ocasión a la juventud catalana el valor del magisterio de Costa y Llobera fue José Carner, uno de los que más han cotizado la influencia de Mallorca en el ennoblecimiento del lenguaje y la forma poética.[16]

---

[16] Quoted by Albert Manent in his excellent book, *Josep Carner i el noucentisme* (Barcelona, 1969), p. 71.

One sign of the times is the series of lectures by Mallorcan writers organized by the *Ateneu Barcelonès* in 1904. It was on this occasion that both Costa and Alcover made their most important critical statements: Costa's lecture contains an impressive attack on Maragall's theory of 'la paraula viva', in favour of conscious craftsmanship and classical balance; Alcover, for his part, emphasizes the artist's need to free himself from the limitations of a particular school, and to communicate with the widest possible audience. Both criteria – lucidity and civic responsibility – were shortly to become guiding principles in a new cultural movement – *Noucentisme* – which in turn was to bring its own limitations. For these, neither Costa nor Alcover can be blamed: their views of art are the direct product of their poetic experience, an example of integrity made possible, perhaps, by the very fact of their isolation.

Chapter 4

THE TWENTIETH CENTURY

I. Noucentisme

The division between centuries is never clear-cut: in Catalonia, *Modernisme* retained its force at least until 1911, the year which saw the death of Maragall and Nonell. In the meantime, however, a new movement had come to the fore – *Noucentisme* – which first made its presence felt a few years earlier, in 1906. Before this, even the most original writers were related in one way or another to the *Renaixença*, even though some of them, like Maragall, were directly concerned with the political and social events of the time. It is, in fact, a new sense of the relations between politics and culture which determines the next phase of literary activity – one which lasts, with certain deviations, until the Civil War. What crystallizes the Catalan political movements of the period is the colonial disaster of 1898: the effects of this on the Catalan economy and the growing sense of alienation from the central government were among the chief motives behind the foundation of the *Lliga regionalista* (1901) and the popular front movement, *Solidaritat catalana* (1906). Under the leadership of Enric Prat de la Riba (1870–1917), eventually to become the first President of the *Mancomunitat* (1913), cultural life comes to be regarded for the first time as an essential component in the political future of Catalonia.[1] Thus 1906 is not only the year of Prat's own manifesto, *La nacionalitat catalana*, but also of the first International Congress of the Catalan Language (followed in 1907 by the foundation of the *Institut d'Estudis Catalans*), and of the first important writings of Eugeni d'Ors (1882–1954) and Josep Carner (1884–1970), the leading figures in the crucial stage of *Noucentisme*.[2]

---

[1] Maurici Serrahima, in his interesting article 'Sobre el Noucentisme', *SdO*, VI (1964), 7–9, describes the movement as 'the first government intervention in the history of our culture'. In fact, Prat de la Riba had a controlling interest in several of the most important intellectual bodies of the time, like the Philological Section of the Institut d'Estudis Catalans (established in 1911), whose original members, among them them Carner, were personally chosen by him. Clearly, the movement involves much more than literature, and is best regarded as a group of mutually dependent programmes, both cultural and political.

[2] *Noucents* means 'twentieth century', but the word *Noucentisme* was probably intended to convey cultural overtones by analogy with Italian *cinquecento*, etc.

The aims of the *noucentistes* were made insistently clear in the *Glosari* which Ors published over a period of twelve years under the name of 'Xènius'. One of Ors's key phrases is 'art arbitrari': the idea that art should be 'arbitrary' in the sense of breaking completely with the existing tradition, with what he calls the 'rusticity' of nineteenth-century Catalan literature. Behind this lies the possibility of reinstating an alternative tradition, the one which had been broken off at the Renaissance. At this point, the qualifications begin: if Martorell and Roiç de Corella are the last classical writers in Catalan, there can be no question of carrying on from them in a literal sense; what is needed is a new type of humanism which will fulfil a similar function in modern terms, and a sense of the language as it might have developed normally after the fifteenth century. In the widest terms, both society and the arts are to share the same concept of urbanity (another key word of the time) and this will be possible precisely because it is to be the guiding principle of official patronage.[3]

In practice, there is a considerable overlap between *Noucentisme* and *Modernisme*, though this is something the *noucentistes* themselves tried to suppress. It is likely, of course, that any new movement in literature or the arts will only succeed by doing a certain amount of injustice to what has gone before, partly to gain energy for its own purposes. In the case of *Noucentisme*, this meant producing a polemical version of *Modernisme*, oversimplifying its Romantic dimension in order to contrast it with a new 'classicism'. So various antitheses begin to take shape: 'classicism' versus 'romanticism', the Mediterranean as against the Nordic, urban values as against the so-called 'rusticity' of the existing literature, and, summing up most of these, 'objectivity' as against 'subjectivity'. It is not difficult to show that most of these contrasts are exaggerated: there is more than a touch of *fin-de-siècle* Romanticism about the criteria of the *noucentistes* themselves; it was the *modernistes* who first saw the need for professionalism; a good deal of the fiction and painting of the 1890s, as well as some of the best essays and poems of Maragall, is concerned with the quality of urban life, and so on. What is more, there is a similarity of aim which runs through the whole period: both *Modernisme* and *Noucentisme* are attempts to create a genuinely European culture, not least by inventing a viable literary language. The first attempts at spelling reform, in fact, go back to the early 1890s, and just over a decade later one finds Josep Carner, the most talented

---

[3]   J.M. Capdevila's study *Eugeni d'Ors, etapa barcelonina (1906–1920)* (Barcelona, 1965) is a useful corrective to the view that Ors was the chief instigator of *Noucentisme*. The 'new classicism' was already well established in the work of Costa i Llobera and Alcover and in the early poems of Josep Carner. In general, as we shall see, the dividing line between *Modernisme* and *Noucentisme* is less clear than many critics assume, and the main effect of the *Glosari* was to set the seal on a number of tendencies which had been gathering weight for some time.

of the younger *noucentista* poets, apparently writing in much the same
spirit:

> Cal que una creació col.lectiva coordinada aconsegueixi per al català ço
> que per als altres grans idiomes ha obtingut: la selecció, l'estabilitat
> bàsica, i la veritable riquesa que consisteix no pas en el nombre de
> paraules, sinó en el nombre de sentits de cada paraula.

> (An organized collective effort must achieve for Catalan what it has
> obtained for the other great languages: selection, a basic stability and that
> true richness which consists not in the number of words but in the number
> of meanings in each word.)

This, one may feel, is Europeanization in its best sense, a plea to build on
what the *modernistes* had already seen as essential to the future of Catalan
literature. Yet, reading between the lines, one senses something else: the
implication that, however rich the writing of the recent past, there is something unstable, something undisciplined, about it; 'true richness', on the
other hand, is a matter of order and refinement, of paying greater attention to
the individual nuances of words. Though this in itself is admirable – no
modernista, surely, would have denied the positive side of Carner's argument – it is only a step from this relatively benign view of *Modernisme* to
the much starker contrast one finds in the writings of Ors, where 'nature',
'rusticity' and 'chaos' are interchangeable terms, to be set against classical
notions of 'measure' and 'control'.

There is another telling phrase at the beginning of Carner's statement,
where he speaks of the need for an 'organized collective effort'. In a way
this points to the crucial difference between *Modernisme* and *Noucentisme*.
The *modernistes* were the first to consider seriously the position of the artist
in contemporary society; yet, however sensitive they were to the conditions
of that society, their attempts to intervene in it were constantly handicapped,
both by internal contradictions and a general lack of cohesion. About the
turn of the century, as we have seen, there is a tendency for *Modernisme* to
merge with the general movement of *Catalanisme* at a time when the political situation in Catalonia is changing very rapidly, culminating in the
triumph of the conservative *Lliga regionalista* in 1901, under the leadership
of Prat de la Riba. And it is this in the first place, rather than any real
aesthetic shift, which determines the rise of *Noucentisme*. Above all, the
state sponsorship of culture, as Carner's statement implies, means institutions. It is not that the *modernistes* had not felt the need for such organiza-
tions – Casellas, as art historian, had struggled for years to raise the quality
of museums – but quite simply that they had lacked the political power to
achieve any positive results.

Now all this changed. Much of what followed was admirable and, given
the circumstances, necessary; nevertheless, like most official programmes,

Noucentisme involved certain sacrifices. Though now the professional writer or artist could count on the backing of official institutions – something the *modernistes* could only have dreamed of – in practice this meant accepting the conservative stance of the *Lliga* or – what it amounted to in most cases – agreeing to leave politics to the politicians. It is this conservatism which underlies the *noucentista* call for order and which accounts for some of its more notorious exclusions, such as its rejection of the *modernista* novel. The *modernistes* themselves were critical of the older, more sentimental kind of rural novel; at the same time, the much grimmer version of country life which appears in the fiction of Casellas and Víctor Català (see below, p. 99) runs directly counter to any concept of order, and so can only be dismissed as 'chaotic'. As Joan Fuster has pointed out, there is a certain 'fear of reality' at work here which helps to explain the *noucentista* hostility to the novel as a whole.[4] And this same fear can be seen in the *noucentista* vision of Barcelona as the Ideal City. As Ors presents it, the idea of Barcelona as a new Athens brings together both the classical and Mediterranean strands of *Noucentisme*. At the same time, of course, it is a deliberately abstract vision, one which can only exist by ignoring contemporary reality. And if it is the contemporary reality we want, we have to go to the painting of the 1890s or to Maragall's reaction to the *Semana trágica*, a vision which, unlike that of the *noucentistes*, can register both the squalor and the grandeur of a living city. And coming back to one of the central beliefs of *Modernisme*, to the idea that the artist is a creator who must *intervene* in reality, we can see how much *Noucentisme* lost by refusing to accept subjectivity as an aesthetic value and by excluding the whole individual, rebellious dimension of *Modernisme*.

From all this, one concludes that *Noucentisme*, however different it may have seemed at the time, is both a continuation and a reduction of *Modernisme*. Marfany puts this more succinctly when he says that '*Noucentisme*, first and foremost, is a *Modernisme*'[5] – not *Modernisme* itself, but '*a Modernisme*': a version which in practice takes up some of the possibilities of *Modernisme* and rejects others, even though this means weakening some of those it *does* adopt. And what this means is that any attempt to differentiate between *Modernisme* and *Noucentisme* on the basis of literary or artistic criteria is bound to fail. The real differences, in short, are political: or, to be more precise, they come from differing interpretations of what, for want of a better word, one calls *catalanitat* – of what it means to be Catalan – something which, as we have seen, involves the whole question of what it is to be a writer or artist in a society which is undergoing a crisis of national consciousness.

---

[4] Joan Fuster, *Literatura catalana contemporània* (Barcelona, 1978), p. 165.
[5] J.-Ll. Marfany, *Aspectes del Modernisme* (Barcelona, 1975), p. 33.

II. Poetry: Noucentisme. Symbolism and Avant-Garde

What *Noucentisme* meant in poetic terms can be seen from Ors's preface to *La muntanya d'ametistes* (The Mountain of Amethysts; 1908), the first book of poems by Guerau de Liost, the pen-name of Jaume Bofill i Mates (1878–1933). The mountain of the title is a real one – the Montseny – whose various aspects are described in a mass of closely observed detail. At the same time, the effect is very different from the impressionistically rendered landscapes of the *modernistes*: the sacramental overtones of the description ('les alzines que cremen en el fumós altar' [the ilexes which burn on the smoky altar] is a typical image) are purely aesthetic in their intention, and the clinical precision of the language and the strict verse forms strengthen the sense of a nature which has been disciplined and reshaped in the interests of art. For Ors, this is the real triumph of these poems: the poet, he explains, has 'imprisoned nature' and judged it by the canons of the City, that is to say, in terms of intellectual rigour and delight in craftsmanship. In one of his later collections, *La ciutat d'ivori* (The City of Ivory; 1918), Guerau de Liost offers his own version of the Ideal City, which reflects very accurately the *noucentista* concern with civility:

> Bella ciutat de marbre del món exterior,
> esdevinguda aurífica dins un esguard d'amor!
>
> Ets tota laborada amb ordenat esment.
> Et purifica el viure magnànim i cruent.
>
> I, per damunt la frèvola grandesa terrenal,
> empunyaràs la palma del seny – que és immortal.

(Beautiful marble city of the external world, turning to gold under the gaze of love! You are made wholly with ordered care. You are purified by the blood of generous living. And, over the trivial grandeur of earth, you will hold up the palm of intelligence, which is immortal.)

This collection, however, is fragmentary, and some, at least, of its poems had been written ten years earlier. With the death of Prat de la Riba in 1917, *Noucentisme* encountered something of a crisis; Guerau de Liost seems to have been aware of this and, as a consequence, was unable to find the right tone for continuing the book. Some years before this, he had already published a second set of verses, *Somnis* (Dreams; 1913), which departed to some extent from the project of *Noucentisme*; in it, the medievalism which seems to have come naturally to him is an important part of the fantasies in which he imagines a series of situations (among them, his own birth and death and a journey to Hell) of which he has no conscious experience. And in the poems he wrote after 1918, he departs even further, in the direction of Symbolism and, occasionally, the avant-garde. In two of his later collections, *Selvatana amor* (Love of the Selva; 1920) and *Ofrena rural* (Country Offering; 1926), there is a gentle Franciscanism in his approach to nature: no longer a 'monster' (Ors's word) but a refuge and a source of energy. And in one of the most moving poems from this last book, 'La nova amor' (The New Love), he describes the husbands who return to their wives in the country at the weekend, and then thinks of his own dead wife:

> Ara sóc al turó.
> No veig senyal de mà ni mocador;
> l'estelada només i la carena,
> i l'alzina de vora el camí,
> ferrenya i pura,
> i una alba de lluna plena,
> i m'estreny la natura,
> odorant de ginesta i romaní,
> amor de nova mena
> humida piament de serení.

(Now I am on the hill. I see no sign of hand or handkerchief, only the stars and the mountain ridge and the ilex beside the road, and the beginnings of a full moon. And nature embraces me, smelling of broom and rosemary, a love of a new kind, piously damp with dew.)

His last published collection, *Sàtires* (1929), is different again. It partly looks back to the humour and rich social and domestic detail of *Somnis*, though its irony is more pointed. By this stage, the vision of the ideal state has succumbed to the realities of the Primo de Rivera dictatorship, and many of these superbly accomplished poems are directed against those members of his own class who have compromised with the times. And to the last, Guerau de Liost retains a moral independence which, though at one stage it is a perfect expression of *Noucentisme*, seems so basic to his whole temperament that it hardly needs a literary programme to support it.

The other poet associated with the beginnings of *Noucentisme* is Josep Carner, a close friend of Guerau de Liost, whose collected poems span almost seventy years of literary activity. Like *La muntanya d'ametistes*, Carner's second volume, *Els fruits saborosos* (The Tasty Fruits; 1906), was an important index to the new sensibility: what the two books have in common is a sense of stylization, of style as something which imposes an aesthetic distance on the subject matter. Carner's own stratagem consists in taking a number of common situations from middle-class life and treating them in the manner of the classical eclogue. The effect is curiously ambivalent: the classical overtones (which extend to the names of the characters) are sentimentalized, and the middle-class world is seen through a haze of pastoral melancholy. Seen in the context of the time, these poems are Carner's contribution to the vision of the Ideal City; in them, literary style is used to indicate a style of living based on intelligence, good sense and elegance. Though the sophistication of his earlier poems seems at times over-fastidious, it would be wrong to think of him as an orthodox exponent of *Noucentisme*: what appealed to him in the aims of the movement, one feels, was the emphasis on clarity of structure and the possibilities it gave for anti-Romantic irony, and much less its conscious attempt to reinstate an interrupted tradition.

The civilized humour of Carner's early poems, much less sharp than that of Guerau de Liost, gave them a balance and an assurance which set the tone for the literary atmosphere of the time. In 1921, however, he entered the Consular Service, a decision which was to take him to Geneva, Costa Rica, Mexico, and finally to Brussels, where he spent the last twenty-five years of his life. The effect on his poetry was very marked. Whatever the motives for his voluntary exile,[6] his new poems show a deeper sense of compassion and a readiness to speculate on metaphysical questions which go far beyond the range of his earlier work. These later poems have not exactly been neglected by critics: at the same time, there is still a tendency to judge them in terms of the earlier *noucentista* verse, rather than on their own, very different, merits. Above all, perhaps, Carner now seems to have learnt how to use his talent for acute observation as the basis for a new kind of realism in which the moral comment is carried into the details of the poem. This in itself is a sign of the increasing moral complexity of the later poems. In *Nabí* (1941), one of the three or four best modern Catalan poems of some length, Carner uses the biblical story of Jonah as a means of focusing some of his deepest preoccupations. Its narrative skill alone would make the poem outstanding: what gives it its real stature, however, is the way in which the alternating voices of faith and doubt are made to coincide, with dramatic inevitability, in the concluding vision of hope:

> Car tota cosa, tret de Déu, és fugissera.
> ¿Qui dirà mai ses menes d'eternes resplendors
> en parla forastera
> i amb llavi farfallós?
> Adéu, però, grans grapes de càstig i avaricia!
> Morir per a la nova naixó, clara delícia!
> Només amor esdevindrà l'home rebel.
> Car ultrapassaràs del Pare la justícia,
> oh maternal condícia
> del brossat, de les pomes i la mel!

(For all things, save God, are fugitive. Who will ever describe his types of eternal brilliance in a foreign tongue and with faltering lips? Farewell,

---

[6] It is clear that the death of Prat de la Riba in 1917 was a severe blow to Carner, and that he felt much less sympathetic towards Prat's successor, Cambó. The need to find a settled career in order to support a growing family must also have played a part in a decision which deprived Catalan literary life of its dominant figure.

though, great clusters of punishment and avarice! The rebel will become wholly love. For you will transcend the justice of the Father, o motherly concern for order of curds, of apples and honey.)

By retelling the story of Jonah, and by adding his own interpretation, Carner has not only re-created an ancient biblical tale for modern readers, but has provided a supreme example of his art at its fullest stretch. Though it is essentially a Christian poem, it is scathing about the effects of religious perversion, and in the widest sense is a poem about the limits of rationality. In this and other poems of his final phase, the nonchalance of Carner's earlier work has resolved itself into an emotional authority which is all the more impressive for its restraint and its sense of collective responsibility in the face of historical circumstances very different from those under which he began to write.

No one faced up more singlemindedly to the cultural implications of *Noucentisme* than Carles Riba (1893–1959), an enormously gifted poet and translator,[7] and beyond question the most intelligent literary critic of his generation. Riba's first mature poems were collected in the two books of *Estances* (Stanzas; 1913–19; 1920–30). The first book has been described as a 'brilliant cultural exercise'. On the surface at least, this seems just: the echoes of Ausiàs March and the *stilnovisti* seem part of a carefully calculated attempt to restore the interrupted tradition, precisely as Ors had recommended. Yet the real value of the poems goes deeper than this: Riba is not so much concerned with an academic kind of eclecticism as with consciously selecting certain models which will help him to express his own preoccupations. Like most of Riba's later work, these are personal poems, not in a confessional sense, but in their consistent attempt to explore real psychological states by means of certain traditional abstractions: mind, soul, desire and the senses. In the second book, the medieval influences give way to those of the German Romantics and the French Symbolists, in particular Goethe, Hölderlin, Mallarmé and Valéry. In these later poems, Riba's mastery of fixed forms is thrown into relief by the extraordinary flexibility of the syntax; and though, in a sense, he is always a reticent poet, these are poems which explore very movingly the vulnerability of human love. Riba's next collection, *Tres suites* (1930–35), is both denser and more restricted in content, a deliberate approach to the notion of *poésie pure* which, for all its apparent hermeticism, probably marked a decisive point in his poetic development.[8] By comparison, his other poems of the thirties, eventually

---

[7] Riba's translations include two separate versions of the *Odyssey* (1919; 1948), the tragedies of Aeschylus and Sophocles, the *Lives* of Plutarch and a selection of poems by Hölderlin. His versions of Cavafy were published posthumously in 1962.

[8] For a detailed discussion of these poems, see Arthur Terry, '*Un nu i uns ulls*: comentari a uns poemes de Carles Riba', in *Sobre poesia catalana contemporània: Riba, Foix, Espriu* (Barcelona, 1985), pp. 33–62.

collected in *Del joc i del foc* (Of the Game and the Fire; 1946), seem hesitant and uncertain in their intention, and there are moments when Riba seems dissatisfied with his own skill.

Any such doubts were interrupted by the Civil War and the period of exile which followed it. The *Elegies de Bierville* (1943) reflect the experience of these years on a scale which one could hardly have imagined from Riba's earlier verse. As poems about exile, they present an account of personal suffering reduced to its basic elements so that it can stand for the collective experience. At the same time, the fact that the later poems in the sequence were written after Riba's decision to return to Catalonia gives them a double movement – exile and return – which appears in various forms: spiritual privation and restoration, the death and rebirth of the soul, a sense of being temporarily withdrawn from the collective life in order to participate in it with greater knowledge:

> [E]ra girat a mi que escoltava crèixer l'anunci
>   de no sé quina mar interior, madurant
> lluny dins meu en illes d'encara impotent melodia;
>   canvi o naixença – era igual: era una mar i el seu vent.

(Turned in on myself, I heard the sound of some inward sea grow nearer, far within me ripening into islands of still powerless music; it was a change or a birth – there was no difference: it was a sea and a sea wind.)

This spiritual exploration is seen in terms both of personal experience and of certain basic mythical patterns (the Orphic adept's descent into Hades, Ulysses's return to Ithaca) which gradually lead to a recognition of the Christian God. This is a new note in Riba's poetry, and in his last two collections, *Salvatge cor* (Savage Heart; 1952) and *Esbós de tres oratoris* (Sketch for Three Oratorios; 1957), the patient speculations of the *Elegies* give way to a more dramatic questioning of the possibilities of religious belief.[9] In this late phase, the conscious acknowledgement of doubt and paradox ends in the affirmation of one of Riba's basic insights: that life, in any real sense, implies generosity and the acceptance of 'risk' (one of his key words) as the only means to salvation.

However, this was not quite the end of Riba's poetic career. At the very end of his collected poems, there is a group of nine poems under the heading of 'For a New Book, as yet Untitled'. The best of these poems are something of a revelation. At various times in his life, Riba had attempted to write a more musical kind of poem, never with complete success, mainly because the texture of his most characteristic poems was too dense. But now,

---

[9]   On *Salvatge cor*, see the excellent study by Joan Ferraté, *Carles Riba, avui* (Barcelona, 1955), pp. 31–77, and also Arthur Terry, 'Alguns sonets de Carles Riba', *Sobre poesia catalana contemporània*, pp. 79–93.

towards the end of his life, he finally achieves what amounts to a new simplicity, partly, it has been argued, under the influence of the American poet Emily Dickinson. Whatever the truth of this, the results speak for themselves: like Dickinson's, these poems are wise in their apparent simplicity, and, above all, have a musical quality – a fusion of words and rhythms – which is quite new to Riba's poetry. Here, for example, is the ending of a poem in which he thinks back on his childhood:

> ¿Qui somriurà dels dos,
> el vell que no preveies
> futur de tu, oh infant,
> o tu, fonda innocència?
> Sols sé que miro el riu
> al llarg de la ribera;
> i sempre sóc al punt
> on l'aigua fa el seu pur
> començament de perdre's.

(Which of the two will smile, the old man you didn't foresee as your future, child, or yourself, profound innocence? I only know that I look at the river along the bank; and I am always at the point where the water makes its pure beginning to lose itself.)

It is difficult to sum up Riba's poetry under a single heading, though he is often referred to as a Symbolist poet. Certainly, he learnt a great deal from Symbolism, just as he himself contributed notably to that tradition. At the same time, there is no doubt that his experience of the Civil War and its aftermath created in him a need for a more human kind of poetry, one which could scarcely have been predicted at the time of writing the *Estances*. In the process, he gave the Catalan language a flexibility and a subtlety which would hardly have been thinkable before he began to write. Yet ultimately, it is for this human quality that one values his work: not because it excludes other types of poetry, but because it shows us a poet who is never content to rest in certainties, but who continues to work on himself and to face up to his own, very human contradictions with an integrity few other Catalan poets have achieved.

Hardly surprisingly, a great deal of the Catalan poetry of the last fifty years reflects the influence of Carner and Riba. One might argue, in fact, that the surest sign of the vitality of Catalan poetry between the wars is the presence, not only of two or three major poets, but also of a dozen or so interesting minor ones, like J.M. Lòpez-Picó (1886–1959), Marià Manent (1898–1988) and Tomàs Garcés (1901–92), all of whom tend to share a similar view of poetry, in which purity of language and precision of imagery are related in varying degrees to the dominant modes of Symbolism.

Not every poet of the period falls into this pattern: the deceptively simple lyrics of Clementina Arderiu (1893–1976), the wife of Carles Riba, seem to come directly from her own spontaneous sense of life, without the mediation of literary models. Similarly, though in other respects they are utterly different, the early poems of J.M. Sagarra (1894–1961) suggest a more traditional and egocentric writer who seems completely untouched by the ideals of *Noucentisme*. And at the other extreme, there is the impact of certain avant-garde movements – Cubism, Futurism and Dada – which roughly coincides with the period of political unrest between the death of Prat de la Riba (1917) and the establishment of the Primo de Rivera dictatorship in 1923.

The crucial figure here is Joan Salvat-Papasseit (1894–1924), an uneven but very original poet about whom critics still tend to disagree. Salvat is the only important working-class poet of the period, though he scarcely fits the usual picture of a proletarian writer. His own statements about poetry are inclined to be confused and anarchistic, though in practice there is very little social protest in his poems. His reputation for subversiveness comes partly from his statements and partly from his early experimental poetry, which makes use of typographical devices in the manner of Apollinaire and Marinetti. These poems now seem the most derivative part of his work: what rebelliousness they contain is generalized and Romantic, and Salvat talks continually of the liberty and dignity of man, without any real awareness of the class struggle. The best of his later poetry, in fact, comes from a clear acceptance of his own social situation: his sense of the texture of everyday life gives his poems a realism which one hardly finds in the middle-class poets of the time, as in these lines from *Nadal* (Christmas):

> Sento el carro dels apis
>   que l'empedrat recolza
> i els altres que l'avencen, tots d'endreça al mercat.
> Els de casa   a la cuina
>   prop del braser que crema
> amb el gas tot encès han enllestit el gall.
> Ara esguardo la lluna, que m'apar lluna plena;
> i ells recullen les plomes,
>   i ja enyoren demà.

(I hear the celery cart jar on the cobblestones, and the others who pass it on their way to market. Those at home, in the kitchen, beside the burning stove, with the gas full on, have prepared the bird. Now I look at the moon, which seems to me a full moon; and they pluck out the feathers, and long for tomorrow.)

And the naturalness of the love poems in *La rosa als llavis* (The Rose in the Lips; 1923) – the most genuinely erotic poetry in modern Catalan – presupposes a kind of security which has nothing at all to do with contemporary literary models.

Salvat-Papasseit died in 1924, when he was only thirty. On the surface, it might seem that *Noucentisme* and the avant-garde were incompatible, yet there is one poet, J.V. Foix (1893–1987), whose work bridges the gap with extraordinary skill. Foix's earliest statements on poetry are very similar to those of Carles Riba: both appear to accept the basic aims of *Noucentisme* and particularly the need to restore the broken tradition of Catalan humanism. What is striking in Foix is that he interprets this general preoccupation both more literally and more widely than any of his contemporaries. One of his best-known lines reads: 'M'exalta el nou i m'enamora el vell' (The new excites me and I love the old). As far as older Catalan poetry is concerned, Foix, significantly, is the only poet of his generation who is prepared to go as far back as Llull. However, it is in his conception of the 'new' that he diverges most sharply from a poet like Riba, who, after his early poems, moves steadily in the direction of the Symbolism which Foix rejects. The spectrum of Foix's poetry is much wider than this: at one end of the scale he goes back through Ausiàs March to the poems of the troubadours, and at the other he is closer to Apollinaire and the Futurists than to Mallarmé.

Something like a third of Foix's published work consists of four collections of prose poems grouped under the general title of *Diari 1918*. The fact that he has chosen to refer this part of his work to a particular year, though many of the individual pieces must have been written later, confirms one's impression that the later work, both poems and prose poems, represents a steady unfolding of the possibilities implied in his very earliest writing. Foix has been loosely described as a surrealist, though this conflicts with his own view of reality. More than once, he has referred to himself as 'un investigador en poesia', not in any clinical or frivolous sense, but simply as an indication that he sees poetry as what he calls an 'objective reality', a reality which is always there, detached from the poet, but always ready to be explored. So he speaks of his poems as 'similitudes' (*semblances*), as deliberate attempts to 'realize his personality' and, characteristically, his use of the word 'semblança' is taken directly from a sentence of Llull: 'De les semblances reals davallen les fantàstiques, enaixí com accidents que ixen de substància' (From real similitudes there derive those of the imagination, as accidents issue from substance).

In the fantastic narratives of many of his poems, details which in isolation seem merely surrealistic fall into place as parts of a personal myth which, because it is detached from any autobiographical intentions, can move easily between individual and collective experience, as in this passage from *Gertrudis* (1927):

> Al capdamunt del carrer més ample, al vèrtex mateix del turó, sota una cortina blau cel, seia, en un tron d'argent, Gertrudis. [...] El grinyol del calçat, em semblava un cor dolcíssim, i la meva ombra esporuguia l'ombra dels ocells presoners de l'ampla claraboia celeste. Quan em creia

d'atènyer el cim, dec haver errat la passa: em trobava en el tebi passadís interminable d'un vaixell transatlàntic. M'han mancat forces per cridar i, en cloure'm la por els ulls, desplegada en ventall, una sèrie completa de cartes de joc em mostrava inimaginables paisatges desolats.

(At the top of the widest street, at the very tip of the hill, beneath a sky blue curtain, Gertrudis was seated on a silver throne. […] The creaking of my shoes was like a sweet choir, and my shadow scared off the shadow of the birds held prisoner in the wide celestial skylight. When I thought I was nearing the top, I must have missed my way: I found myself in the warm, interminable corridor of a transatlantic liner. I had no strength to shout and, as fear closed my eyes, a complete pack of playing cards showed me unimaginable landscapes of desolation.)

However much his poems approach the condition of waking dreams, Foix insists that the poet is a kind of magician who retains the power to manipulate the elements of his vision. In his later volumes of poetry, *Les irreal omegues* (The Unreal Omegas; 1948) and *On he deixat les claus ...* (Where I have Left the Keys ...; 1953), the emotional authority with which he is able to write of the Civil War depends precisely on this ability to control the anecdotal elements of a situation in order to raise it to the status of myth. So in 'Fronteres' (Frontiers), one of the most moving poems to have come out of the war, Foix questions his own identity, not in any narcissistic sense, but as a guarantee of his right to speak for others in a common situation:

> Pel corriol, entre flames de tinta,
> El no-res augur;
> Oscil.la en cels antics llàntia extinta
> I una ombra en el mur.
>
> Avanç, enllà, però una mà m'atura
> I, clara, una veu
> Molla dels rous d'antany, clama segura:
> – De tot crim ets reu.
>
> I en cloure els ulls per contemplar el paisatge
> De la mort carnal,
> Abandon en els glaços el bagatge
> Del país natal.

(Along the narrow path, among flames of ink, I sense nothingness; in ancient skies an extinct lantern sways and a shadow on the wall. I go on, beyond, but a hand stops me and, harshly, a voice soft with dew of bygone years, cries firmly: You have committed every crime. And as I close my eyes to contemplate the landscape of bodily death, I leave behind in the ice the baggage of my native country.)

The relative lack of development, which in a different kind of writer might be a weakness, seems natural enough in a poet who sees his task as the exploration of a single truth, which is both unique and indivisible. As a result, Foix has remained extraordinarily faithful to the themes and technique of his early work, while at the same time he has experimented constantly with new material in a way which makes him both the least literary and the most frequently exciting poet of his generation.[10]

III. Drama and Fiction before 1936

Perhaps the greatest limitation of *Noucentisme* was that it encouraged poetry at the expense of other kinds of writing. Such an effect was partly deliberate and partly the natural consequence of a movement which placed so much emphasis on the need to purify the language itself. This helps to explain the relative poverty of the Catalan theatre before the Civil War: the types of audience which supported the plays of Rusiñol (see above, p. 75) or the working-class drama of Ignasi Iglèsies (1871–1928) remained untouched by the most important literary movement of the time. In the 1920s and 30s, the commercial theatre went its own way; the one really talented dramatist of these years, J.M. Sagarra (see above, p. 94), achieved his success through a series of Romantic plays, sometimes of considerable lyrical power, which were completely divorced from any kind of social reality. This is not to say that serious writers were not aware of the need for a more responsible type of theatre; in terms of practical results, however, there is little to show beyond the first plays of Joan Oliver (1899–1986), a writer whose full importance does not emerge until after 1936.

The situation in fiction is more complex. In 1925, Carles Riba delivered a famous lecture, *Una generació sense novel.la*, in which he argued that the absence of mature novelists was due, not so much to lack of talent, as to the moral poverty of contemporary Catalan society.[11] Significantly, he did not

---

[10] See Pere Gimferrer, *La poesia de J.V. Foix* (Barcelona, 1974). Also Arthur Terry, 'Sobre les *Obres poètiques* de J.V. Foix', *Sobre poesia catalana contemporània*, pp. 97–111, and *Readings of J.V. Foix,* ed. Arthur Terry (Sheffield and Barcelona, 1998).

[11] Carles Riba, *Obres completes,* II, pp. 314–20. Critics often write as if Riba's lecture were an isolated occasion. There had, in fact, been something of a revival in the novel from 1917 onwards, though mainly at the level of popular reprints. By 1925, the influence of *Noucentisme* had clearly weakened, and writers like Sagarra and Pla were showing an increasing interest in the economics of novel publishing. The two articles which Sagarra published in *La Publicitat* in the spring of 1925, though relatively unoriginal, did have the effect of reviving a debate which was in danger of becoming sterile. Riba's lecture, which is partly a reply to Sagarra, runs counter to the general lines of the debate, to which it now seems an anachronistic postscript. The real mistake is to suppose that the interventions of Sagarra and Riba were directly responsible for a revival of novel writing itself. For a full discussion of the debate, see Alan Yates, *Una generació sense novel.la?* (Barcelona, 1975), pp. 147–200.

mention Narcís Oller; what he was hoping for, clearly, was a type of society which would measure up to the ideals of *Noucentisme*: 'cal, doncs, un llarg temps, perquè una atmosfera d'humanisme envolti i impregni el cos social' (it will, therefore, take a long time for an atmosphere of humanism to surround and penetrate the body of society).

Looking back to the beginning of the century, one sees yet again the inhibiting effect of *Noucentisme*. As we have seen, Oller's last novel, *Pilar Prim* (1906), departs to some extent from the realism of his earlier work. A few years before, the deaths of Yxart and Sardà had put an end to the period of rational, positivist criticism which had sanctioned his previous novels, leaving the way open to the intuitive subjectivism of the *modernistes*. In its way, the originality of *Pilar Prim* is an index to the change in literary mood: it seems no coincidence that its hero, Deberga, is a reader of Nietzsche, and much of the writing is 'poetic' in a *modernista* sense. These are perhaps minor aspects of a novel which still owes its success to the study of individual psychology and environment, yet they suggest Oller's growing doubts as to the validity of the realist novel and his difficulties in finding an alternative solution.

The fragmentary nature of *modernista* prose – echoed in poetry by Maragall's theory of 'la paraula viva' – was basically at odds with the idea of an organically constructed novel. One effect of this is a revival of the *quadre de costums*, a type of writing which easily lent itself to the *fin-de-siècle* sensibility, whether as prose poem or short story. The novels of Santiago Rusiñol, for example, are invariably composed of a number of these smaller units. As we have seen, only once does he succeed in turning his weaknesses into strengths. This is in *L'auca del Senyor Esteve* (1907), a minor comic masterpiece which, in its way, is a serious, though unrepeatable, solution to the problems of the *modernista* novel.

After *L'auca del Senyor Esteve*, Rusiñol's fiction suffers increasingly from the contradictions which he himself had diagnosed in his most successful work. In other novelists of the beginning of the century, a different kind of tension can be seen, which will eventually help to bring about the collapse of the *modernista* novel as a whole. In general terms, the problem of such writers is to find a means of reconciling the basic principles of realism with the demands of the new subjectivity. One result of this is an insistence on the more 'decadent' aspects of Romanticism. The erotic mysticism one finds in the early novels of Prudenci Bertrana (1861–1942) – *Josafat* (1906) and *Els nàufrags* (The Shipwrecked; 1907) – is only one attempt to break through the limitations of conventional narrative into a more subjective and 'poetic' world. In other novelists, this accounts for the powerful fantasy element contained in what, on the surface, often appears to be naturalistic writing, and it is precisely in this area that the most impressive achievements of the *modernista* novel are to be found.

The dominant mode of fiction between 1900 and 1907 is the rural novel, whose chief exponents are Ramon Casellas (1855–1910), Marià Vayreda (1850–1903), Josep Pous i Pagès (1873–1952) and Víctor Català (the pen-name of Caterina Albert (1869–1966)). The best-known work of this group is Víctor Català's novel *Solitud* (1905), a story of great power and psychological penetration, which seems deliberately to play off the *modernista* attitude to nature against the determinism of the Naturalists.[12] Its most distinguished predecessor is Ramon Casellas's *Els sots feréstecs* (The Wild Hollows; 1901), with which it has a good deal in common. Both Casellas and Víctor Català are exploiting a tendency which is already established in the earlier, more conventional fiction of the *costumista* variety. But where earlier *costumisme* had tended to be idyllic and sentimental, the new version of ruralism is altogether grimmer. The nearest parallel here is with the rural dramas of Guimerà: in fiction, however, such a vision of nature involves a partial reassessment of narrative form, and it is here that one sees most clearly how the deliberately fragmented structure encouraged by *Modernisme* leads in the direction of fantasy and Symbolism. Both novelists, in fact, are engaged in the same task: the transformation of the older type of realism through an awareness of *modernista* aesthetics. Neither of their novels can be judged in realistic terms. In *Els sots feréstecs*, the effect is that of an extended metaphor: the story of a single obsession in which the neurotic terrors of the protagonist – a country priest whose fear of being 'buried alive' in the mountains hovers frighteningly on the borders of reality – are presented in purely artistic terms. *Solitud*, by comparison, is less insulated from real life, and its symbolism is richer, if less coherent. The emergence of the central character, Mila, from adolescence into womanhood involves two conflicting views of nature. One is the Rousseauesque vision of the earlier Romantics, symbolized by the figure of the shepherd, Gaietà; the other feeds on a sense of violence and evil, and it is this which prevails. In such a setting, Mila's development becomes an initiation into the darker reaches of the imagination, a recognition of the disturbing and powerful forces which lie beneath the *modernista* faith in intuition. Ultimately, both novels are highly personal solutions to a problem which underlies the *modernista* novel as a whole. It is difficult to see how the rural novel, conceived in these terms, could have developed further: as it was, Casellas wrote no more novels and, significantly, all Víctor Català's important books – *Solitud* and the three collections of stories – *Drames rurals* (1902), *Ombrívoles* (Shadowy Things; 1904) and *Caires vius* (Living Aspects; 1907) – were published within a space of six years.

Several other novelists of the time do, in fact, continue to work in this manner, though more often than not in the form of the short story. One notable exception to this is Josep Pous i Pagès, the author of *La vida i la*

---

[12] On this point, see Alan Yates, '*Solitud* i els *Drames rurals*', *SdO*, XI (1969), 54–6.

mort d'En Jordi Fraginals (1912), a novel which seems quite deliberately to mark the passing of *Modernisme*. Curiously enough, the first four parts of the novel read like a serious and well-executed attempt to reinstate the more conventional and objective type of rural novel. The last part, however, is different: the final illness and suicide of the chief character imply the total collapse of the reality which has been so carefully built up in the earlier stages of the book. One suspects that Unamuno's praise of *Jordi Fraginals* – 'la novela es novela, toda una novela y no más que una novela'[13]– was directed particularly at these closing chapters: the 'tragic sense of life' which they convey comes not only from the final dissolution of a strong-willed protagonist, but also from the sense in which the author himself appears to accept the final impasse of the *modernista* sensibility.

Another exception, though of a different kind, is the one novel by Miquel de Palol (1885–1965), *Camí de llum* (Path of Light; 1909). This is in no sense a rural novel, though part of its action takes place in the country. There are only two protagonists, Carles, whose wife has died of tuberculosis, and his daughter Maria, for whom he fears a similar fate, and who eventually dies of the same disease.Though it has something in common with the other novels I have mentioned – the characters, for instance, exist on the margins of society – what strikes one most is the refined nature of the writing: the subtle descriptions of atmosphere and states of mind in the Symbolist manner. What holds the novel together, on the other hand, are the protagonists's journeyings in search of the daughter's health, of the 'path of light' which is ultimately denied to them. And at certain points the relationship between father and daughter comes close to incest, as the latter is made to incorporate the image of the dead wife.[14]

As a genre, then, the rural novel hardly survived the first impact of *Noucentisme*. One of the basic attitudes of the new movement was its anti-ruralism, its desire to impose order on what it regarded, justly or otherwise, as a source of Romantic imprecision. Combined with this, however, was an attack on the novel as a whole, on the grounds of its irrelevance to the creation of the Ideal City whose achievement still lay in the future. The phrase of Carles Riba already quoted – 'cal, doncs, un llarg temps, perquè una atmosfera d'humanisme envolti i impregni el cos social' (it will, therefore, take a long time for an atmosphere of humanism to surround and penetrate the body of society) – merely echoes an argument which had first appeared nearly twenty years before. To ignore the achievement of Oller

---

[13] Miguel de Unamuno, 'Sobre la literatura catalana', *Obras completas* (Madrid, 1958), V, p. 672.
[14] See Alan Yates's preface to his excellent edition of this novel (Barcelona, 1976), pp. 5–18.

and the *modernistes* now seems perverse, though at the time the confrontation with *Modernisme* was a necessary condition of success in other directions. As we have seen, the *modernista* novel itself suffered from the more
general crisis of Naturalism; at least by 1912, the novel as a genre was
discredited as part of the new orthodoxy, and there are few signs of a serious
revival before the mid-1920s. There are occasions, even, when the sense of
disorientation which Riba describes in his lecture seems to be confirmed by
the novelists themselves: in an interview given in 1926, Víctor Català refers
to the Catalan novel as a 'nineteenth-century genre'; two years later, Joan
Puig i Ferrater (1882–1956), in his confessional novel *Vida interior d'un
escriptor* (Inner Life of a Writer), reveals his sense of frustration at the intellectual superiority of the *noucentistes*.

This feeling of alienation is partly a matter of language, of the inability to
achieve the degree of linguistic refinement demanded by the most influential
critics of the time.[15] For the majority of the *noucentistes*, on the other hand,
prose is something to be cultivated separately from the novel, either in the
form of the short story or of translations of foreign classics. The few
attempts at a more extended type of fiction are novels in name only: the
most celebrated, Eugeni d'Ors's *La ben plantada* (The Well-Rooted
Woman; 1912), is, as Unamuno said, 'un pequeño evangelio estético
político', a rhetorical meditation on an ideal woman who symbolizes the
coming of the new classicism.

The one prose writer of an older generation to be accepted by the
noucentistes was Joaquim Ruyra (1858–1939). The reasons for this are
partly literary, partly linguistic. Ruyra's first volume of stories, *Marines i
boscatges* (Seascapes and Woodscapes; 1904), already shows a concern for
style and precision of language which sets it apart from the contemporary
rural novel. This is all the more striking since Ruyra's subjects are invariably rural: his descriptions of the landscape and inhabitants of the Costa
Brava and its interior have an authority which comes partly from the accurate registering of local idiom and partly from sympathetic observation. It is
this last feature which gives his stories their peculiar distinctiveness: where
the rural novel is often violent and pessimistic, Ruyra's whole vision is
based on a religious sense of goodness and simplicity. The compactness of
his stories (his one attempt at a full-length novel was never completed)[16] is

---

[15] The *Normes ortogràfiques* of 1913, which now form the basis of modern Catalan
spelling, were one of the great achievements of the grammarian Pompeu Fabra (1868–1948)
and the *Institut d'Estudis Catalans*. At the time, however, they created a good deal of
scandal, and helped to widen the rift between the *noucentistes* and the older writers.

[16] This novel, *La gent del mas Aulet* (The People from Mas Aulet), occupied Ruyra for
almost thirty years, and shows a total inability to integrate the smaller units of his short
stories into a larger whole. Its microscopic technique, though entirely in keeping with the
criteria of *Noucentisme*, is one of the principal reasons for its failure.

partly a question of tone: even in those which are not told in the first person, one is aware of the narrator's voice which controls the series of events. The characteristic temper of this voice is gently ironical, and Catalan critics have often spoken of Ruyra's 'Franciscanism' – a term which several of his best stories, notably 'Les coses benignes' (The Friendly Things; 1925), seem deliberately to invite. As the preface to one of his later collections makes clear, Ruyra was very conscious of the linguistic aims of *Noucentisme*, and it is this, as much as anything, which explains the extraordinary modernity of his prose.[17]

Though by 1925 the novel had begun to revive, it was precisely this sense of artistry which was lacking in the more substantial novelists of the period – writers like Puig i Ferrater and Prudenci Bertrana, whose books all too often give the impression of thinly fictionalized autobiography. In the late 1920s and early 30s, however, there are signs of a more serious approach to fiction in the early novels and stories of Miquel Llor (1894–1966), Llorenç Villalonga (1897–1980), Joan Oliver (1899–1986), Xavier Berenguel (1905–1990), Francesc Trabal (1898–1957) and Salvador Espriu (1914–85). The work of all these writers is fairly modest in scale, but in each of them one is aware of a poise and a sense of the complexity of human life which had been lost to Catalan fiction since Narcís Oller. The work of Trabal, for instance, which culminates in *Vals* (Waltz; 1935), is the first serious attempt at erotic fiction in Catalan, and at the same time reflects the general atmosphere of the period with remarkable accuracy.

Of all these novelists, the most important is Villalonga: in him, poise takes the form of a consciously aristocratic snobbery through which the semi-feudal society of Mallorca is filtered with affectionate irony, a note which he has sustained with great brilliance through a whole series of books, from *Mort de dama* (Death of a Lady; 1931) to *Bearn* (1961) (see below, p. 111), one of the most outstanding novels published since the Civil War.

Mort de dama is part satire, part elegy, though it is the satire which predominates. The action, such as it is, revolves round the death of an elderly aristocratic woman, Dona Obdúlia, who represents 'the soul of a society which is disappearing'. This society is being replaced for the worse by the onset of tourists and hotels. Despite his nostalgia for the 'world of his infancy', Villalonga caricatures many aspects of it, from the mental limitations of Dona Obdúlia to the provincialism of the local poets, symbolized by the triumph of their leading poetess, Aina Cohen.

In many ways, the latter is the most interesting character in the book: she is basically a frustrated person, not without talent, who has willed herself to conform to the mediocre tastes of her contemporaries, with the result that

---

[17] As a member of the Philological Section of the *Institut d'Estudis Catalans*, Ruyra collaborated with Pompeu Fabra in the preparation of the *Diccionari general de la llengua catalana* (1932), the great normative dictionary of modern Catalan.

she finally goes mad. And, standing on the sidelines, there is the figure of Maria Antònia, Baroness of Bearn, the only character who is not satirized, a kind of idealized aristocrat who will play a much greater part in Villalonga's later, more elegiac novels.

In some of the best writers of the 1930s there is an obvious widening of scope. One example of this is the trilogy *Novel.les de l'Ebre* (*Terres de l'Ebre* [Lands of the Ebro; 1932]; *Camins de nit* [Roads of Night; 1935]; *Tino Costa* [1947]) by Sebastià Juan Arbó (1902–84), which demonstrates very forcefully the continuing relevance of the rural novel as a means of presenting unfamiliar areas of life. But the most striking reminder of the geographical and social variety of Catalonia is the work of Josep Pla (1897–1981), an extremely prolific writer who, though to some extent he shares the *noucentista* prejudice against the novel, is beyond doubt the most gifted social observer of the last century. Though he wrote biographies and a certain amount of fiction, Pla's favourite form was the personal travel diary. The title of one of his earliest books, *Coses vistes* (Things Seen; 1925), could stand for most of his work: his endless curiosity and apparently spontaneous capacity for verbalizing his experience are conveyed in a style whose sheer readability conceals a great deal of literary skill. In many ways, Pla was the most professional of modern Catalan authors: though a strong, and at times pessimistic, personality comes through his books, one's main impression is of normality – the normality of a writer who confidently accepted a partic- ular literary situation and whose work itself, in its unfailing regularity, helped to keep alive a whole tradition of writing and communication through the difficult circumstances of the 1940s and 50s.

IV. After 1936

(a) Poetry

The Civil War of 1936–39 brought about the complete collapse of Catalan political institutions and to a great extent of the cultural tradition which had been patiently built up over the previous forty years. The war itself produced a few fine poems, notably by two gifted poets who died young, Bartolomeu Rosselló-Pòrcel (1913–38) and Màrius Torres (1910–42). Rosselló-Pòrcel's early poems show the influence of the Spanish Generation of 1927, though the precision of their language is already very evident. However, it is his last, posthumous collection, *Imitació del foc* (Imitation of Fire; 1928) which demonstrates his real originality, in which echoes of the Spanish Baroque and French Surrealism combine with a real feeling for popular poetry. Torres, on the other hand, is a poet who writes strictly within the bounds of Symbolism, influenced no doubt by Carles

Riba, though his poems on love and death, many of them composed in the course of a terminal illness, are both moving and technically accomplished.

After the Republican defeat, many writers went into exile, in some cases permanently. For those who remained or returned in the early 1940s, the literary situation could hardly have been more discouraging: the banning of Catalan in schools, the severe restrictions on publication and the general vindictiveness of the central government towards any manifestations of Catalan culture made this a period of ephemeral little magazines and other clandestine publications. By the mid-1950s this situation had eased a little,[18]and one could begin to observe two distinct types of reaction on the part of Catalan writers. On the one hand, there was a high-minded though anachronistic attempt to write as if circumstances were still normal, and on the other, there were the beginnings of a more socially conscious kind of writing, represented by the two most influential poets of the post-war period, Salvador Espriu (1913–85) and Pere Quart (1899–1986). In this situation, the death of Carles Riba in 1959 seemed like the end of an epoch: though the *Elegies de Bierville* had been the finest poems to come out of the Civil War, the Symbolist tradition seemed to have come to an end with its most distinguished practitioner.

Neither Espriu nor Pere Quart was exactly a new writer. Pere Quart is the pseudonym of Joan Oliver (see above, p. 97), a writer who had published fiction and verse in the 1930s and had begun to make a name as a dramatist during the Civil War with plays like *Allò que tal vegada s'esdevingué* (What Perhaps Happened; 1936) and *La fam* (Hunger; 1938) (see below, p. 118). Basically, Pere Quart is a serious moralist who is also a superb entertainer: a middle-class writer whose dislike of bourgeois complacency made him the most accomplished satirist of his generation. His poetry, particularly in collections like *Vacances pagades* (Holidays with Pay; 1961) and *Circumstàncies* (1968), breaks every rule of 'fine writing': it is colloquial, often to the point of coarseness, realistic, totally unrhetorical, and full of self-mockery. As he says in one of his prefaces:

> Pere Quart, pel que sembla prefereix avui – i també en poesia – el desordre creador i la dolorosa inquietud esperançada.
>
> (Pere Quart, it would appear, nowadays prefers – in poetry too – creative disorder and a painful, yet hopeful, anxiety.)

Espriu is the more complex of the two writers, and the finer poet. Like Joan Oliver, he has worked in more than one genre. (For his fiction and theatre, see pp. 112 and 118–20.) The maturity of his first two books of poems,

---

[18] For a well-documented discussion of the publishing situation and other related questions, see Francesc Vallverdú, *L'escriptor català i el problema de la llengua* (Barcelona, 1968).

Cementiri de Sinera (1946) and *Les cançons d'Ariadna* (1949), probably reflects his earlier experience as a prose writer. Like his prose, these already show what was to become a basic polarity in his work: a controlled anger at the false values of the urban middle classes (an attitude he shares with Oliver) and an elegiac tenderness towards the vanishing rural and mercantile community of Arenys de Mar, the 'Sinera' of his poems and fiction.

In his poems, Espriu has meditated constantly, through both elegy and satire, on the need to come to terms with death, without losing faith in the value of life. After the war, he extended the range of his writing in the direction of public issues. This is particularly clear in his best-known collection, *La pell de brau* (The Bull's Hide; 1960), a sequence in which the collective situation of the Peninsular peoples is focused through themes and images taken from the history of the Jews in exile. There is no doubt that this book did more than anything else to establish Espriu as the spokesman of the post-war generation, sometimes at the expense of his other writing. But it is equally obvious that his view of the collective situation is also an intensely personal one, and that failure to realize this can only over-simplify an achievement of great integrity and emotional complexity.

Espriu's last major collection, *Setmana santa* (Holy Week; 1971), is different again, and forms an impressive climax to the meditation on death which runs through the whole of his work. In it, he sets out to strip the significance of Holy Week of all the false conceptions and dogmatisms it has accumulated in the course of time. Thus Christ appears, not as a semi-supernatural being, but as someone who has suffered the ultimate sacrifice in order to provide the supreme example of human dignity. This version of things is hardly orthodox, and this is the point: Espriu's vision is essentially man-centred, and this means a constant questioning of fixed beliefs in order to arrive at a truer understanding of man's place on earth. Or as Espriu himself puts it:

> Mai no podrem, però, deixar
> el lliure dret d'examinar
> lleis, fonaments, límits, raons,
> rengles d'enigmes, sense fons ...

(But we can never give up the free right to examine laws, foundations, limits, reasons, rows of unfathomable enigmas ...)

In the early 1960s, the poetry of Espriu and Pere Quart was often used to justify the arguments for 'social realism' which ran through the critical statements of the time. In so far as they amounted to a literary programme, these arguments tended to be over-rigid and more limiting than the post-Symbolist tradition they often attacked. Looking back over the new poetry of the next ten years, however, one can see that the demand for greater contemporary awareness was worth making. What is most valuable in the 'realist' attitude is the stress which it places on personal experience, and this is exactly what one finds, for example, in the best of the new poets, Gabriel Ferrater (1922–72). Ferrater's three volumes of poems, later collected in *Les dones i els dies* (Women and Days; 1968), are fluent and intelligent, and it is precisely the strength of his private convictions and the sense of the individual's struggle to achieve some kind of happiness which set him apart from lesser poets who have tried too consciously to assume a public voice. At the same time, it is hardly enough to call Ferrater a 'poet of experience': what really distinguishes him is his persistent attempt to show how experience itself is constantly reshaped in the mind, and how this process adds up to the sense of an individual life. It is clear, also, that his moral attitudes do not depend on any large-scale system of beliefs. Like Thomas Hardy, a poet he particularly admired, Ferrater wrote simply from a sense of his own life, from a feeling that the suddenly surfacing perceptions of life can fit whole and without compromise into poems. Or, as he puts it in the preface to his first collection, *Da nuces pueris* (1960):

> Entenc la poesia com la descripció, passant de moment a moment, de la vida moral d'un home ordinari, com ho sóc jo [...] Quan escric una poesia, l'única cosa que m'ocupa i em costa és de definir ben bé la meva actitud moral, o sigui la distància que hi ha entre el sentiment que la poesia exposa i el que en podríem dir el centre de la meva imaginació.

> (I take poetry to be a step by step description of the moral life of an ordinary man like myself [...] When I write a poem, the only thing which concerns me and gives me trouble is to define as clearly as possible my moral standpoint, that is to say, the distance which separates the feeling the poem expresses from what one might call the centre of my imagination.)

Critics sometimes say that a writer has 'created a world of his own'. To this we might reply that we don't want any world but the one we live in, and that what we ask of a poet is a few good poems about it. Ferrater, I think, would have agreed: more than anything else, his poems are a serious and varied attempt to show what it is like to live in the world which is available to anyone who has the perceptions to see it. This is why he is so concerned with the sense of what makes an individual life. If in the end his honesty left him with only a few certainties, these at least seem infinitely worth having. Or, as he put it in a poem from his last collection, 'Oci' (Leisure):

> Ella dorm. L'hora que els homes
> ja s'han despertat, i poca llum
> entra encara a ferir-los.
> Amb ben poc en tenim prou. Només
> el sentiment de dues coses:
> la terra gira, i les dones dormen.

Conciliats, fem via
cap a la fi del món. No ens cal
fer res per ajudar-lo.

(She is asleep. At this hour men are already awake, though as yet only a little light strikes in to them. A little suffices us: the awareness, merely, of two things: the earth revolves, and women sleep. Assenting, we travel on to the end of the world. We need do nothing to assist it.)

In the meantime, several good minor poets had been consolidating their reputations, notably Rosa Leveroni (1910–85), Joan Teixidor (1913–92) and Joan Vinyoli (1914–84). Writing under the influence of Carles Riba, but also of the great fifteenth-century poet Ausiàs March, Leveroni balances the fear of death against the Christian belief in immortality with a complete lack of self-pity. Teixidor, though he had begun to publish before the Civil War, only reached his full maturity in the 1950s, with the appearance of his best collection, *El príncep* (The Prince; 1954), a moving series of elegies on the death of his first son which is also a scrupulous examination of his own identity. Both these poets are thoroughly disillusioned with the world in which they are compelled to live, and the same is true of Vinyoli, who, after some Symbolist beginnings, concentrates on more fundamental themes – love, sickness, the coming of old age – with a good-humoured resignation in which poetry itself is the only possible means of salvation. In all these poets, unpretentiousness is in no sense a negative quality; the inventiveness which more often than not goes with it is a large part of the attraction of their poems, no more so than when they are dealing with the kind of themes on which many less talented writers have foundered.

One poet who escapes most kinds of classification – a major writer by any standards – is Vicent Andrés Estellés (1924–93). Because he is a Valencian, he has tended be underrated in the rest of Catalonia, though there are signs that this situation is changing. What makes a critical reading of his work difficult is its sheer quantity as well as its range. Estellés has been described as a 'visceral' writer, yet, though this captures the direct tone of his poems, it overlooks his technical mastery in many different kinds of verse-form. As an 'inner émigré' during the Franco régime, he delayed the publication of his early poems until much later, though these include a great deal of his most powerful patriotic poetry. More justly, Joan Fuster has called him a 'poet of realities', rather than a 'poet of realism', and this means that he writes of love and death as one who has experienced them at first-hand. In this, he is the heir of Ausiàs March and Joan Salvat-Papasseit: poets who deliberately question conventions, and with whom he engages in a dialogue throughout his work. Above all, he is a master of colloquial language, often to the point of obscenity, as in his rewritings of the pastoral eclogue:

NEMORÓS

Escriuran el meu nom,
però no és el meu nom. I sols em moriré
si tu em crides, em dius, com em deies llavors.

CORINNA

Nemorós, Nemorós! (No m'esgarres les bragues,
que m'han costat vint duros ...) Nemorós ...

(NEMORÓS: They will write my name, but it is not my name ... And I
shall only die if you call to me, speak to me, as once you spoke.
CORINNA: Nemorós, Nemorós! [Don't tear my knickers; they cost me
twenty *duros* ...] Nemorós ...)

But as well as echoing the native tradition, Estellés also carries on a
dialogue with classical Greek and Latin poets – Horace, Ovid, Catullus,
Homer – which centres on the theme of exile and alienation and ultimately
questions his own role as poet. And in one poem in particular, he uses Ulysses' strategy for escaping the Cyclops as a means of reflecting his own situation and that of his people:

Jo sóc Ningú, i Ningú m'anomene
Ho he dit i mai ningú no em va fer cas.
He proclamat un propòsit tenaç
d'ésser ningú pels camins del meu poble.
La meua veu s'extingirà en la pols.
La meua veu serà pols i sols pols.
Perdurarà tan sols allò que diu.
I diu, només, la voluntat d'un poble.
Poble sotmés, sacrificat, sofert!

(I am No One and am called No One. I have said it, and no one ever paid
me attention. I have announced a stubborn proposal: to be no one on the
roads of my people. My voice will be extinguished in dust. My voice will
be dust and only dust. Only what it speaks will endure. And it only speaks
the will of a people. Subdued, sacrificed, suffering people!)

Agustí Bartra (1908–92) is another major poet who, for different reasons
– his long exile in Mexico and New York, the sheer range of his verse – has
tended to be undervalued. Though he began to write before the Civil War,
he came to dismiss this early work:

Abans de la guerra jo no existia com a poeta. Neixo amb la guerra, en una
situació límit. Els meus primers poemes surten de la tragèdia que
m'envolta i de la qual formo part.

(Before the war I didn't exist as a poet. I was born with the war, in an extreme situation. My first poems come from the tragedy which surrounds me and of which I am part.)

Bartra's stance is essentially prophetic: throughout his exile, he never loses hope in a better future for Catalonia, a process which leads inevitably to the *Poemes del retorn* (Poems of Return; 1971). Though he has written some good short poems, the bulk of his work consists of long sequences – *Màrsias i Adila* (1948), *Quetzalcòatl* (1971), *Soleia* (1977) – in which his re-creation of existing myths strips them of their religious dimension in order to focus on the situation of man on earth. The vast scope of these poems, with their seemingly endless flow of imagery, makes them difficult at times to take in. Nevertheless, their sheer inventiveness is impressive, as is their scale of reference: though he is essentially a Romantic poet – the parallels with Maragall are particularly striking – his other influences set him apart from any other Catalan poet of his time. Though there is a considerable debt to Whitman, there are also echoes of Russian poets – Blok and Maiakovski – and of the German Romantic tradition from Novalis to Rilke. All this is brought together in what is possibly his masterpiece, *Ecce Homo* (1968), a semi-autobiographical poem in which Bartra's own story is presented as that of a man of his time. For once, there is no reference to an existing myth: the poet himself, in his outward projection, becomes his *own* myth, in a fusion of the lyric and the epic which runs through practically the whole of Bartra's work.

Joan Brossa (1919–98) is another major author to whom recognition came relatively late. As poet, dramatist and creator of visual poems, he is beyond question the most versatile of recent Catalan writers. (For Brossa's theatre, see pp. 121–22.) Two things are unique to Brossa: his working-class origins and his full-time dedication to poetry. To the first he owes his liking for popular entertainments – music hall, circus, conjuring – as well as his extraordinary ear for everyday speech; the second accounts for the sheer bulk of his work, which, however impressive, makes it difficult to assimilate as a whole. One guiding thread is his relation to Surrealism: though his affinities with Surrealism are clear throughout his career, he himself prefers to speak of 'Neosurrealisme', a way of consciously building on the discoveries of the Surrealists, with, as he puts its it: 'un peu a l'abstracció i l'altre a la realitat' (one foot in abstraction and the other in reality). What is particularly interesting is that Brossa – like Foix, one of his early mentors – finds precedents for Surrealism within the Catalan tradition itself. Speaking of popular Catalan poetry and folktales, for instance, he says:

Tota aquesta mitologia popular [...] a mi m'agrada moltíssim; tots aquests trencaments per a produir efectes no habituals, contrastos i salts al buit; descoberta de nous nivells de sensibilitat amb el material més humil ...

(All this popular mythology [...] delights me; all those sudden cuts to produce unusual effects; contrasts and leaps into empty space; the discovery of new levels of sensibility by means of the humblest material.)

Though much of Brossa's work consists of poems in fixed forms – sonnets, formal odes and, most recently, sestinas – these are largely concerned to destroy the notion of the 'traditional poem' by playing off technical mastery against the free associations characteristic of Surrealism. As early as 1950, however, Brossa began to publish what, on the surface at least, was a very different kind of poetry: one which seemed deliberately to exclude any obvious 'poetic' effects and to reduce any kind of verbal artifice to a minimum, as in 'Nota':

> Aquest sonet
> el divideixo en tres parts per aclarir-ne
> millor el sentit. A la primera
> explico com em sembla que les muntanyes
> desprenen la nit dels murs; a la segona
> dic que un carboner va per la neu amb
> un fanal, referint-me a l'experiència
> humana, La tercera és la sobtada visió
> de la vida com una tómbola fantàstica.
> La segona comença aquí: La soca que englotia
> el vegetal; i la tercera aquí: Crestallut, surt
> de la mar un cavall.

(This sonnet I have divided into parts to make the meaning clearer. In the first, I explain how the mountains seem to detach the night from the walls; in the second, I describe how a charcoal burner walks through the snow with a lantern, thus referring to human experience. The third is a sudden vision of life as an imaginary sweepstake. The second begins here: The tree-stump, devoured by the vegetation; and the third here: With rigid mane, a horse rises from the sea.)

Since these are genuine poems, however unconventional, they inevitably raise certain obvious, though difficult, questions: what are we doing when we write a poem? What is involved in reading a poem? How does a poem relate to truth? And more specifically, what is the relation between words themselves and the objects they designate: not only the actual words of the poem, but also the way in which the reader is made to realize these words in his or her own imagination? Hence, as Pere Gimferrer has remarked: 'El primer tema de la poesia d'en Brossa – de fet, el primer tema de qualsevol poeta – és la paraula mateixa'[19] (The main theme of Brossa's poetry – in fact, the main theme of any poet – is the word itself). Ultimately, then, many

---

[19] Pere Gimferrer, '*Poesia rasa* de Joan Brossa', in *Guia de literatura catalana contemporània*, ed. Jordi Castellanos (Barcelona, 1973), p. 434.

of Brossa's poems are a form of mental hygiene: each of them represents what Edwin Morgan, speaking of concrete poetry, calls a 'jolt into perception',[20] a way of sharpening the reader's reactions to any combination of words whatsoever.

(b) Fiction

The Civil War produced one outstanding novel, Joan Sales's *Incerta glòria* (Uncertain Glory; 1956, expanded 1970). Though partly based on the author's own experiences as a soldier fighting for the Republicans, this is much more than a simple chronicle: the narrative is divided between three protagonists, each of whom speaks from his or her point of view, and their accounts are extended into the post-war period, thus giving a certain objectivity to the whole. And beyond the actual reporting of events, there is a concern for the human condition in general, for how one may live with integrity in a world in which all moral values are at risk. As one of the characters puts it, one can only do this by living the moment to the full, in a passage which reflects on the title of the book:

> No és altra cosa, és això, i és per això que la busquem, ¡una cosa que tingui plenament sentit! ¡que valgui per ella mateixa, que sigui absoluta! El nostre error és buscar-la en aquesta vida; no pas que no s'hi pugui trobar, però no podríem suportar-la més que un instant; ens aniquilaria. Si no ens aniquila és perquè es dissipa; o bé es transforma en monotonia i finalment torna a l'absurd [...]. La glòria en aquest món es transforma en monotonia si dura més d'un instant.

> (It's nothing else, it's this, and that's why we seek it, something which makes complete sense, which is self-sufficient, absolute! Our mistake is to seek it in this life; not that it can't be found, but that we couldn't bear it for more than a moment, it would annihilate us. If it doesn't annihilate us, it's because it vanishes, or else becomes monotony and finally the absurd [...] Glory in this world becomes monotony if it lasts for more than a moment.)

Several writers who began publishing in the 1930s went on to achieve their greatest successes after the Civil War. One such is Llorenç Villalonga, whose early novel, *Mort de dama*, was referred to in the previous section (see p. 102). In 1961, after a series of minor novels in Catalan and Castilian, he published what is beyond question his masterpiece, *Bearn*. Villalonga's entire production has been described as a series of personal memoirs, and in a sense this is true. However, in *Bearn*, the central character, Don Toni de Bearn, though partly based on himself, is set back in the second half of the

---

[20] Edwin Morgan, 'Into the Constellation: Some Thoughts on the Origin and Nature of Concrete Poetry', in *Essays* (Manchester, 1974), p. 32.

nineteenth century, and seen through the eyes of a priest who only partly approves of his way of life. If *Mort de Dama* was mainly satire, *Bearn* is cast in an elegiac mode: by setting the novel in the nineteenth century, Villalonga is creating a myth which concerns the decadence and ultimate extinction of the kind of semi-feudal society represented by Don Toni and his wife.

As might be expected, their world is re-created with great affection, though because of the different point of view of the priest who tries to reconstruct their story, the whole novel is rich in ambiguities. As the priest himself exclaims at one point: 'Qui arribarà a conèixer mai la veritat?' (Who will ever know the truth?), and the reader is left to wonder whether Don Toni will achieve salvation after his death.

Salvador Espriu is another writer who only gained his full stature, both as poet and prose writer, after the Civil War, though he began to publish remarkably early. *El doctor Rip* (1931), the monologue of a doctor who is dying of cancer, was written at the age of sixteen, though the revised version which appeared in 1979 is virtually a new book. A year later, Espriu published the first version of a short novel, *Laia*, which he continued to revise in later editions. This is the story, told in the third person, of an enigmatic young girl brought up in a fishing village and eventually unhappily married: an essentially solitary creature who is both deceiving and deceived, and whose life has all the inexorability of tragedy. And the fact that Espriu repeatedly returned to it suggests that it formed a kind of nucleus in his production, a novel which, though powerful in itself, contained the seeds of some of his later work.

After the Civil War, Espriu only published a few stories, of which 'Tres sorores' (Three Sisters) is a small masterpiece, the nearest thing in Catalan to Joyce's 'The Dead'. But a few years before his death, he produced one of his most remarkable works, *Les roques i el mar, el blau* (The Rocks and the Sea, the Blue; 1981), a sequence of a hundred prose pieces based on Greek myths and other figures from Greek antiquity. Espriu's method here is characteristically oblique: some of the stories are told by Aristocles, a Greek fisherman who is also something of a philosopher, to his son, Euforió; others are placed in the mouth of an impersonal narrator or of one or other of the inhabitants of Sinera, most of them familiar from earlier works of Espriu's. Yet, as is made clear in Aristocles's prologue, all of these, including himself, are merely puppets, and behind them is the voice of the poet, modulating his voice with supreme skill and using all the possibilities of the language. And many of the pieces are oblique in another sense, in their intermingling of past and present.

Thus Aristocles is no ordinary fisherman: though he lives in the world of the Greek myths, he is curiously timeless: he knows the paintings of Goya and has read a book by Camus. The same applies to some of the Greek characters: Ismene lives in a world of crime novels and television, and Nausica has read the play by Maragall. And this suggests something else which is very characteristic of Espriu: the idea that human nature does not change, so that the characters of the Greek myths are 'immortal' in a very special way. What I have said gives only a faint idea of the book's richness and inexhaustibility. In a very real sense, it gathers together most of the themes and many of the characters of Espriu's previous writing, often in new combinations and surprising juxtapositions. And it ends with a moving, though deeply ironical description of the funeral of Salom – Espriu's *alter ego* whom he claimed to have died at the beginning of the Civil War – and we are left with the final sentences, spaced out in a solemn, definitive cadence:

> La senyora Magdalena Blasi no va respondre. Els del modern baiard rodat funerari sortien amb el taüt, i rera cap dol. El sacerdot es retirava.. Els llums s'apagaven. La solemne cerimònia havia acabat.

> (Senyora Magdalena Blasi didn't reply. The men with the modern wheeled hearse brought out the coffin, with no mourners behind. The priest withdrew. The lights went out. The solemn ceremony had ended.)

Mercè Rodoreda (1909–83) had also begun to write before the war, but her first mature novel, *Aloma*, dates from 1938, and was drastically revised for a later edition (1969). In this early novel – possibly the most autobiographical of her writings – one already sees many of the characteristics of her later work: the interest in individual psychology, the use of atmospheric symbolism, and, above all, the contrast between the innocence of childhood and the difficulties of being an adult woman. In 1939, she went into exile, eventually settling in Geneva, where she wrote a number of remarkable short stories, experimenting with different types of narration, and subsequently produced what is generally agreed to be her masterpiece, the novel *La Plaça del Diamant* (1962). This story of a working-class woman in the Barcelona of the 1930s and 40s is perhaps the finest work of fiction to have appeared since the Civil War. The book has been justly praised, both for its rendering of the details of ordinary life and for its moments of poetic intensity. Yet the latter are in no sense pieces of 'fine writing': the first-person narrative remains firmly rooted in the consciousness of the central character, Natàlia, whose own experience is allowed to create the simple, but moving, symbols – the doves, the tree – which give shape to her story. Roughly, this concerns her marriage to Quimet, who is killed in the war, her subsequent thoughts of suicide, and her eventual second marriage to Antoni, an impotent pharmacist who acts partly as a father-figure and partly as a reminder of her happy childhood. And Natàlia's final monologue is open-ended in a manner which recalls the conclusion of Joyce's *Ulysses* – a novel which Rodoreda greatly admired:

[Els ocells] es ficaven al toll, s'hi banyaven estarrufats de ploma i barrejaven el cel amb fang i amb becs i amb ales. Contents ...

([The birds] went into the puddle, they bathed in it with puffed up feathers, and mixed sky with mud, beaks with wings. Contented ...)

Rodoreda's last major novel, *Mirall trencat* (Broken mirror; 1974), is at first glance very different: unusually, it is told in the third-person and follows the history of two upper middle-class families united by marriage. However, the development avoids any linear pattern; as the author explains in her preface:

Jo en tot el que tenia escrit de la novel.la d'una família, només en reflectia trossos. El meu mirall al llarg del camí era, doncs, un mirall trencat.

(In all that I had written of the novel of a family, I only reflected pieces of it. My mirror on the road [she is echoing a famous phrase of Stendhal's] was, then, a broken mirror.)

Though it contains many passages of atmospheric beauty, this is one of Rodoreda's most pessimistic novels: in the end, most of the members of the family are dead, and the family house in the suburbs, one of the central symbols of the novel, is destroyed and its site overrun by rats – a sure sign that the way of life so lovingly described is no longer possible in the aftermath of the war.

Two slightly younger novelists, Pere Calders (1912–94) and Manuel Pedrolo (1918–90), only began to publish fiction after the Civil War. Calders first came to public notice as the author of *Unitats de xoc* (Shock Troops; 1938), the chronicle of his experiences as a Republican soldier, seen from the point of view of a man who is fighting to restore civic dignity. After the war, he spent twenty-three years of exile in Mexico, where he began to write the short stories which made his reputation. He has been seen, with some justice, as a precursor of 'magic realism'. Most of his stories show what happens when some fantastic event impinges on the life of a quite ordinary man: thus, someone finds a tiger in his kitchen, or another person returning home discovers that his house has moved eight kilometres from where it should be. Calders's humour – and some of the stories are very funny indeed – comes out above all in the course of describing his protagonists' reactions; almost inevitably they fail to rise to the occasion and try to assimilate the fantastic event to their lives of dull routine. And the moral is clear: Calders believes that life is not worth living unless it is prepared to admit the irrational on its own terms. Or, as he sadly admits at one point:

Els fets s'han d'ajustar a les coses que sabem i no a les que ignorem, oblidant que aquesta darrera actitud ens obriria un món molt més ample.

(The facts must be adjusted to the things we know and not to those we don't know about, forgetting that this last attitude would open up a much wider world for us.)

Though Calders is best known as a writer of short stories, he has written several novels, notably *Ronda naval sota la boira* (Ship Circling in the Mist; 1966). This has been described with some justice as an 'anti-novel'; certainly one of its concerns is to test the viability of writing a novel, as is shown by its narrative construction. On the surface, the book is a parallel version, or even a parody, of the sinking of the *Titanic*: an ocean liner is caught in a whirlpool in the midst of thick fog and eventually sinks as the captain goes down with his ship. But already there are complications: the novel purports to be the diary of one of the passengers, Oleguer Sureda – an 'ordinary man', like those in the stories – but at the end of each section there are notes added by the 'real' narrator, glossing and sometimes correcting Oleguer's account. And behind all this there is the author who is inventing the story – Calders himself. What all this amounts to is a profound mistrust of absolutes, including truth itself. This is particularly evident in the case of the captain, Maurici, whose fixed idea of heroism demands that he goes down with his ship, even if it means sacrificing the rest of the passengers and crew. Though most of the passengers are quite unreal – mere caricatures – Calders's sympathies are clearly with the survivors: the true heroes, one might say, who are faced with the problem of remaking their lives. And all through the novel, we – both author and reader – are faced with what Calders calls 'imprevistes certeses' (unforeseen certainties): the sense in which fate can only work its effects because humans are incapable of abandoning their fixed attitudes.

Pedrolo is a difficult writer to get into focus, partly because of the extent of his work – he published over a hundred titles – and partly because of the sheer range of his material. (For Pedrolo's work in the theatre, see p. 120.) Though to a great extent he is a realist writer, his work ultimately escapes any conventional definition of realism, partly through the intense moral concern reminiscent at times of existentialism. This comes out in one of his many reflections on the novel:

Una novel.la és més que una història ben o mal contada: és sempre un testimoni de la nostra condició, una presa de posicions i, en definitiva, un acte de protesta.

(A novel is more than a story told well or badly: it is always a witness to our condition, a taking of positions and ultimately an act of protest.)

In his early novels, this protest is largely political – something which led him into difficulties with the censorship – though, interestingly, this is linked to the theme of sexual repression. Like Calders, Pedrolo is concerned with the obstacles which separate us from reality; but where Calders sees a failure to recognize the irrational, Pedrolo, in his existential mode, finds a tendency to ignore, or comply with, injustice. And his way of approaching reality is to use a great variety of narrative techniques in order to reveal a series of partial truths. Thus, in *Estrictament personal* (Strictly Personal; 1955), he employs interior monologue; in *Balanç fins a la matinada* (Balance until Morning; 1963) retrospective narration; and in *Avui es parla de mi* (Today There is Talk of Me; 1966) a series of autobiographical snap-shots, linked only by similar words or phrases, is framed by an absurd, though realistically rendered, situation in the present.

One of Pedrolo's finest novels is *Totes les bèsties de càrrega* (All the Beasts of Burden; 1967), where the contrast between the central character – an anonymous man – and the absurdity of the setting is very marked. The novel may be read as an allegory: it opens with a horrific scene in which an unidentified woman – the man's mother? – is undergoing a ludicrous opera-tion which she can hardly be expected to survive, in full view of a group of ordinary citizens. Later, there are rumours that she *has* survived, and the rest of the novel describes the man's ineffectual search for her through a series of grotesque situations – a judicial trial carried out in a latrine, a cemetery, a barracks, a brothel and so on – ending with a return to another – or is it the same? – operation. In terms of the allegory, the body in the operating theatre represents the state of the Catalan nation, and the man himself, in the course of his odyssey, is made to undergo all kinds of violation to his human dignity. Paradoxically, this is one of the more compassionate of Pedrolo's works, though it raises certain questions which surface more crucially in his later novels. Is the allegory really valid, or is it merely a projection of the man's own filial shortcomings? And why does the mother herself seem at times to become a source of oppression?

The fact that such questions arise hardly detracts from the disturbing power of the novel. However, by the 1980s, the kind of social and political evils Pedrolo is concerned with have become more diffuse; the result is a greater concentration on the sexual theme, often in disconcerting ways, and these, one suspects, have more to do with the author's individual psychology than with anything in the world around him.[21]

Lastly, a writer who died young, Montserrat Roig (1946–91), the author of five novels as well as a considerable amount of non-fiction. On the

---

[21] For another interpretation of *Totes les bèsties de càrrega,* see Kathryn Crameri, *Language, the Novelist and National Identity in Post-Franco Catalonia* (Oxford, 2000), pp. 84–7. Louise Johnson's article 'Some Thoughts on Pedrolo: Estrangement, Mothers and Others', *Tesserae,* 5. 11 (1999), 37–47, skilfully analyses the complications of Pedrolo's sexual attitudes.

surface, the sequence of novels which begins with *Ramona, adéu* (Goodbye, Ramona; 1972) and ends with *L'hora violeta* (The Violet Hour; 1980) constitutes a family saga, centred on several middle-class generations in a particular area of Barcelona. This in itself has great documentary value, but what makes these books outstanding is their sure grasp of personal relationships and the way these change according to historical circumstances. And in *L'hora violeta*, her concerns with feminism lead her to question the nature of gender and the narrative voice in a particularly subtle way.

In the course of the novel, Roig uses diaries, letters and various first-person voices, combined with a third-person narrative which seems to go deeper than any of these. The result is a certain inconclusiveness in the story which reflects the lives of the women concerned. All of these are in some sense waiting – the Penelope of the *Odyssey* is a constant point of reference – but, unlike Penelope, their expectations, for various reasons, remain unfulfilled. At the same time, none of them is allowed to become a 'character': their several illusions, one of which is a conventional feminism, never permit them to acknowledge a Self. Something similar happens to the men in the story: in their dealings with Communism, they fail to achieve the heroic status they desire and consequently remain one-dimensional. And this affects the relationships between the sexes: for all their efforts, the women, with one exception, fail to avoid the trap of patriarchy. The exception is Agnès, who at the end of the novel rejects her husband and thus takes control of her destiny.

This novel has often been read autobiographically, as if the various women were versions of Roig herself. To some extent, this must be true, yet the fact is that she is writing a fiction, whose links with autobiography are, to say the least, tenuous. So, as Helen Wing puts it: '[T]he artist herself, Roig, by conflating the notions of gender and individuality through the interplay of autobiographical voices, becomes both subject and object of her art.'[22]

Roig's last novel, *La veu melodiosa* (The Melodious Voice; 1987) is very different from the preceding ones and seems to indicate a new phase in her work. Though the observation of the social context is as acute as ever, the story has a fable-like quality which is reflected in the economy of the writing. It concerns a young boy, l'Espardenya, who is brought up by his grandfather in complete seclusion from the world outside, but is eventually forced to come to terms with a group of fellow students. At first these only accept him as a figure of fun – he is both ugly and gauche – but when they find he has a second life helping families of immigrants and is sent to prison, though innocent, they come to respect and, finally, to love him. Thus this central character, who has something of both Candide and Prince

---

[22] Helen Wing, 'Deviance and Legitimation: Roig's *La hora violeta*', *BHS*, LXXII (1995), 87–96 (p. 95).

Muishkin, has a perception of life – the 'melodious voice' – which his friends do not possess, and he finally becomes a poet, with the prospect of being united with the female narrator.

(c) Theatre

The theatre suffered more than any other genre from the Civil War: the professional staging of plays in Catalan was prohibited up to 1946, and translations of foreign plays were not allowed until the 1950s. And when Catalan plays eventually appeared, these were more often than not revivals of third-rate plays of the 1930s. The decisive moment came, however, with the foundation of the Agrupació Dramàtica de Barcelona (Barcelona Theatre Group, or ADB) in 1955, followed by the Escola d'Art Dramàtic Adrià Gual (Adrià Gual School of Dramatic Art, or EADAG) in 1960. Thus the 1960s saw the production of a number of foreign plays, from Molière to Brecht, together with the emergence of several native dramatists, among them Espriu, Maria Aurèlia Capmany, Manuel de Pedrolo, Baltasar Porcel and Joan Brossa. Nevertheless, the situation was still fairly precarious: all too often, the production of a new play was limited to a single performance, and opportunities of seeing plays in Catalan outside Barcelona were still very restricted. In fact, it was not until the death of Franco in 1975 that theatre was firmly institutionalized, a process which culminated in the creation of the Centre Dramàtic de la Generalitat (Theatre Centre of the Generalitat, or CDG) in 1981.[23]

The War itself produced one outstanding play, Joan Oliver's *La fam* (Hunger; 1938). Based on the recent conflict between anarchists and communists, it presents a revolutionary situation in which two contrasting characters – Samsó, a brave but egotistical man who is incapable of serious planning, and Nel, a good, rational person who is over-analytical and reluctant to act – are played off against one another. Samsó, despite his defects, is shown to be someone of great humanity; at the end of the play, he returns to his life of freedom, but not before opposing those opportunists who are planning a counter-revolution.

Oliver's play, though acclaimed at the time, had no sequel, and the author himself went into exile for the next ten years. Espriu, on the other hand, remained in Catalonia and, perhaps more eloquently than any other writer, reflected the mood of these years. His first play, *Antígona*, was written in 1939 and revised in 1963 and 1967. In its original version, it is a

---

[23] For a more detailed account of this process and much else, see *Contemporary Catalan Theatre: an Introduction*, ed. David George and John London (Sheffield, 1996). This also includes a useful bibliography of translations of plays published in periodicals.

bitter response to the Civil War: Antigone sacrifices herself in order to put an end to civil discord, but in the end it is Creon, the tyrant, who prevails. Espriu's treatment of the theme is highly original, no more so than when he adds the character of Eumolp, the hunchbacked slave – something of a buffoon – who accompanies Antigone in her death. When one remembers that Espriu claimed to have 'died' at the beginning of the Civil War, it is not difficult to see Eumolp as a version of himself: someone who, quite disinterestedly, gives up his life for Antigone, without in the least detracting from her heroism. And in the revision of 1963, Espriu adds another character, the 'Lúcid conseller' (Lucid Counsellor), who appears towards the end of the play, embodying Espriu's more recent reflections on the injustice of Antigone's death, as well as casting a sceptical eye on Creon himself.

The full complexity of Espriu's reactions to the War, however, appeared in his 'improvisation for puppets', *Primera història d'Esther* (First Story of Esther; 1948). Here, by imagining the performance of a puppet play on the biblical episode of Esther in the small Catalan town of Sinera, Espriu is able to superimpose the Old Testament story on the world of his own childhood – a world which has been destroyed by the War. In the course of the action – which is witnessed by the inhabitants of Sinera – the biblical characters constantly refer to local people and events, thus creating a wonderful mixture of past and present. Like all his best work, this depends for part of its effect on the extraordinary linguistic agility with which he creates a situation in which the barriers of time and place are abolished, and where the dead generations of Sinera are as real to the biblical characters as they are to the author himself. And in the final speech of the showman to the audience, the contemporary reference becomes even clearer:

> Eviteu el màxim crim, el pecat de la guerra entre germans. Penseu que el mirall de la veritat s'esmicolà a l'origen en fragments petitíssims, i cada un dels trossos recull tanmateix una engruna d'autèntica llum.

> (Avoid the greatest crime of all, the sin of war between brothers. Remember that in the beginning the mirror of truth was broken into tiny pieces, and that each one of these pieces nevertheless reflects an atom of true light.)

Espriu only published one other play, *Una altra Fedra, si us plau* (Another Phaedra, Please; 1977), a slighter piece than the two previous ones, but interesting in the context of his other work. By presenting the actress who is to play the role of Phaedra before she goes on stage, in conversation with the three women from Sinera who are to witness her performance, Espriu is deliberately creating a distance between ourselves and the familiar action. And in doing so, he replaces tragedy by inevitability; the whole play is overshadowed by the figure of Death, who does not speak, and it ends *before* the deaths of Phaedra and Hippolytus, as if we knew all too well what is to come.

Pedrolo, best known as a novelist, is the author of thirteen plays, several of which have remained in the repertoire. As he says himself: '[N]o sóc un dramaturg, sóc un novel.lista que circumstancialment ha escrit unes quantes peces dramàtiques' (I am a novelist who happens to have written a few plays.) This is over-modest: the fact is that he made a considerable contribution to the Catalan theatre of the 1950s and 60s at a time when other talents were hard to seek.

Though his plays vary a good deal in technique, their essential aim is clear:

> [La meva obra dramàtica] sempre dóna voltes entorn del mateix problema. L'examina o el presenta, des d'angles diferents i, per tant, hi va profunditzant, però el problema sempre és, fonamentalment, el de la lliberat.
>
> ([My dramatic work] always revolves round the same problem. It examines or presents it from different angles and thus goes into it more deeply, but the problem is always, fundamentally, that of freedom.)

This appears quite clearly in his best-known play, *Homes i No* (Men and No; 1957). Though it has been described as an absurdist drama,[24] this is only partially true: even if the situation itself may be classed as absurd, it is followed through with absolute coherence. In many of Pedrolo's plays, the stage is seen as a cage or a room: here, two groups of three characters are imprisoned in cells on either side of No, their gaoler. In the first act, the older prisoners try to escape, but fail; in the second, which takes place some years later, the younger generation – Feda and Sorne – resume the search for freedom, acting more intelligently than their parents. In the end, they discover a curtain at the back of their cells which, despite No's protests, they pull down, revealing more bars. This means that No himself is a prisoner, and the process, it seems, will be repeated to infinity. But this is deceptive: if Feda and Sorne have broken down one barrier only to find another, they have nevertheless achieved a kind of victory through language, through their ability to analyse the situation in which they find themselves. Not only this: the second set of bars does not necessarily imply an infinite repetition, but may merely represent one more obstacle in the search for freedom which must never be abandoned. Or as Pedrolo himself once put it:

> [Feda i Sorne] s'han desfet, doncs, d'un tabú, d'una limitació primera, immediata. Amb el temps, més enllà de la peça, ells mateixos o els seus fills faran un altre progrés.

---

[24] Martin Esslin, *The Theatre of the Absurd* (Harmondsworth, 1968), p. 285.

([Feda and Sorne] have rid themselves, then, of a taboo, a first, immediate limitation. In the course of time, beyond the play, they themselves or their children will make further progress.)

Joan Brossa, though he remained faithful to what he called 'Neo-surrealism', openly rejected the Theatre of the Absurd: 'Res de res! m'interessen més els germans Marx i tots els pallassos (menys en Dalí).' (I don't like it at all. I'm more interested in the Marx Brothers and all the clowns [except for Dalí].) If his poetry is hard to assimilate because of its sheer bulk, this is even truer of his theatre, or what he liked to call his 'scenic poetry', which runs to six volumes in the collected edition. Never-theless, certain features stand out. One is its anti-literary bias:

> Jo sempre he cregut que l'ingedient bàsic del teatre [...] no és la literatura, sinó el carnaval. En aquest sentit profund el teatre no morirà mai perquè la gent el porta ben endins i és tan vell com la humanitat. Arlequí, Pierrot i Colombina, aquesta és la essència del teatre. Vull dir que el teatre és un mitjà que treballa damunt la imaginació i no pas solament damunt l'intel.lecte.

> (I've always believed that the basic ingredient of the theatre [...] is not literature but the carnival. In this profound sense, the theatre will not die because the people carry it deep within them, and it is as old as humanity itself. Harlequin, Pierrot and Columbine, this is the essence of the theatre. I mean that the theatre is a means which works on the imagination and not just on the intellect.)

Another is his extreme care for language: not just the way individual characters are made to speak the appropriate idiom, but also the sense in which speech works on the audience. And this accounts for the difficulty of much of his work: time after time characters come out with statements or images which make perfect sense in themselves; the trouble is to recognize an overall meaning. In one of his early full-length plays, *Or i sal* (Gold and Salt; 1959), for example, there are different characters in each of the three acts: the action goes from an apparently nonsensical conversation between three men to a second act in which the various characters are dressed in sixteenth-century clothes, and finally to a seemingly ordinary couple, the husband of which is obsessed with killing dragons. At the level of plot, then, the three acts are unconnected. As in most of Brossa's work, meaning comes as much from gaps and juxtapositions as from logical statement. But, looking back over the whole play, there are a number of thematic and tech-nical links: implicit criticism of religion, the relevance of history to modern times, the suggestion of a modern witch-hunt.

Brossa left off writing full-length plays fairly early on, partly because of difficulties of getting them produced, partly because of incomprehension on the part of the public. Almost to the end of his life, however, he continued to produce a vast number of short pieces, ranging from a few pages to two or three lines. Most of these are intended to undermine conventional notions of theatre and also to fulfil a social purpose, and many of them read like sketches for longer plays. Some of them are frankly satirical – covert and not so covert attacks on the Franco régime; others are a tribute to his master, the transformist Fregoli, while yet others, as John London has said, are an attempt to 'elevate striptease from the sordid to the surreal'.[25] In all of them, Brossa aims to undermine the audience's stock reactions, as in the following piece:

STRIPTEASE

Fons taronja, A intervals de deu segons cauen del sostre totes les peces de roba amb què es vesteix una dona. Finalment caurà una sabata i, en esperar que caigui l'altra, baixarà el teló.

(Orange backdrop. At ten-second intervals all the pieces of clothing a woman wears fall from the ceiling. Finally a shoe falls and, while we are waiting for the other one to fall, the curtain drops.)

In such pieces, the precision of the stage directions – 'Orange backdrop. At ten-second intervals ...' – suggests that Brossa is watching his own play. And at the back of these sketches, there is always the feeling that he is exploiting, with great sensitivity, the basic forms of popular entertainment – the circus, conjuring, the *commedia dell'arte* and vaudeville – in a way no other Catalan writer has done.

---

[25] John London, 'The Theatrical Poetry of Joan Brossa', in *Joan Brossa: Words are Things* (London, 1992), pp. 21–4 (p. 23).

Chapter 5

THE PRESENT

All the authors I discuss in this chapter are still alive at the time of writing. Some, like Martí i Pol and Perucho, produced the bulk of their work in the last century but are still continuing to add to it; others, like Moncada, have only begun to write in the last twenty years or so and have a promising career ahead of them. Moreover, I have had to be very selective: at the moment, there are at least two dozen poets worth reading, and the same goes for the novelists and, to a slightly lesser extent, for the theatre writers. To have mentioned all of these would have prolonged this chapter out of all proportion; alternatively, to have reduced them to mere lists would hardly have enlightened the reader and only served to confuse him. In the end, therefore, I have been forced to compromise: I have concentrated on what seem to me the most interesting writers, all too conscious that others would have deserved mention in a longer account.

I. Poetry

Miquel Martí i Pol (b. 1929) has often been associated with the mode of 'social realism' fashionable in the 1960s, but this is far too limiting and in many ways inaccurate. After an early religious phase which came to a crisis in the poems of *El fugitiu* (The Fugitive; 1952–7), he began to write about ordinary people, and in particular those otherwise anonymous men and women he saw as trapped in the routines of industry. This is the closest he comes to 'social realism', but even here there are differences: above all, as is clear from the two sequences entitled *La fàbrica–1959* (The Factory; 1958–9) and *La fàbrica* (1970–1), he writes as one who works in the factory himself and, as a result, can empathize with his fellow-workers in a way which is foreign to most other 'social realist' poets. Nevertheless, there is a certain distancing which enables him to avoid the faults – sentimentality, paternalism – of much poetry of this kind. As he himself once said:

> El pitjor pecat de l'artista és l'autocontemplació. Això demostra que el distanciament és absolutament necessari. Distanciament d'allò que fa i, sobretot, distanciament de si mateix. [...] L'home és el substrat necessari

de l'artista. Però no és l'artista, per més que visqui com a tal. Per això és imprescindible el distanciament i la recerca.

(The artist's worst sin is self-contemplation. This means that distancing is absolutely necessary. Distancing from what he does and, above all, distancing from himself. [...] The man is the necessary substratum of the artist. But he is not the artist, however much he lives as such. This is why distancing and research are essential.)

In 1970, Martí i Pol fell victim to an illness – multiple sclerosis – which immobilized him and forced him to give up his work. References to this illness recur throughout the rest of his poetry, though with a complete absence of self-pity. From now on, this follows three lines of development: the personal lyric, with its characteristic mixture of elegy and irony, love poetry, and poetry about collective concerns, frequently satirical. His personal poems, which often overlap with the love poems, are introspective in a quite new way, as if his illness had made him seem a stranger to himself. And in his dealings with death, the easy irony conceals a courageous determination to survive:

> De tant en tant la mort i jo som u,
> mengem el pa de la mateixa llesca,
> bevem el vi de la mateixa copa
> i compartim amicalment les hores
> sense dir res, llegint el mateix llibre.
> [...]
> Després les coses tornen al seu lloc
> i cadascú reprèn la seva via.

(From time to time death and myself are one, we eat the same slice of bread, we drink wine from the same glass and we share the hours in a friendly way, not speaking, reading the same book. [...] Afterwards, things return to their places and each of us goes his own way.)

What is perhaps surprising in these later poems is his continuing concern for collective issues. The three lines of development I have mentioned come together, in fact, in one of his finest collections, *Estimada Marta* (Dear Marta; 1978). Some of these poems must count among the best love poems in the Catalan language – equalled only in modern times by Salvat-Papasseit and Gabriel Ferrater. But apart from this, Martí i Pol uses his own illness as a metaphor for the ills of society under Franco, together with the chances of recuperation. Thus his own indomitable fortitude acts both at a personal level and as an assurance that civil themes – not merely 'social realism' – will never be far from his work.

Unlike Martí i Pol, Ramon Xirau (b. 1924) came to poetry relatively late. Since he has spent most of his working life in Mexico, where he teaches philosophy, he writes at one remove from the majority of Catalan poets.

This makes for considerable independence, as well as a certain neglect among his contemporaries. This is entirely undeserved: his three most substantial collections, *Les platges* (The Beaches; 1974), *Graons* (Steps; 1979) and *Dit i descrit* (Said and Described; 1983), show him to be that rare thing: an openly Christian poet who draws fully on the resources of modern poetry. Moreover, the fact that he is also a philosopher has a direct bearing on his poems; for him, the two things are complementary, or as he once said: '[P]orque la filosofía – quiero decir la metafísica – y la poesía son dos formas de una expresión más alta: la expresión religiosa.' Hence the importance of metaphor for Xirau. Its real significance is metaphysical: if it implies a fusion, one must ask what it is which is fused, and in what way this affects our sense of reality. Thus 'platges' (beaches), a key metaphor in the first two collections, is both a reference to an actual landscape and an image of harmony, a 'place' where the celebration of God may take root.

One striking feature of Xirau's poems is the way language is apparently made to generate itself. Sometimes the syntax seems to deconstruct itself and create a new dimension:

> Prou, el silenci parla. Prou. Silenci,
> parla. Prou el silenci calla
> calladiu, calladament Et diu.

(Enough, silence speaks. Enough. Silence, speak [or, 'it speaks']. Enough: silence falls silent, silent, silently it speaks You.)

At other times, he will coin a new word which is rich in associations. Thus, 'gregoriosament' in 'gregoriosament el cant neix de la barca' (gregoriously the song is born from the boat) is a reference to Gregorian chant, but also suggests 'gloriosament' (gloriously) and possibly also 'gregàriament' (gregariously) as a symbol of collective faith.

The interpenetration of poetry and philosophy appears at its most subtle in 'L'anyell' (The Lamb), the long poem which forms the centre piece of *Dit i descrit*. In this meditation on the Apocalypse, as Octavio Paz has written in his preface to *Graons*:

> [L]es idees són formes que podem veure, tocar, sentir; les imatges, al seu torn, posseeixen una vibració que no és física sinó espiritual. Tornem a pensar amb els ulls, amb el cos.
>
> (The ideas are forms we can see, touch, feel; the images, in their turn, possess a vibration which is not physical, but spiritual. We go back to thinking with the eyes, with the body.)

This emphasis on seeing – on seeing the world as it is – is central to *Dit i descrit*. Not only is God 'un Déu del veure' (a God of seeing), but description itself – a way of using words so that you *see* exactly what they are describing – becomes a means of deciphering the world. As Xirau recognizes, such an enterprise is strictly impossible, though it must always be attempted: the most language can do is to lead one to the edge of the unsayable and then fall silent. But what it has 'said' and what it has 'described' are part of the conditions of poetic language itself. Or as Xirau himself has said: 'El poema no trata de significados; *es* el significado; no trata del mundo: es el mundo transfigurado en lengua y habla.'

Two poets made their mark in the 1950s and early 60s: Jordi Sarsanedas (b. 1924) and Francesc Vallverdú (b. 1935). Though he has continued to write good poems, notably in *Postals d'Itàlia* (Postcards from Italy; 1965), Sarsanedas's reputation as a poet rests mainly on his second collection, *La Rambla de les Flors* (The Rambla of Flowers), published in 1955. This came out at a crucial time: roughly the transition from a Symbolist aesthetic to a more socially orientated poetry. Sarsanedas's allegiance to Salvat-Papasseit – the addressee of one of the best poems in the book – struck a new note in the poetry of the time, a willingness to celebrate ordinary lives and events. Thus one poem, 'Novetat del món', ends:

> Deixem els vells records, que siguin pedres
> a la ciutat dels morts, que tota tomba és pia.
> I baixem al carrer.

> (Let us leave old memories, that they may be stones in the city of the dead, for every tomb is pious. And go down into the street.)

Nevertheless, this desire to reflect social reality largely avoids the banalities of 'social realism', partly through humour and partly through the workings of a vivid, at times almost surrealistic, imagination, as in these earlier lines from the same poem:

> El groc del taxi és un xiscle d'ocell,
> un tremolor de plomes.
> El vermell del tramvia és un lladruc de gos.
> Passo la mà per les testes amigues
> d'un món tendre i manyac.
> El camió cantàbric que torna de nits altes
> és un bou solemníssim.

> (The yellow of the taxi is the cry of a bird, a trembling of feathers. The red of the tram is a dog's bark. I pass my hand over the friendly heads of a tender, docile world. The Cantabrian lorry which returns from deep nights is a most solemn ox.)

Vallverdú is another poet who has been loosely associated with 'social realism' but is considerably more complex. His first collections, *Com llances* (Like Lances; 1961) and *Qui ulls ha* (Who Has Eyes; 1962), are more directly political than those of any other poet of his generation, and at times one detects the influence of Pere Quart and Espriu. The deliberately aggressive nature of such poems is designed to shock; what strikes one most, however, is their rejection of elitism and at the same time their avoidance of stock responses. In later collections, like *Somni, insomni* (Sleep, Insomnia; 1971), there is a more indirect, though increasingly subtle political dimension, as when he glosses a series of statements by the great fifteenth-century writer Bernat Metge in contemporary terms. And this suggests what, by and large, is true, that for all the modernity of his satire, Vallverdú is fully aware of his medieval predecessors, Ramon Llull, Jaume Roig (in the verse form of certain poems) and Ausiàs March, to whom he dedicates one of his best sonnets:

> Poeta enter, ensenyes el dolor
> que hi ha en el fons de tota vida humana:
> la teva veu ressona com campana
> des del passat a l'esvenidor.
>   Poeta amic, quin secret les paraules
> serven avui que ens puguin concitar?
> Tens el poder de fer sobresaltar
> els nostres ulls embadalits pels saules.
>   Poeta aspriu, difícil de tenir,
> card entre llirs, en el que vagis dir
> ¿descobrirem un dia el teu misteri?
>   Però què hi fa? El que importa és el setge
> per tu bastit, Ausiàs March, heretge,
> que ha perdurat al mateix encanteri.

(Complete poet, you show us the pain which lives in the depths of every human life: your voice resounds like a bell which rings out from the past to the future. Dear poet, what secret do words hold today that they can still stir us? You have the power to shock our eyes as they gaze distractedly at the willows. Rough-diamond poet, difficult to handle, thorn among lilies, shall we one day discover your mystery in what you said? But what does it matter? What is important is the siege you laid, Ausiàs March, you heretic, which has outlived enchantment itself.)

Of the poets born since 1940, three are outstanding: Pere Gimferrer (b. 1945), Narcís Comadira (b. 1942) and Francesc Parcerisas (b. 1944).

Gimferrer's first collections of poems were written in Spanish. In them he shows a remarkable freedom from contemporary influences; instead, he adopts a much more cosmopolitan range of models, from Rimbaud and Darío to Eliot, Wallace Stevens, Saint-John Perse and Octavio Paz. Cinema is also important: in many of these poems – and this is to persist into his Catalan poetry – the use of certain cinematic techniques – montage, abrupt transitions – is combined with a kind of metapoetry in which the poem is made to reflect on its own composition. From 1970 onwards, all Gimferrer's poetry is written in Catalan, a transition which he describes as the need to write in a language in which the 'I' of the poems can coincide with himself. In his first three collections in Catalan, *Els miralls* (The Mirrors; 1970), *Hora foscant* (Darkening Hour; 1972) and *Foc cec* (Blind Fire; 1973), the preoccupations of the earlier poems – notably, the search for identity – are continued, along with an exploration of those elements in the Catalan tradition – popular poetry, the Baroque – which are still valid for a contemporary poet. Like Foix, Gimferrer is acutely aware of the menacing aspects of reality and of the dangers involved in attempting to go beyond conventional categories. So, in 'Solstici' (Solstice), from *Foc cec*, the inner conflict – the confrontation between man and reality – is conveyed in military images which suggest both a remote historical past and a timeless, self-renewing cosmic myth. In the last third of the poem, however, the highly metaphorical language becomes self-reflecting:

> ... Els mots
> celen un clos pregon, i l'escriptura
> llatzera el cos del tigre. Escrit amb foc
> i escrit amb llum, a la lunar contrada,
> pasturatge dels morts. L'amant albira,
> enllà dels membres contorçats, l'obscur.
> I les arrels no es mouen. Com els cossos,
> s'han nodrit de silenci. Llur país
> de sequedat i de centelles obre
> els ulls, esbatanats. El crit del corb
> sagna el cel moradenc. Fusta i safirs:
> l'últim fulgor, convuls, de llum terrestre.

(Words conceal a deep enclosure, and writing lacerates the body of the tiger. Written with fire and written with light, in the moon's domain, pasture of the dead. The lover glimpses darkness beyond the twisting limbs. And the roots do not move. Like bodies, they have fed on silence. Their land of dryness and sparks opens its eyes wide. The cry of the raven bleeds in the purple sky. Wood and sapphires: the last convulsive brilliance of earthly light.)

Thus, words can suggest silence – the silence before language from which any true sense of the nature of reality must come – and writing itself may be a means of opposing the forces which threaten to destroy man in his search for reality. The poem itself, of course, expresses this much less abstractly; what is crucial, however, is the link which emerges between language and sexual love. Both, sooner or later, must come to terms with silence and the darkness of the unknown. And words, like plants, have their 'roots'; like the bodies of the lovers, they are capable of violence and conflict, but also of the kind of silent, unconscious knowledge which comes from their place in the natural process.

A great deal of Gimferrer's poetry is concerned with the senses' attempt to penetrate the inflexible world of conceptual language in order to reveal what he calls the 'other face of reality':

> Només el real pot ser sublim o terrífic, vehicle de revelació d'ell mateix o del sobrereal; però és precisament propi del creador descobrir el veritable rostre del real, posar en moviment les relacions inesperades, les associacions brusques, els trànsits ocults.

> (Only the real can be sublime or terrifying, the vehicle by which it reveals itself or the superreal; but it is precisely the task of the creator to discover the true face of the real, to set in motion the unexpected relationships, the sudden associations, the hidden transitions.)

One such means of access to a higher reality is sexual love, which from now on plays a central part in Gimferrer's work. This theme combines with others in L'espai desert (Deserted Space; 1977), his most ambitious poem to date. Here, for the first time, he investigates the possibilities of poetry within the context of a specific time and place. Much of this investigation depends on language itself; Gimferrer sees the poem as an activity, rather than as a means of expression: the complex transformations of the poem are brought about by the pressures of the actual language in such a way that the identity of the poet is destroyed and re-formed through glimpses of a truer reality.

In Aparicions (Apparitions; 1981), the long sequence which followed L'espai desert, the question of individual identity is approached from a more inward direction, from the connection between the act of writing and the possibility of living an authentic life. Thus the poem moves between a state of pre-consciousness associated with dream to a 'centre of consciousness' in which individual identity is merged in a reciprocal movement between particular lives and the life of the earth.

Since Aparicions, Gimferrer has published four further collections, El vendaval (The Whirlwind, 1988), La llum (The Light; 1991), Mascarada (Masquerade; 1996) and El diamant dins l'aigua (The Diamond in the Water; 2001). In contrast to the free verse of much of the earlier poetry, many of the poems in the first two collections are strict sonnets, in which Gimferrer's virtuosity reaches new heights. He himself has described these poems as 'Symbolism taken to its final limits': if they constantly lament the gap which separates words from the objects they attempt to designate, their formal perfection serves to undermine what, at first sight, might seem a depressing conclusion. This technical virtuosity is also carried over into his most recent collection, where the title poem runs to forty-five quatrains, all of which use only the same two rhymes. Again, in this same collection, there are signs that Gimferrer is still extending his range in the direction of public events: hence his moving poem on Sarajevo and the fine epitaph on Maria-Mercè Marçal, another good poet who died young. As for *Mascarada*, this is on one level a homage to Paris, with shades of Aragon and Baudelaire, but more specifically to an experience of Paris which is now in the past and will never be repeated. But at a deeper level, this is a love poem addressed to his wife, his companion in that earlier experience. Despite its title, this is the most personal of Gimferrer's poems: the love he describes is both intense and astonishingly frank. Yet the passages on coprophilia which have so disconcerted many critics need to be read in their context, where they take on a certain sacred quality which raises them above mere pornography and makes them one more expression of a love which is never less than absolute. (For Gimferrer's one novel, see p. 136.)

Narcís Comadira is a very different kind of poet. His early poems, many of them sonnets, show a concern for form which he inherits from Carner and the Foix of *Sol, i de dol.* Or, as he himself has said:

> Per a nosaltres, la poesia era un artefacte lingüístic que ha de funcionar per si mateix i que podia ser molt bona i tenir un contingut trivial.

> (For us, poetry was a linguistic artefact which must funcion on its own and which could be very good, though its content were trivial.)

What saves Comadira's own poetry from being trivial, however, is his constant attempt to relate poetry to life, and more specifically, to the search for happiness. And in this, art is central:

> [N]omés l'art pot oferir, com a món ideal que és, i per tant capaç de ser perfecte, una terra on viure val la pena i morir pot tenir un sentit.

> (Only art can offer, as the ideal world it is, and thus capable of perfection, an earth where life is worth living and death has a meaning.)

Or as he puts it in 'Un passeig pels bulevards ardents' (A Walk down the Burning Boulevards; 1974):

> El món és moviment i tot ordre impossible.
> Només l'ordre de l'art et donarà el repòs.

> (The world is movement and all order impossible. Only the order of art will give you respite.)

This last poem, a long sequence in nine sections, is much more ambitious than anything Comadira had previously written and is a decisive turning-point in his development. Though it has a distinct narrative thread – it begins with a journey on the London Underground – it builds on a contrast between the real city and the 'unreal city' of the writer's imagination. Thus

the contradiction between art and life is set in a specific context, and the
poem ends with an appeal to Beauty:

> Fugissera Bellesa sempre incontaminada,
> vine tu amb el fuet d'un somriure o d'uns ulls.
> Sacseja'ns en la fosca de la monotonia,
> desafia el passat, el present i el futur.

(Ephemeral Beauty, never corrupted, come with the whip of a smile or of
eyes. Unnerve us in monotony's darkness, challenge past, present and
future.)

This, however, makes the poem sound too abstract; what it represents,
above all, is a freeing of Comadira's imagination: the sudden leaps from one
image to another often have the effect of collage, as do the intertextual allusions to other poets, from Jordi de Sant Jordi to Baudelaire and Eliot, whose
The Waste Land acts as a point of reference for the whole sequence. And the
confusion between the two cities – the real and the unreal – reflects a more
intimate confusion within the lyric self: not so much a personal self as one
which is created for the sake of the poem.

Àlbum de família (Family Album; 1980) is an attempt to come to terms
with the past – Comadira's own past and the past of those who are
connected to him. However, the book – one of his best – is more subtle than
might appear at a first reading. Surprisingly, it is neither nostalgic nor
elegiac; at the end of the title poem, he wonders why he is so drawn to these
photographs of the past:

> Passaran una a una i les tems,
> infant poruc, tantes fotografies,
> dansa fatal de fantasmes efímers.
> Però t'atreu el contratemps monòton,
> el compàs, la feixuga melodia,
> els acords plens i les gràcils cadències,
> la llibertat i el terror del silenci.

(They will go past one by one and you are afraid, fearful child, of so
many photographs, the fatal dance of ephemeral ghosts. But you are
attracted by the monotonous counterpoint, the beat, the ponderous
melody, the full chords and the delicate cadences, the freedom and the
terror of silence.)

Reduced to its basic terms, this descent into the past is a descent into
nothingness (*no-res*) – hence the 'terror of silence'. However, it is only by
confronting this state of negation that the poet can encounter his authentic
self, or, in the poem's own terms, can experience life as opposed to mere
existence. Nevertheless, as the final poem makes clear, this life, however
precious, is always under threat:

Fas foc d'afectes vells i t'aconsolen.
Algun captard, el cel encara és net
i, en cercles grans, ocells de presa hi volen.

(You set fire to old affections and they console you. Some evening, the sky is still clear and birds of prey fly there in great circles.)

Comadira's most recent collection, *L'art de la fuga* (The Art of Fugue; 2002), shows him still at the height of his powers, not concerned to construct an *œuvre*, but writing sensitively, and with a certain stoicism, about the passing of the seasons, the ephemeral beauty of flowers and about several artists who are close to him. And in his poem on Tàpies – not for nothing is he a painter himself – he writes what amounts to a justification of his own work:

No
no pas el que veuen els ulls
sinó el que deleja l'ànima.
Però a tothora
amb el pes de dolor que el cor constreny.
Un cor humà
marcat pel sempre insaciable
desfici del misteri.
La mà és qui hostatja l'ull.
La mà que hi veu
mentre traça
sobre la crosta de la carn del món
els signes de la persistència.

(No, not what the eyes see but what the soul desires. But at all times with the weight of pain which constrains the heart. A human heart marked by the always insatiable anxiety of mystery. It is the hand which accommodates the eye. The hand which sees with it while it traces the signs of persistence on the crust of the world's flesh.)

Parcerisas's first collection, *Vint poemes civils* (Twenty Civil Poems; 1967), published when the poet was in his early twenties, is astonishingly mature. With the exception of the eroticism which is to figure largely in his later work, most of his basic themes are already here: solidarity with common people, anti-imperialist invective (Vietnam), the attack on false morality, solitude and disillusionment. And running beneath all this, there is a wish to distance himself from the deceptive 'innocence' of childhood and to experience the truer realities of the present.

Of all the poets I am concerned with here, Parcerisas is the one most deeply influenced by English and American poetry: not only Eliot and Auden, but also Allen Ginsberg and the 'Beat' poets. This is very evident in his second collection, *Homes que es banyen* (Men Bathing; 1970), where his reading of other poets is perfectly assimilated into his own increasingly subtle poetic language. What is more, he greatly extends his range, especially in the direction of love poetry, as in the poem 'Bruts d'amor' (Dirty with Love), where he compares his wife to a house:

> És font, deu, una pàtria petita on amagar errors.
> I el pes nocturn del meu cos penetrant el seu
> és el darrer maó que crema les mans.
> No espereu la teulada que clogui la casa,
> jo obro a la nit la construcció futura,
> que és com dir que ara, tot just comença la feina.

(It is a fountain, a spring, a little homeland where one can hide one's errors. And the nightly weight of my body penetrating hers is the last brick which burns the hands. Do not expect the roof which will close the house, I work by night on the future construction, which is to say that now, just now, the work begins.)

And as well as an acceptance of 'hippy' ideology – anti-war, pro sexual freedom – there is an ironic rejection of Romanticism in favour of the rational materialism which comes to a head in *Discurs sobre les matèries terrestres* (Discourse on Earthly Matters; 1972) and *Latituds de cavalls* (Horse Latitudes; 1974). By now, Parcerisas has partly abandoned the formal structures of his earlier poems – perhaps influenced by *The Waste Land* and the *Cantos* of Pound – and resorts to collage and near surrealist imagery. These experimental techniques reflect a sense of disorientation: the inability to make sense of the world and the imperfect nature of human communication. At the same time, many of these poems are concerned with introspection, not in a systematic sense, but through a network of concealed allusions and silences which, better than words, reveal the transitoriness of earthly things. And the eroticism which appeared intermittently in the earlier poems now becomes central: the idea of love as centred on the sexual act in what amounts to a writing of the body.

In *L'Edat d'Or* (The Golden Age; 1983), Parcerisas leaves behind his period of experimentation and finds what now seems to be his true 'voice': the 'voice', both restrained and mature, which will persist into his most recent poems. From now on, his poetry will successfully enact the criteria he once expressed in an interview:

> El poeta encara pot parlar a favor de la felicitat, però ha de dur un màxim d'exigència a la seva obra, ha d'aprofundir en la seva experiència del món, i ha d'aprofundir en els recursos de la llengua i de l'estil. Cap obra d'art no existeix si no és en virtut d'allò que materialment és i, per tant, només en la riquesa, en la complexitat, en l'humor o en la intel.ligència del poema, és a dir, de la seva construcció formal, podrem trobar aquesta comprensió autèntica que dóna sentit al món.

(The poet can still speak in favour of happiness, but he must make the greatest demands on his work, he must deepen his experience of the world, and must delve into the resources of language and style. No work of art exists except by virtue of what it *is*, materially speaking, and thus, only in the richness, the complexity, the humour or the intelligence of the poem, that is to say, of its formal construction, can we find the true understanding which makes sense of the world.)

This is a highly moral poetry which often takes off from some everyday occurrence – shaving, a chance encounter in the street, the sight of a tree – in order to reflect seriously on life itself. And even when he contemplates some relic of the past, as in 'Testes romanes' (Roman Heads), there is an obvious implication for the present:

> Tant és que cerquessin el bé o el mal,
> i ho sabem: les passions es glacen en el marbre.
> Les seves testes impàvides i immortals
> en la pedra són, tan sols, la pàtria naufragada.

(It does not matter whether they sought good or evil, and we know it: passions are frozen in the marble. Their impassive, immortal heads in the stone are merely our wrecked homeland.)

In his most recent collection, *Natura morta amb nens* (Still Life with Children; 2000), perhaps his best so far, Parcerisas continues to write well-shaped poems, more concerned than ever with the passage of time and, as the title suggests, with what his children will be like when he is no longer there. Time, in these poems, implies dispossession, but also the only chance we have of experiencing beauty. The theme of *ubi sunt* had appeared earlier in his work, but now it is brought to a climax in the long autobiographical poem 'Els morts' (The Dead). This is an impassioned, and at times anguished, meditation on those friends who have died or otherwise disappeared from his life, summed-up in the line 'El record cada dia em buida una part de mi' (Memory each day empties a part of me). Yet the ending is not without hope: the dead are in a sense still alive, and what will survive of the poet himself is love, even after death:

> La meva mà
> te n'ofereix aquests records. La vida
> dels meus morts i una vida amb tu
> – foc, crit i migdia – quan jo no hi sigui.

(My hand offers you these memories. The life of my dead and a life with you – fire, cry and midday – when I am no longer there.)

II. Fiction

Two of the writers I consider here – Joan Perucho (b. 1920) and Jordi Sarsanedas (b. 1924) – began to publish fiction in the 1950s. Perucho, after a promising beginning as a poet, went over to prose, in an astonishing series of books, beginning with *Llibre de cavalleries* (Book of Chivalry; 1957.) This already contains many of the features of his later work: the re-elaboration of an existing genre – in this case, the novel of chivalry – , the deliberate mixing of time scales, and the skilful blending of the real and the imaginary. It is tempting, though not quite right, to call this kind of writing 'fantastic'; only rarely does he produce what could be called 'science fiction', and his extraordinary powers of invention seldom run to the irrational. What is certain is his sense of the marvellous, something which aligns him with Borges and Calvino, with whom he shares a liking for curious erudition. This means that he hardly ever writes 'stories' in a conventional sense: he deliberately mixes the genres – narrative, essay and encyclopedia – in what is essentially a poetic view of reality. Again, the reference to other types of fiction is crucial; in his second novel, *Les històries naturals* (Natural Histories; 1960), he combines an impression of early nineteenth-century Barcelona with a story of vampires based on the Gothic novel, and in *Pamela* (1983), he takes a character from Richardson's novel of that name and invents a future for her, partly based on the epistolary nature of the original.

This last novel, I think, is one of Perucho's greatest achievements, a *jeu d'esprit* based partly on history, partly on an existing fictional character. And to complicate matters, the story runs on two levels: some letters of Pamela's (reproduced in the text) have come to the notice of the real-life scholar, Menéndez y Pelayo who, assisted by his fictitious disciple, Ignasi de Siurana, sets out to investigate the life of a subversive woman who has introduced the ideas of the Enlightenment into what for him is the authentic, traditional Spain. The mixture of the real and the imaginary does not stop here: there are historical anachronisms – Pamela, at the beginning of the nineteenth century, is seen reading a sonnet of Elizabeth Barrett Browning's – and Pamela and Ignasi fall in love with one another across the gap in time. And at the end, just before her death by firing squad, Pamela renounces her subversive past and embraces Christianity – a sure sign of the idealism which runs through much of Perucho's work.

Sarsanedas's first work of fiction, the novella *Contra la nit d'Oboixangó* (Against the Night of Oboshango; 1953), already shows a firm sense of plotting, together with a subtle and flexible use of language. This was followed shortly afterwards by *Mites* (Myths; 1954), a far more original work, in which the narratives seem to take place half way between dream and reality. The absence of logic in several of these stories clearly owes a debt to surrealism; reality is distorted as if seen from a great distance, and it is this 'literary space' which gives them their dimension of 'myth'. And running through them all is a sense of alienation: a meditation on man's search for an ideal in the midst of a hostile world where his attempts at communication – both emotional and rational – are doomed to failure.

The stories which came after this are more realistic, though by no means straightforward narratives. In one of the best, 'Dues noies' (Two Girls), two twin-like girls are shown, first, in the course of a promising adolescence, and later as adults, where their paths diverge, though each in her own way suffers a kind of failure. Sarsanedas, in fact, is particularly good at female psychology; in another story, 'Plou i fa sol' (It Rains and Shines), he describes a woman who spends some days alone in her husband's family home, trying to redirect her life towards simple people and things. This she does, partly through her relationship with a young country boy, and this time the result is quite positive. As she says at one point:

> De les poques coses que he après a la vida, una n'hi ha que em sembla tenir un cert preu: el respecte que es mereix qualsevol cosa que és. La sola manera decent d'atansar-se a un objecte és reconeixent-li la seva participació a la dignitat de l'existència.

> (Of the few things I have learnt in life, there is one which seems to me to have a certain value: the respect deserved by anything which exists. The only decent way of approaching an object is by recognizing its share in the dignity of existence.)

Sarsanedas's two full-length novels, *El martell* (The Hammer; 1956) and *Una noia a la sorra* (A Girl on the Beach; 1981), are very different from one another, though neither is a straightforward narrative. *El martell* plays with the conventions of the crime novel, but in the end the murder remains unsolved and its motives unexplained. In the meantime, the narrator, who is the victim's nephew, is engaged in a game of identity, attempting to integrate his various lives with the help of a mysterious girl, Sabina, and trying out various literary solutions. *Una noia a la sorra* also revolves around a crime – a girl is found dead on a beach – but this serves as an event which centres the lives of a number of other people, all of whom suffer from a lack of ideas and ideals. The parallel with life under Franco is very obvious, yet their situation is described with a good deal of humour, and the prose, though used for more realistic ends than in the other novel, has the lyrical quality which marks the whole of Sarsanedas's work.

Gimferrer's one novel, *Fortuny* (1983), is something of a *tour de force*. Rather than a novel in the conventional sense, it is a series of impressions linked together by the history of the real life Fortuny family, notably the painter Marià Fortuny i Marsal and his son, Marià Fortuny i Madrazo – painter, photographer, impresario and fashion designer. Countless historical characters appear in the course of the text, ranging from Henry James and D'Annunzio to Hitler, Mussolini, Charlie Chaplin and Rudolph Valentino. The action, such as it is, takes place mainly in three cultural capitals, Paris, Venice and Vienna, and spans roughly the first half of the twentieth century. Much of this action is elliptical: everything is understated, and it is left to the reader to make the fleeting connections which constantly hover over the narrative. There are resemblances here to the French *nouveau roman* – Gimferrer himself has referred to Claude Simon, Marguerite Duras and, surprisingly, Azorín, as possible models – but what holds the novel together is something different: a fascination with an essentially decadent aesthetics, with the high priests of beauty, from Henry James to Fortuny i Madrazo himself, and with forms of luxury which contain the seeds of their own destruction.

One writer, Terenci Moix (b. 1943), created something of a sensation in the 1960s. His first books, the short story collection *La torre dels vicis capitals* (The Tower of Capital Vices; 1968), and the two novels, *Onades sobre una roca deserta* (Waves on a Deserted Rock; 1969) and *El dia que va morir Marilyn* (The Day Marilyn Died; 1969 [revised in Castilian, 1993]), mark a clear break with the prevailing realism of the contemporary Catalan novel, though some of the stories, at least, have affinities with Sarsanedas and Perucho. But what makes them disturbing is the deliberate attempt to undermine the conventional moral values of the bourgeoisie. This is particularly evident in the stories, where episodes from the past – seen through a Hollywood version of history – are made to confuse the usual distinctions between vice and virtue by recourse to sadism, masochism and outright cruelty.

The outstanding work of these years is the long novel *El dia que va morir Marilyn*. On one level, this is an immensely subtle account of what it was like to grow up in Barcelona in the aftermath of the Civil War. (Here, the crucial year is 1962, the year in which Marilyn Monroe committed suicide, and when the principal narrator, Bruno, and his companions reach the age of twenty.) Compared with other Catalan novels of the period, one is struck by the sheer range of the experience involved, above all by the incorporation of the Pop culture – comics, American films and music – in which Bruno and his generation grow up. Moreover, the kaleidoscopic technique gives the story great density: it is divided between four narrators, Bruno, his mother, his father and his best friend Jordi, a homosexual, so that we get differing accounts of the same events. The homosexual theme, in particular, is treated with great sensitivity, as in all of Moix's novels, and the eventual flight of Bruno and Jordi from Barcelona in 1962 – the year in which they have finally become adults – is both a rejection of the values of their parents' generation and a realization that homosexuality has no place in this society.

Another homosexual is at the centre of *Siro o la increada consciència de la raça* (Siro or the Uncreated Conscience of the Race; 1972), the first novel in an uncompleted trilogy. Siro, the character in question, has returned from abroad after the death of his lover, to find himself involved in the upper middle-class society of Port Serrat (a thinly disguised version of Port de la Selva). The plot itself is minimal, but one's interest is sustained, partly by Siro's own search for a workable identity and partly by his dialogues with the young historian, Narcis Llaudó, who, in contrast to his own would-be optimism, persists in his vision of a Catalonia which is frustrated by its own glorious past. And in the end, Siro's Europeanism is forced to yield to the pressures of:

> [A]quella generació intermèdia, que barrejà la grisor de la postguerra i les il.lusions de la nova prosperitat sense cap altre període entremig que no fos, simplement, la renúncia.

> (That intermediate generation, which mixed the greyness of the aftermath of the war with the illusions of the new prosperity without any period in between which was not, simply, renunciation.)

Between 1976 and 1992 Moix published no more works of fiction in Catalan. However, in 1992 he brought out what in many ways is his most ambitious novel, *El sexe dels àngels* (The Sex of Angels). The plot itself is fairly simple: it makes use of flashbacks (dialogues and tape recordings) to portray the life of a young author who died in the late 1960s – in many ways a description of the writer's own youth. By means of this literary device Moix is able to examine cultural, political and social life in Barcelona during that period, often by presenting well-known personalities from real life. But much of the book's success is stylistic: the skilfully crafted prose veers with great authority from the deliberately ornate rendering of present-day episodes to the colloquialisms and sarcasms of the flashbacks. And above all, like all great fiction, it transcends its immediate milieu by its continuous expressive energy and by its ability to create human portraits which are universally valid.

Like Moix, Quim Monzó (b. 1952) is deeply familiar with the world of Pop culture. His first novel, *L'udol del griso al caire de les clavegueres* (The Howl of the Icy Wind at the Edge of the Drains; 1976) is divided between the London rock scene and the events of May, 1968 in Paris. The latter are rendered with great vividness and the former with considerable humour, but in both cases the result is disenchantment. As well as this, however, there is a deliberate attempt to catch the reader off guard. The most obvious example of this is the way the narrative sections are inter-spersed with imagined encounters between some of the heroes of the time: Orson Welles, Jean-Luc Godard, Jimi Hendrix, Jim Morrison and others. This is more than just a rhetorical device: rather, it is a means of giving the reader a different perspective on events, and hence on reality itself.

In his later work, this disillusionment takes on different, less localized forms. *Benzina* (Benzine; 1983), his second novel, is set in an imaginary New York, among a group of artists, writers and fashion designers. On the surface, the plot reads like a comedy of sexual errors, but beneath this, there is a more serious theme: the way in which the attempt to create a world apart is constantly undermined by the demands of everyday life – hence, for example, the way in which the would-be independence of art is compromised by the activities of buyers and dealers.

Almost from the beginning of his career, Monzó's main activity, apart from his prolific journalism, has been the writing of short stories. His increasing mastery of the form is undeniable, as even a cursory reading of *Vuitanta-sis contes* (Eighty-Six Stories; 1999) shows. Most of the stories are far from conventional, and, rather than following European models, have more to do with the *avant-garde* fiction of Cortázar and North American writers like Robert Coover and Donald Barthelme. There is very little characterization: most of Monzó's protagonists are stereotypes who reflect the conventions of their society, and in this he shows himself to be an acute critic of contemporary mores. Many of these stories are based on an initial *aperçu* – often a joke – which is then pursued to its logical conclusion. Thus in one of them, 'Sobre la futilitat dels desitjos humans' (On the Futility of Human Desires), a modern-day Robinson Crusoe is 'rescued' by the arrival of a ship, only to find that the crew are intending to set up a commune on his island. But others, like 'Benzina', amount to a serious comment on the possibilities of artistic creation. Thus, in 'Oldeberkoop', writing itself is seen as a means of transcending conventional reality: when the person who is speaking stops, the interlocutor who is transcribing her speech is left without any more material, and the story comes to a sudden end.

The Mallorcan writer Biel Mesquida (b. 1947) is the most problematic of all these novelists. To begin with, his first book, *L'adolescent de sal* (The Adolescent of Salt; 1975) is a deliberate attempt to destroy the conventional novel in favour of a writing which crosses all the accepted genres. Thus, in the course of the text, he makes use of diaries, critical essays, newspaper cuttings, *graffiti*, a film script, a theatre piece, as well as innumerable references to other writings. What gives a kind of unity to all this is the fact that everything is filtered through the voice of the 'narrador-actor-autor', something which accounts both for the undoubted power of the book and also for certain distortions. Despite the deliberately chaotic nature of the text, certain themes begin to emerge, notably what Mesquida calls 'colonization'. This includes most aspects of contemporary culture: Catalonia is 'colonized' by Franco's Spain, Mallorca by the hordes of foreign tourists, and women by the current patriarchal hierarchy. (Most of the women in the book are essentially passive and tend to collaborate in their own dependency. The one partial exception is Cheska, though she is made to serve largely as the author's Muse.) Mesquida's resistance to all this takes two forms: homosexuality and language; homosexuality because it contravenes the norms of bourgeois society, and language because it offers the only possible means of escape from the clichés of contemporary existence. Here he is consciously indebted to the theories of Julia Kristeva, and particularly to her distinction between the symbolic and the semiotic. Though the symbolic – the weight of conventional meanings – can never be fully overcome, Mesquida admits that, in order to attempt this, he would need to be:

> [M]és foll, internat en una bogeria per poder cercar les combinacions, necessàries, de les frases, de les estructures, de les estètiques, per tal de copejar i commocionar el sistema nerviós del qui ho llegesqui.

> (More insane, entering into a madness in order to seek the necessary combinations of phrases, structures and aesthetics, so as to strike and upset the reader's nervous system.)

Nevertheless, to do so would mean risking unreadability, something he only just avoids at various points in his text. This said, there is no denying the value of *L'adolescent de sal* at the time of its publication; as Kathryn Crameri puts it: '[It was important] because it challenged the Catalan literary establishment to produce great modern literature rather than mediocre regional homilies to the way the Països Catalans could be, given the chance'.[1]

Unfortunately, the same could not be said of Mesquida's next book, *Puta-Marès (ahí)* ([untranslatable]; 1978),[2] which is notably inferior in artistic terms. Here, there is a logical progression from *L'adolescent de sal*, in that Mesquida now proclaims the need for a 'llengua lliure' (free language) which will avoid all local or geographical connotations. Language, in fact, is central to the novel, both to its structure and as a theme. In contrast to the previous book, it includes what at first appear to be two clearly differentiated narratives: the story of a young nun, Catalina, and the narrator's own attempt to solve the murder of three friends. However, both narratives run into the sands: the apparently innocent Catalina turns out to be a murderess herself, and the murder of the friends is never solved. Instead, what we have is an account of the narrator's difficulties in writing about it – something to which language itself is clearly crucial. Yet, despite the interest of certain parts of the book – again, it is fascinating to see how Mesquida attempts to put Kristeva's theories into practice – the effort is ulti-

---

[1] Kathryn Crameri, *Language, the Novelist and National Identity in Post-Franco Catalonia* (Oxford, 2000), p. 150.

[2] The title is virtually untranslatable: 'puta' = 'whore' in both Castilian and Catalan; 'marès' contains Catalan 'mare' = 'mother', but is also an adjective from 'mar' = 'sea' and a noun indicating a kind of rock found in Mallorca; 'ahí' means 'there' in Castilian. However, none of this helps very much; perhaps it is more important to note Mesquida's intention of writing, not *one* language, but *a* language, i.e. any language.

mately self-defeating, and even the most open-minded reader comes away with the feeling of having been unduly imposed upon.

Of the many good novelists who have begun to publish in the last twenty years or so, the most outstanding, to my mind, is Jesús Moncada (b. 1941). His first appearance in print, however, came some years earlier, with a poignant essay on the destruction of Mequinensa, the small town on the Ebro where he was brought up.[3] This contains the seeds of his later fiction, which began with two excellent volumes of short stories, some of which in turn build towards his first novel, *Camí de sirga* (The Towpath; 1988). On the surface, this is an elegy for his lost town, now sunk beneath the waters of a hydroelectric dam; reading it, however, one becomes increasingly involved in the lives of its inhabitants – miners, bargees, factory owners – and their relationships. Moncada has, in fact, created the sense of a community comparable to García Márquez's Macondo or Faulkner's Yoknapatawpha County. Above all, he is a great story-teller: his style – often ironic, though with an undercurrent of sadness – has strong roots in the oral tradition, not least in its tendency to tell things from different points of view. His use of time and space is equally skilful: the gradual destruction of the town is conveyed through a constant shuttling between past and present, and external events – the coming of the Republic, the Civil War, the concentration camps – are lightly, but effectively, sketched in.

His second novel, *La galeria de les estàtues* (The Gallery of Statues; 1992) shows many of the same features; the rich language, the interplay of past and present and the ability to turn real places into fiction. Nevertheless, there are differences: for once he moves beyond Mequinensa to include Torrelloba (a city based on Zaragoza). The action now takes place in two different places and times: Mequinensa during the Civil War and Torrelloba in the post-war Franco years. Moreover, there is a tendency to concentrate more on individual characters: Inspector Melquíades Serrador and the student teacher Dalmau Campells. Some of the minor characters are frankly bizarre, like the blind pilgrims on their way to Lourdes who are the sole witnesses to a murder. It has to be said that Moncada's interest in developing minor episodes occasionally takes away from the coherence of the main plot. Nevertheless, there is no denying the strength of the irony with which he dissects the ruling classes in the provincial towns of Franco's Spain, or the vividness of his predominantly oral style.

Moncada's most recent novel, *Estremida memòria* (Trembling Memory; 1997) is set in the Mequinensa of around 1877. In that year, a crime was committed and the supposed perpetrators – one of them innocent – executed. The town is divided between feelings of outrage and shame, and discussions

---

[3] Jesús Moncada Estruga, 'Crònica del darrer rom', *SdO*, 138 (March, 1971), 17–19.

of the events have continued until the present day. Once again, Moncada excels at re-creating the lives and behaviour – often sexual – of the inhabitants of Mequinensa. However, the narrative is by no means straightforward, and this is one of the book's great strengths. To begin with, Moncada claims to have used a contemporary account by one Agustí Montolí, a minor civil servant who is one of the principal characters in the book. This account has been supplied by a friend of the author's (real or fictitious?), Arnau de Roda, to whom Moncada sends chapters of the book as he writes them. Arnau, now an old man with family connections to the original events, then corrects and in many cases elaborates on Moncada's account, though he dies at the end of the novel. This perspectivism is highly effective: not only does it add depth to the story, but it re-creates the atmosphere of uncertainty which was prevalent at the time, and which still continues. And by means of this technique, Moncada succeeds once again in perpetuating an image of a town which is still very much alive, despite its physical disappearance.

III. Theatre

There is no doubt that the death of Franco in 1975 marked a turning-point in the development of the Catalan theatre: the relaxing of censorship, greater institutionalization and a general feeling of growing integration. However, despite all the obstacles, distinctly new kinds of play had begun to emerge before this. In 1961, for instance, Baltasar Porcel (b. 1937), also well-known as a novelist, had produced La ximbomba fosca (The Dark Zambomba), a play much misunderstood at the time, but one which remains an honourable contribution to the Theatre of the Absurd. Though it owes something to Beckett and Ionesco, it is a genuine piece of Catalan theatre. The action, such as it is, is very simple: the inmates of a boarding-house are disturbed by the death of their landlady. They discuss what to do with the corpse – one of them, in a typical Ionesco touch, suggests they eat it – and in the course of their discussions various metaphysical implications emerge. Above all, perhaps, Porcel makes full use of the stage as a space: several of the scenes have a ballet-like quality and there are moments of significant silence.

The greatest success of these years, however, was El retaule del flautista (The Legend of the Piper; 1968), by Jordi Teixidor. This is a re-telling of the Pied Piper of Hamelin story in a deliberately Brechtian manner, a mixture of music hall and farce with interpolated songs and a number of 'distancing' effects. The story begins in the traditional way: a fourteenth-century German town is infested by a plague of rats, and a stranger arrives who says he can spirit them away. From this point on, however, events take a different course: his offer is rejected; the local priest sees the plague as a divine punishment and preaches resignation; the makers of rat traps and poison fear that it will go against their economic interests. So the piper is imprisoned as a wizard, despite the protests of the people, who are eventually quelled by the army. In the end, the mayor weakens: he frees the piper and is prepared to accept his offer, but the latter refuses and goes away, leaving the town at the mercy of those who are only out for financial gain. On one level, then, the play denounces the unholy combination of the army, big business and religion, with obvious contemporary resonances. But in the end, it is the people themselves who are spurred on to greater efforts by the female narrator:

> Vilatans, si ensenyem forats, els apedaçaran; si demanem remeis, ens donaran calmats. Ben mirat, sempre pegats. Caldrà trobar la manera d'imposar les solucions expeditives.

> (Fellow townspeople, if we show them holes, they fill them up, if we ask for cures, they give us tranquillizers. One way or another, we always get beaten. We've got to find more effective solutions.)

After the success of *El retaule*, Teixidor continued to write for a time in what might be called the epic tradition. *La jungla sentimental* (The Sentimental Jungle; 1973) centres on the world of big business: two rival firms, one involved in a strike, are locked in tension; the situation gives rise to spying and counter-espionage, and finally to murder. Against these barbarities – the 'jungle' of the title – is played out a love affair between the son and daughter of the two rival magnates. In a note to the play, Teixidor claims to have deliberately mixed two apparently incompatible genres, as the title itself indicates. And his ultimate aim, as in all epic theatre, is to involve the spectator as critic and interpreter, instead of a merely passive observer.

Since then, Teixidor seems to have lost a certain sense of direction. This may, however, be misleading. Certainly, in 1988 he appeared with what by any standards is a strong play, *Residuals* (Residuals), quite different from anything he had previously written. What strikes one here, above all, is the relative freedom of the language, the move away from direct verisimilitude towards a more poetic way of writing. The play consists of two monologues, which may or may not be allowed to intersect. These are spoken by two characters in old age, Mr and Mrs V, between whom there is no love lost. Instead, they are each witness to the other's decline, and consequently to his or her own decline, and ultimately to the mediocrity of the piece of history they have been compelled to live through. There is nothing here of the didacticism which figured so largely in Teixidor's earlier work, and the language is less direct and less rational. The effect is oddly moving, and suggests a promising new direction which it still remains for Teixidor to pursue.

The most impressive theatre writer of the last forty years is Josep Maria Benet i Jornet (b. 1940). His early plays, as Rodolf Sirera has observed,[4]

---

[4]   In *Contemporary Catalan Theatre: an Introduction*, ed. David George and John London (Sheffield, 1996), p. 51.

tend to alternate between a realist and a more symbolic mode. Thus, in *Una vella, coneguda olor* (An Old, Familiar Smell; 1963), he portrays the miserable lives of the Catalan lower classes after the Civil War in the manner of Buero Vallejo. His more symbolic plays, on the other hand, and especially the *Drudània* trilogy – *Cançons perdudes (Drudània)* (Lost Songs [Drudània]; 1966), *Marc i Jofre o els alquimistes de la fortuna* (Marc and Jofre or the Alchemists of Fortune; 1968) and *La nau* (The Ship; 1969) – are strongly influenced by Brecht, though with debts to the adventure story (*Marc i Jofre*) and science fiction (*La nau*). Drudània is an imaginary country which reflects the situation in Catalonia and, as in Benet's later plays, there are recurring themes: cowardice, punishment, the need for people to face up to society, and childhood as a place of refuge.

In his preface to *Berenàveu a les fosques* (You Were Having Tea in the Dark; 1971), his most ambitious play to date, Benet sets out what amounts to a credo:

> [...] el fet teatral té un camp molt ampli per a manifestar-se de maneres ben diverses, i l'experimentació, la recerca, és en ell, com en qualsevol art, absolutament necessària. En principi no m'interessen, però, les possibles solucions derivades de l'irracionalisme. Les possibilitats de coneixement que proporciona la raó són, ho accepto, dèbils i insuficients, però malgrat tot crec que la raó és el mitjà més elaborat que posseïm per a continuar la nostra problemàtica aventura humana. No renego de la imaginació ni de la intuïció, però penso que és la raó qui, millor o pitjor, pot ordenar-les, codificar-les i donar sentit a llurs aportacions.

> (... the theatrical act has a very wide field in which to show itself in very different ways, and experimentation, research, as in any art, is absolutely necessary. In principle, though, I'm not interested in possible solutions which come from irrationalism. The possibilities of knowledge which reason offers are, I grant, weak and insufficient, but in spite of everything I believe that reason is the most elaborate means we have of continuing our problematic human adventure. I don't reject imagination or intuition, but I think it is reason, for better or for worse, which can order and codify them and make sense of their contributions.)

In *La desaparició de Wendy* (The Disappearance of Wendy; 1973), fantasy is strictly under the control of reason, exactly as in the above statement. It has been described as a 'love song to the theatre',[5] and this is surely right: the theatricality of the play is emphasized, both by the presence of an audience within the audience – one composed of characters from popular mythology – and by the final reference to the toy theatre the protagonist delighted in as a child. This protagonist – a version of the author himself – is

---

[5] By Rodolf Sirera, in David George and John London (ed.), *Contemporary Catalan Theatre*, p. 53.

a combination of Cinderella and Peter Pan. As the action develops, the past – the writer's own infancy – is seen from the present, and undergoes a kind of demythification. Reduced to its simplest terms, the play concerns Cinderella / Peter's attempts to escape from the authoritarianism of others, especially his father, while at the same time he is baffled by a complex reality he cannot understand. And in the end, in the Presenter's final speech, he is accused of being too inward-looking, something which has come from his childhood theatre:

> A punt de donar l'ordre, un instant abans de decidir-la, contemplaves l'escenari, com el contemples ara, i resolies que el bullit incipient de volums, de colors i de figures podia ser la més bella cosa del món. I va ser així com et vas perdre, perquè t'havies ficat massa endins, i quan el teló va caure, com ho fa ara, va caure darrera teu.

> (About to give the order, a moment before deciding it, you looked at the stage, just as you are looking at it now, and determined that the potential mixture of volumes, colours and figures could be the most beautiful thing in the world. And that's how you lost yourself, because you had gone too far in, and when the curtain fell, as it does now, it fell behind you.)

Descripció d'un paisage (Description of a Landscape; 1978) is a more straightforward play, but no less powerful. Essentially, it is a modern version of the story of Hecuba, Queen of Troy, a narrative of vengeance, cowardice and sticking to one's principles. And contemporary resonances are not far to seek, above all the sense that power, even in a so-called democracy, never fails to corrupt. The action takes place in a modern Arab country governed by a dicta-torial Emir who has begun to relax his former severity. It begins with the return from exile of the two daughters of Dr Munàdil, a one-time opponent of the Emir's, who was killed in the course of an abortive revolution. But beneath the daughters' adaptation to new circumstances there lies a desire to avenge them-selves on Bassir, the former lover of Zahira, whose cowardice forced him to kill his mistress's son. This they do by blinding him and killing his own son. But in the end, he achieves a kind of Pyrrhic victory: though sightless – and this is the ultimate meaning of the title – he is able to 'see' the landscape of which the others are deprived:

> No heu aconseguit res, Zahira! El vostre enemic ha vençut i ara per sempre més Zahira, tinc davant meu el paisatge! I el veig! Em sents? És gràcies a tu, Zahira […] Zahira, estic distingint cadascun dels colors del paisatge.

> (You've achieved nothing, Zahira. Your enemy has won, and now for ever. Zahira, I have the landscape before me! And I see it! Do you hear me? It's thanks to you, Zahira… Zahira, I can distinguish each of the colours of the landscape.)

One of Benet's virtues is that he hardly ever repeats himself. In a more recent play, *Desig* (Desire; 1989, first performed in 1991), he achieves what amounts to a new austerity. In it, four unnamed characters, two men and two women, utter laconic dialogues or monologues reminiscent of Beckett, and move in an undefined space, with a suggestion of highways and bars, as in a road-movie. None of the characters is able to relate to the others, and there is a sense in which they may belong to different levels of reality. The whole play, in fact, is based on the conflict between reality and desire, and its interest lies in watching its characters attempting to attain the unattainable, in other words, happiness.

The development of the Valencian theatre since the Civil War owes almost everything to the work of the Sirera brothers, Rodolf (b. 1948) and Josep Lluís (b. 1954). In Valencia, the status of Catalan was quite different from that in the rest of Catalonia: the upper classes spoke Spanish for preference, and Catalan, for literary purposes, was restricted to works of a sentimental, folkloristic nature. Starting from this unpromising situation, the Sireras succeeded in establishing Catalan as the language of the stage, while at the same time rejecting the outmoded nineteenth-century tradition.

Rodolf Sirera's first full-length play, *La pau (retorna a Atenes)* (Peace [Returns to Athens]; 1973) breaks completely with this tradition: though loosely based on Aristophanes's *Peace*, it is an essentially Brechtian play, complete with songs and cinema projections, though it is often much funnier than Brecht. Much of this fun comes from intentional discrepancies: the ancient Greek characters listen to Radio Athens and speak on the telephone. However, beneath all this there is a serious anti-military satire: Trygaeus, an honest citizen who has lost his son in the war, flies to Olympus to bring back Peace, but the Peace with whom he returns to earth is a false one, who eventually turns out to be War. And in the end it is the arms manufacturers who prevail, since war is necessary in order to keep them in business.

The Sireras' next play, *Homenatge a Florentí Montfort* (Homage to Florentí Montfort; 1971, though not produced in full until much later) was much more openly satirical: the commemoration of a fictitious nineteenth-century writer who represents the very tradition they deplore. Again, the presentation is highly unconventional: a typically florid lecture on the poet is followed by six of his truly awful poems and a numbingly traditional piece of drama. But the real sting comes in the tail: an epilogue in the form of a documentary which reflects on the backwardness of Valencian culture:

> Malgrat que no es vullga, la Renaixença ens ha llastrat amb les seues concepcions d'una cultura jocfloralista, per a una burgesia urbana, ben isolada del context cultural català, i el que és pitjor completament d'esquena a la realitat i la problemàtica del que constitueix el nostre País.

(Though it may not have intended to, the *Renaixença* has burdened us with its concept of a culture of *Jocs Florals*, for an urban bourgeoisie, quite isolated from the Catalan cultural context and, what is worse, completely alien to the reality and problematics of what constitutes our Country.)

After some rather heavy-handed historical plays, Rodolf Sirera returned to the Brechtian manner in *L'assassinat del Doctor Moraleda* (The Assassination of Doctor Moraleda; 1978), a late nineteenth-century political mystery, perhaps over-plotted, but nevertheless full of carefully calculated tensions. But his greatest success of these years is *El verí del teatre* (The Poison of [the] Theatre; 1978), a short but extremely powerful piece in which not a word is wasted. There are only two characters: the Marquis de … (based on the Marquis de Sade?) and the actor Gabriel de Beaumont. The Marquis invites the actor to perform the death of Socrates. His first performance is unsatisfactory – too consciously 'acted'; for his second performance, the Marquis makes him believe that the wine he drank earlier was poisoned, and that he will only be given the antidote if his performance comes up to scratch. After this second performance, the Marquis gives him another drink, which this time *is* a deadly poison for which there is no antidote. And the actor finally dies after the play has ended. All this may sound merely ingenious, yet the real force of the play comes from the dialogue between the two characters, partly based on Diderot's *Paradoxe sur le comédien*, concerning whether real emotions can be acted on the stage. At the beginning, the Marquis acts the part of a servant so convincingly that Gabriel is taken in, and we are left wondering who is the better actor. And later on, when the Marquis transgresses the bounds of theatre by making the actor really die, Sirera takes his reflections on his art to the extreme: if a dramatist cannot actually kill someone onstage, then, by a strange sort of paradox, he can make one of his characters do so, though the death itself will be hidden from the audience.

Since then, the Sireras have written a number of plays, either singly or jointly, one of the best of which is *Cavalls de mar* (Seahorses; 1986). This is an ambitious play which incorporates a number of cinematic techniques, notably in blending episodes from the Civil War with scenes from earlier in the century. (Part of the action, indeed, involves the beginnings of the Valencian cinema industry.) Also, as in the Epilogue to *Homenatge a Florentí Montfort*, there are comments on how twentieth-century modernization might affect Valencia. And in contrast to the political background, there is a plot concerning unfulfilled love, never very pronounced, but showing a fusion of political and personal strands more complete than anything the Sireras had previously achieved.

Sergi Belbel (b. 1963) is by far the youngest of these writers, though by now he has a considerable body of work behind him. His early plays, like *Elsa Schneider* (1987), already show some of the constants of his later work: the concern for personal relationships, an uninhibited treatment of sexuality and an extreme linguistic precision. In his best plays, everything is reduced to a minimum, as in *Dins la seva memòria* (1987), where a character called simply 'Ell' (He) is accompanied by three internal voices, 1, 2 and 3, who enable him to relive the death of his twin brother. One striking feature of the dialogue is the way this is divided between the different voices:

1. Recordaràs
2. també
3. aquell rostre seu
1. desfigurat, sang del front, venes obertes.
2. A partir d'ara
1. odiaràs
3. sobre totes les coses
2. aquell rostre de mort
1. desfigurat, sang del front, venes obertes.

(1. You will remember 2. also 3. that face of his 1. disfigured, blood on the forehead, opened veins 2. From now on 1. you will hate 3. above everything 2. that dead face 1. disfigured, blood on the forehead, opened veins.)

This incantatory tone, along with other kinds of repetition, gives the text a distinctive poetic quality which owes something to the later Beckett. Characters which are hardly characters emerge from an undefined space, or as one of them puts it:

Les quatre parets del meu cap [...], espai buit omplint-se de fantasmes sorgits d'un temps que ja no hi és. Però no, fantasmes no. Són provocacions. Sí: escenes que la meva ment reviu per qüestionar el meu cos i desvetllar-lo, moure'l, retorçar-lo.

(The four walls of my head ..., an empty space filling with phantoms which come from a time which no longer exists. But no, not phantoms. They're provocations. Yes: scenes which my mind relives in order to question my body and awaken it, move it, distort it.)

In *Carícies* (Caresses; 1991), Belbel leaves behind the semi-abstract settings of his previous plays and sets his action in a distinctly Catalan milieu. As always, the play is tightly structured: each of the 'ten scenes and an epilogue' brings together a pair of unnamed characters, some of whom are eventually seen to be related to one another. Some of the scenes are quite violent: Belbel does not hesitate to present the world of drugs and unnatural sex in a way that had never before been seen on the Catalan stage. Yet his intention is not to shock, but rather to convey a vision of contemporary society as based on lack of understanding, the inability to communicate and an essential solitude.

This play was followed by *Després de la pluja* (After the Rain; 1992), one of Belbel's several incursions into farce, though in a sense he is mocking the genre itself. Again, the setting is contemporary: a microcosm of human relationships in an office block where smoking is forbidden, and where the smokers secretly gather together on the roof-top in the midst of a city which is suffering the effects of a drought. The farcical elements are very obvious – each of the secretaries is distinguished by the colour of her hair; a man falls from the roof only to be restored to life a moment later – yet the epilogue is quite different in tone. A year after the main action, which has ended with the coming of the rain, the Computer Programmer and the Brown-Haired Secretary, who are now living together and expecting a child, revisit the office block which is shortly to be demolished. The roof-top is deserted and practically in ruins, and the scene ends with the sun coming out after a year of rain. A mildly optimistic ending, then, though we, like the two characters themselves, cannot put out of our minds the action which took place during the drought.

No account of contemporary Catalan theatre would be complete without at least a brief reference to the various performance groups which have grown up since the 1960s. Though most of their work is not strictly literary, their influence on stage design and their success in creating a non-theatrical audience have been immense. The oldest of them, *Els joglars* (The Minstrels), was founded in 1962, under the directorship of Albert Boadella. In its early days, it followed the pattern of Marcel Marceau's mime performances, though it soon came to criticize the more absurd aspects of the Franco régime – something it could get away with by being classified as variety theatre or music-hall. Its greatest achievement – and in this it has been followed by later groups – is to have taken theatre away from the commercial stage into various small-scale venues: universities, village halls and in some cases the streets themselves.

This tendency towards street theatre was accentuated in the early 1970s by the formation of another group, *Els comediants* (The Comic Actors; founded in 1971). Though its work by now involves television performances, its real originality lies in its revival of carnival, particularly in the context of the recently reinstated *Festes majors*. Thus one of their most successful productions, *Dimonis* (Devils; 1982), both uses traditional carnival material and directly involves the audience in the action.

La fura dels baus, founded in 1979,[6] takes over the tradition of street theatre and points it in an altogether more provocative direction. All their

---

[6] A nonsense title. *Fura* means 'ferret' and a *bau* is the beam of a ship.

productions have a strong visceral quality: their actors are equally skilled in tightrope walking and the manipulation of fireworks, and the emphasis falls more and more on their actual bodies. Or, as Mercè Saumell puts it: '[T]he performers' bodies act as seismographs, registering the different states of tension throughout each production.'[7]

---

[7] Mercè Saumell, in David George and John London (ed.), *Contemporary Catalan Theatre*, p. 120.

Chapter 6

EPILOGUE

A book like this must inevitably be open-ended. Within its obvious limits, I have tried to show the variety of Catalan literature and also something of its historical background. Yet 'variety' is perhaps not quite the right word, in so far as it implies a kind of studied neutrality, or, worse still, that the whole of Catalan literature is a set of variations on a single stem. Nothing, in fact, could be further from the truth; 'variety', in this context, implies contradictions and alternatives, writers who positively refuse to be fitted into the neat schemes of conventional histories of literature. These tend to present literature as a smooth evolution: Romanticism to *Modernisme*, *Modernisme* to *Noucentisme*, *Noucentisme* to Social Realism and so on. Yet to contemporaries things must have looked rather different, and hindsight, whatever its other advantages, always runs the danger of oversimplification. Recently, however, this has begun to change; Pere Gimferrer, for instance, speaks of an 'alternative tradition', something to which *Noucentisme* was largely blind:

> Ordre? Diafanitat? Classicisme? Potser sí; però també recerca torturada, oratges interiors, sequedat, combats, tenebra.[1]
>
> (Order? Transparency? Classicism? Yes, perhaps; but also tortured investigation, inner storms, dryness, combats, darkness.)

This 'alternative tradition' gives full value to the irrational as well as to the rational and allows for the subversive as well as the conformist. Above all, perhaps, it goes against the idea of a steady evolution and makes connections across the centuries, the kind of connection Foix implies when he links Ramon Llull with his own avant-garde techniques. It is this darker side of the imagination which *Noucentisme* tends to overlook: not only the medieval tradition of mysticism and the occult, but the more tormented, apocalyptic passages of Ausiàs March and, in the nineteenth century, the turbulent landscapes of Verdaguer with their suggestions of inner conflict. Nowadays, to be sure, we read the *modernista* novel from a different perspective from the *noucentistes*, one more responsive to their dark, Gothic strain. And it is

---

[1] Pere Gimferrer, *Antoni Tàpies i l'esperit català* (Barcelona, 1974), 36.

also true that the *noucentistes* themselves evolved: it is no coincidence, I
think, that Carner, in his last great poem, *Nabí*, should use the biblical story
of Jonah to express the kind of emotional uncertainties that would have been
unthinkable in his earlier *noucentista* phase, or that Carles Riba, in his last
two collections of poems, should measure himself for the first time against
the examples of March, Foix, and the Carner of the poem I have just
mentioned. In their context, these are crucial readjustments, acts of recognition which, however belated, point to continuing sources of renewal. And
this perhaps helps to suggest the more general image of Catalan literature I
have been trying to create: that of a body of writing which, for all its objective achievement, refuses to settle once and for all into the fixed patterns of
histories of literature but remains a constant challenge to writers and readers
at the present day.

As for the future of Catalan literature, one can, of course, only speculate.
Certainly, there is a great deal of talent around at the moment, and the kind
of resourcefulness I have just described seems a good guarantee for the
years to come. However, one must not be complacent: more than one
contemporary writer has suggested that all is not well, and what is at stake is
always the Catalan language itself. So Narcís Comadira, in the course of
defending Catalan as the only possible medium for a Catalan poet, writes:

> És la llengua que ha nascut aquí i que s'ha configurat en un país que s'ha
> anat configurant amb ella. És la que ha batejat cims i valls, rius i cales,
> pobles i ciutats. És la que ha rebut de la idiosincràsia dels seus parlants, la
> seva diferència i les seves peculiaritats. És la que és viva – malgrat que
> malalta – en el país que l'ha fet nèixer, en el país on està arrelada, on
> encara pot florir i granar.[2]

> (It is the language which has been born here and which has taken shape in
> a country which has taken shape along with it. It is that which has given
> names to mountains and valleys, rivers and bays, towns and cities. It is
> that which has drawn its difference and peculiarities from the idiosyncra-
> sies of its speakers. It is that which is alive – though sick – in the country
> which has given birth to it, in the country in which it is rooted, where it
> still may flourish and seed.)

He is thinking here of the constant pressure of Spanish, of the way
Catalan itself has suffered at the hands of the mass media, and the effect this
has had on the nature of Catalan speech. These, for sure, are obstacles to be
reckoned with; at the same time, one hopes he is being too pessimistic. What
is certainly true, and Comadira says as much, is that language itself must
never be taken for granted, but must always be worked for, and as long as

---

[2] Narcís Comadira, 'Ser poeta i ser-ho avui a Catalunya', in *Sense escut* (Barcelona,
1998), 65–77 [71].

writers are aware of this, the future of their literature seems assured. The best Catalan literature, as I have tried to show, has an enormous capacity for remaking itself while remaining intensely Catalan, and, taken as a whole, it seems to bear out as clearly as any the words of the Irish poet, W.B. Yeats:

> You can no more have the greatest poetry without a nation than religion without symbols. One can only reach out to the universe with a gloved hand – that glove is one's nation, the only thing one knows even a little of.

SELECT BIBLIOGRAPHY

The following abbreviations have been used for standard series of texts: *AC* 'Antologia catalana', Edicions 62 (Barcelona); *LMO* 'Les millors obres de la literatura catalana', Edicions 62 (Barcelona); *ENC* 'Els nostres clàssics', Barcino (Barcelona). As far as possible, I have tried to list cheap editions as well as standard works.

General histories of literature and works covering particular periods

Martí de Riquer, Antoni Comas and Joaquim Molas, *Història de la literatura catalana*, 11 vols (Barcelona: Ariel, 1964–88).

Jordi Rubió i Balaguer, *Literatura catalana*, in G. Díaz-Plaja, ed., *Historia general de las literaturas hispánicas* (Barcelona: Barna, 1949–), Vol. I, pp. 643–746; Vol. III, pp. 727–930; Vol. IV, i, pp. 493–597; Vol. V, pp. 213–337.

Joaquim Molas, *Literatura catalana antiga* (Barcelona: Barcino, 1961–63), Vol. I (segle XIII); Vol. III (segle XV, i).

Josep Romeu, *Literatura catalana antiga* (Barcelona: Barcino, 1961–64), Vol. II (segle XIV), Vol. IV (segle XV, ii).

J. Ruiz i Calonja, *Història de la literatura catalana* (Barcelona: Teide, 1954).

Jordi Rubió i Balaguer, *De l'Edat Mitjana al Renaixement* (Barcelona: Aymà, 1948).

——— *La cultura catalana del Renaixement a la Decadència* (Barcelona: Edicions 62, 1964).

(Various authors), *Un segle de vida catalana, 1814–1930*, 2 vols (Barcelona: Alcides, 1961). Contains chapters on most aspects of Catalan history and culture, including literature.

Joan Fuster, *Literatura catalana contemporània* (Barcelona: Curial, 1978).

Anthologies

Joan Triadú, ed., *An Anthology of Catalan Lyric Poetry* (Oxford: Dolphin, 1953).

J.M. Castellet and J. Molas, ed., *Poesia catalana del segle XX* (Barcelona: Edicions 62, 1963).

Joan Triadú, ed., *Nova antologia de la poesia catalana* (Barcelona: Selecta, 1965).

J.M. Castellet and J. Molas, ed., *Ocho siglos de poesía catalana* (Madrid: Alianza, 1970). Bilingual text.

Joaquim Marco and Jaume Pont, ed., *La nova poesia catalana* (Barcelona: Edicions 62, 1980).

Language and history

W.D. Elcock, *The Romance Languages* (London: Faber, 1960).

P. Russell-Gebbett, *Medieval Catalan Linguistic Texts* (Oxford: Dolphin, 1965).

Joan Coromines, *El que s'ha de saber de la llengua catalana* (Palma de Mallorca: Raixa, 1954).

A.M. Badia i Margarit, *Llengua i cultura als països catalans* (Barcelona: Edicions 62, 1964).

J.Vicens Vives, *Notícia de Catalunya* (Barcelona: Ancora, 1954); Spanish translation: *Noticia de Cataluña* (Barcelona: Destino, 1954).

Joan Fuster, *Nosaltres els valencians* (Barcelona: Edicions 62, 1962).

Editions and more specialized anthologies

Chapter 1

Poesia catalana medieval, ed. J. Ll. Marfany, *AC* (Barcelona, 1966).

Ramon Llull, *Obres essencials*, 2 vols (Barcelona: Selecta, 1957).

────── *Llibre d'Evast e Blanquera*, *LMO* (Barcelona, 1982).

────── *Llibre de les bèsties, AC* (Barcelona, 1965).

────── *Poesies*, ed. Josep Romeu i Figueras (Barcelona: Selecta, 1958).

Arnau de Vilanova, *Obres catalanes*, ed. M. Batllori and J. Carreras Artau, 2 vols, *ENC* (Barcelona, 1947).

Jaume I, *Libre dels feyts*, ed. J.M. de Casacuberta, 9 vols (Barcelona: Barcino, 1926–62).

────── *Crònica o llibre dels feits*, ed. Ferran Soldevila, *LMO* (Barcelona, 1982).

Bernat Desclot, *Crònica*, ed. M. Coll i Alentorn, 5 vols, *ENC* (Barcelona, 1949–51).

────── *Crònica,* ed. M. Coll i Alentorn, *LMO* (Barcelona, 1982).

Ramon Muntaner, *Crònica*, ed. J.M. de Casacuberta and M. Coll i Alentorn, 2 vols (Barcelona: Barcino, 1927–52).

Pere III, *Crònica*, ed. Amadeu J. Soberanas (Barcelona: Alpha, 1961).

Francesc Eiximenis, *Terç del Crestià*, ed. P.P. Martí de Barcelona and Norbert d'Ordal, 3 vols, *ENC* (Barcelona, 1929–32).

────── *Lo Crestià (selecció)*, ed. Albert Hauf, *LMO* (Barcelona, 1983).

────── *La societat catalana al segle XIV* (anthology), ed. Jill Webster, *AC* (Barcelona, 1967).

Sant Vicenç Ferrer, *Sermons*, ed. J. Sanchis Sivera, 2 vols, *ENC* (Barcelona, 1932–34).

Anselm Turmeda, *Disputa de l'ase*, ed. Marçal Olivar, *ENC* (Barcelona, 1928).

Ramon de Perellós, *Viatge ... fet al purgatori nomenat de Sant Patrici*, in *Viatges a l'altre món*, ed. Arseni Pacheco, *AC* (Barcelona, 1973).

Bernat Metge, *Obres completes*, ed. Martí de Riquer (Barcelona: Selecta, 1950).

―――― *Obres completes*, ed. L. Badia and X. Lamuela (Barcelona: Selecta, 1976).

―――― *Lo Somni*, ed. A. Vilanova (Barcelona: CSIC, 1946).

Antoni Canals, *Scipió e Aníbal, De providència*, etc., ed. Martí de Riquer, *ENC* (Barcelona, 1935).

J.Ll. Marfany, ed., *Poesia catalana del segle XV*, *AC* (Barcelona: 1967).

Jaume March, *Obra poètica*, ed. Josep Pujol, *ENC* (Barcelona, 1994).

G. de Próixita, A. Febrer, M. de Gualbes, J. de Sant Jordi, *Obra lírica*, ed. Martí de Riquer, *LMO* (Barcelona, 1982).

Jordi de Sant Jordi, *Poesies*, ed. Martí de Riquer (Granada: Universidad de Granada, 1955). Bilingual edition.

―――― *Les poesies*, ed. Martí de Riquer and Lola Badia (Valencia: Tres i Quatre, 1984).

Ausiàs March, *Poesies*, ed. Pere Bohigas, 5 vols, *ENC* (Barcelona, 1952–59).

―――― *Antologia poètica*, ed. Joan Fuster (Barcelona: Selecta, 1959). With modern Catalan versions.

―――― *Les poesies*, ed. Joan Ferraté (Barcelona: Quaderns Crema, 1979).

―――― *Poesia*, ed. Joan Ferraté, *LMO* (Barcelona: Edicions 62, 1979).

―――― *Cinquanta-vuit poemes*, ed. Robert Archer (Barcelona: Edicions 62, 1989).

―――― *Obra completa*, ed. Robert Archer, 2 vols (Barcelona: Barcanova, 1997).

Jaume Roig, *Llibre de les dones, o Spill*, ed. F.Almela i Vives, *ENC* (Barcelona, 1928).

―――― *Espill o llibre de les dones*, ed. Marina Gustà, *LMO* (Barcelona, 1978).

Roiç de Corella, *Obres*, ed. R. Miquel i Planas (Barcelona: Biblioteca Catalana, 1913).

―――― *Obres completes I: Obra profana*, ed. Jordi Carbonell (Valencia: Albatros, 1973).

―――― *Tragèdia de Caldesa i altres proses*, ed. Marina Gustà, *LMO* (Barcelona, 1980).

Curial e Güelfa, ed. R. Aramon i Serra, 3 vols, *ENC* (Barcelona, 1930–33).

Joanot Martorell, *Tirant lo blanc*, ed. Martí de Riquer (Barcelona: Selecta, 1949).

―――― *Tirant lo blanc*, ed. Martí de Riquer and Maria Josepa Gallofré, *LMO* (Barcelona: 1983).

―――― *Tirant lo blanc*, ed. Albert Hauf, 2 vols (Valencia: Generalitat Valenciana, 1990).

Teatre hagiogràfic, ed. Josep Romeu, 3 vols, *ENC* (Barcelona: 1957).

Teatre profà, ed. Josep Romeu, 2 vols, *ENC* (Barcelona, 1962).

Teatre medieval i del Renaixement, ed J. Massot i Muntaner, *LMO* (Barcelona, 1983).

Chapter 2

Pere Serafí, *Antologia poètica*, ed. A. Bover i Font (Barcelona: Edicions 62, 1987).
Vicenç Garcia, Rector de Vallfogona, *Sonets*, ed. G. Grilli, *AC* (Barcelona, 1979).
Francesc Fontanella, *Lo desengany*, ed. Anna M.Torrent, *AC* (Barcelona, 1968).
———— and Joan Ramis, *Teatre barroc i neoclàssic*, *LMO* (Barcelona, 1982).
Fra Joan Gaspar Roig i Jalpí (Bernat Boades), *Libre de feyts d'armes de Catalunya*, ed. E. Bagué, 5 vols, *ENC* (Barcelona: 1930–48).
Romancer català (Milà i Fontanals), ed. Joan Antoni Paloma, *LMO* (Barcelona, 1980).
El pensament il.lustrat a Catalunya, ed. E. Moreu-Rey, *AC* (Barcelona, 1966).
Rafael d'Amat i Cortada, *El col.legi de la bona vida* (anthology), ed. Alexandre Galí (Barcelona: Selecta, 1954).
Joan Ramis, *Lucrècia*, ed. Jordi Carbonell, *AC* (Barcelona, 1968).
Poesia neoclàssica i pre-romàntica, ed. Joaquim Molas, *AC* (Barcelona, 1965).

Chapter 3

Poesia catalana romàntica, ed. Joaquim Molas, *AC* (Barcelona, 1965).
Josep Robrenyo, *Teatre revolucionari*, ed. J.Ll. Marfany, *AC* (Barcelona, 1965).
El teatre català anterior a Pitarra, ed. M. Font (Barcelona: Barcino, 1928). Includes three plays by Robrenyo.
Jacint Verdaguer, *Obres completes* (Barcelona: Selecta, 1943).
———— *L'Atlàntida* (Barcelona: Selecta, 1973).
———— *Canigó*, ed. Narcís Garolera (Barcelona: Quaderns Crema, 1995).
Àngel Guimerà, *Obres selectes*, 2 vols (Barcelona: Selecta, 1948).
———— *Antologia poètica*, ed. Pere Gimferrer (Barcelona: Selecta, 1974).
Emili Vilanova, *Obres completes* (Barcelona: Selecta, 1949).
Narcís Oller, *Obres completes* (Barcelona: Selecta, 1948).
———— *Contes*, ed. Alan Yates, *LMO* (Barcelona, 1979).
Santiago Rusiñol, *Obres completes* (Barcelona: Selecta, 1947).
Poesia catalana de la Restauració, ed. Joaquim Molas, *AC* (Barcelona. 1966).
Joan Maragall, *Obres completes*, 24 vols (Barcelona: Edimar, 1929–55).
———— *Obres completes*, 2 vols (Barcelona: Selecta, 1960–61).
———— *Antologia poètica*, ed. Carles Riba (Barcelona: Selecta, 1954).
———— *Antologia poètica*, ed. Arthur Terry, *LMO* (Barcelona, 1981).
———— *Visions i cants*, ed. Enric Bou (Barcelona: Edicions 62, 1984).
———— *Enllà*, ed. Glòria Casals (Barcelona: Edicions 62, 1989).
———— *El comte Arnau*, ed. J.Ll. Marfany, *AC* (Barcelona, 1974).
———— *Elogi de la paraula i altres assaigs*, ed. Francesc Vallverdú, *LMO* (Barcelona, 1978).
Josep Lluís Pons i Gallarza, *Poesies*, ed. J.M. Llompart (Palma de Mallorca: Moll, 1975).
Joan Alcover, *Obres completes* (Barcelona: Selecta, 1964).
———— *Cap al tard / Poemes bíblics*, *LMO* (Barcelona, 1989).
Miquel Costa i Llobera, *Obres completes* (Barcelona: Selecta, 1947).
———— *Horacianes i altres poemes*, *LMO* (Barcelona, 1982).

Chapter 4

Eugeni d'Ors ('Xènius'), *Obra catalana completa: Glosari 1906–1910* (Barcelona: Selecta, 1950).
Guerau de Liost, *Obra poètica completa, Proses literàries* (Barcelona: Selecta, 1948).
────── *Antologia poètica*, ed. Enric Bou, *LMO* (Barcelona, 1981).
Josep Carner, *Obres completes: poesia* (Barcelona: Selecta, 1957).
────── *Poesia 1957* (Barcelona: Quaderns Crema, 1992).
────── *Nabí* (Barcelona: Edicions 62, 1971).
────── *Llegendari*, ed. Jaume Coll (Barcelona: Quaderns Crema, 1992).
Carles Riba, *Obres completes: I (Poesia i narrativa)*, ed. J.Ll. Marfany (Barcelona: Edicions 62, 1965).
────── *Obres completes: I (Poesia)*, ed. Enric Sullà (Barcelona: Edicions 62, 1984).
────── *Tres suites*, ed. Jordi Malé i Pegueroles (Barcelona: Edicions 62, 1993).
J.M. López-Picó, *Obres completes: I (Poesia)* (Barcelona: Selecta, 1948).
Marià Manent, *Obra poètica* (Barcelona: Selecta, 1956).
────── *La ciutat del temps* (Barcelona: Ossa Menor, 1961).
Tomàs Garcés, *Poesia completa* (Barcelona: Columna, 1986; 2nd edition, 1993).
Clementina Arderiu, *Antología poética* (Madrid: Rialp, 1961). Bilingual Catalan-Spanish edition.
────── *L'esperança encara*, *AC* (Barcelona, 1969).
Josep Maria de Sagarra, *Obra poètica (1912–37)* (Barcelona: Selecta, 1947).
Joan Salvat-Papasseit, *Poesies* (Barcelona: Ariel, 1962).
──────, Bartolomeu Rosselló-Porcel, Màrius Torres, *Poesia*, *LMO* (Barcelona, 1982).
J.V. Foix, *Obres poètiques* (Barcelona: Nauta,1964).
────── *Obres completes: I (Poesia); II (Prosa)* (Barcelona: Edicions 62, 1974; 1979).
────── *Obra poètica*, ed. Jaume Vallcorba, 14 vols (Barcelona: Quaderns Crema (1983–1997). This is now the best edition and contains variants.
────── *Diari 1918*, *LMO* (Barcelona, 1981).
────── *Darrer comunicat* (Barcelona: Edicions 62, 1970).
Prudenci Bertrana, *Josafat*, ed. Jordi Castellanos (Barcelona: Edicions 62, 1977).
Ramon Casellas, *Els sots feréstecs*, ed. Jordi Castellanos (Barcelona: Edicions de 1984, 2001).
Víctor Català, *Solitud*, ed. Núria Nardi (Barcelona: Edicions 62, 1990).
Josep Pous i Pagès, *La vida i la mort d'En Jordi Fraginals*, *LMO* (Barcelona, 1979).
Miquel de Palol, *Camí de llum*, ed. Alan Yates, *AC* (Barcelona, 1976).
Joaquim Ruyra, *Obres completes* (Barcelona: Selecta, 1949).
Llorenç Villalonga, *Obres completes: I (El mite de Bearn)* (Barcelona: Edicions 62, 1966).
────── *Mort de Dama*, *LMO* (Barcelona, 1981).
────── *Bearn*, *LMO* (Barcelona, 1980).

—— *Desenllaç a Montlleó*, ed. Glòria Mas (Barcelona: Barcanova, 1990).

Xavier Berenguel, *Obres completes: I* (Barcelona: Nauta, 1967).

Sebastià Juan Arbó, *Obra catalana completa: I (Novel.les de l'Ebre)* (Barcelona: Edicions 62, 1966).

Josep Pla, *Obres completes* (Barcelona: Destino, 1966–). Over thirty volumes have so far appeared.

Bartolomeu Rosselló-Porcel, *Obra poètica* (Palma de Mallorca: Moll, 1975).

Màrius Torres, *Poesies* (Barcelona: Ariel, 1964).

(For Rosselló and Torres, see also above under Salvat-Papasseit.)

Pere Quart (Joan Oliver), *Obra* (Barcelona: Fontanella, 1963).

—— *Circumstàncies* (Barcelona: Ossa Menor, 1968).

—— *Poemes escollits, LMO* (Barcelona, 1983).

Joan Oliver, *Tres comèdies* (Barcelona: Selecta, 1960).

—— *Biografia de Lot i altres proses* (Barcelona: Fontanella, 1963).

Salvador Espriu, *Obres completes: I i II (Poesia)* (Barcelona: Edicions 62, 1985).

—— *Obres completes: III (Narrativa)* (Barcelona: Edicions 62, 1986). Contains the final versions of *El Doctor Rip* and *Laia*.

—— *Narracions, AC* (Barcelona, 1965).

—— *Antígona*, ed. Alfred Badia (Barcelona: Edicions 62, 1990).

—— *Primera història d'Esther, AC* (Barcelona, 1966).

—— *Les roques i el mar, el blau* (Barcelona: Llibres del Mall, 1981).

Gabriel Ferrater, *Les dones i els dies, LMO* (Barcelona, 1979).

Rosa Leveroni, *Poesia* (Barcelona: Edicions 62, 1981).

Joan Teixidor, *Una veu et crida* (Barcelona: Edicions 62, 1969).

——, Agustí Bartra and Joan Vinyoli, *Poesia* (Barcelona: Edicions 62, 1984).

Joan Vinyoli, *Poesia completa (1937–75)* (Barcelona: Ariel, 1975).

—— *Vers i prosa*, ed. Ferran Carbó (Valencia: Tres i Quatre, 1990).

Vicent Andrés Estellés, *Obra completa*, 10 vols (Valencia: Tres i Quatre, 1972–90). Vol. I contains the *Primer llibre d'èglogues* and Vol. II *Llibre d'exilis* and *Horacianes*.

Agustí Bartra, *Obra poètica completa*, 2 vols (Barcelona: Edicions 62, 1971; 1983).

—— *Rapsòdia de Garí* (Barcelona: Edicions 62, 1972).

Joan Brossa, *Poesia rasa* (Barcelona: Ariel, 1970).

—— *Poemes de seny i cabell* (Barcelona: Ariel, 1977).

—— *Rua de llibres* (Barcelona: Ariel, 1980).

—— *Viatge per la sextina* (Barcelona: Quaderns Crema, 1987).

—— *Antologia poètica*, ed. Pere Gimferrer, *AC* (Barcelona, 1980).

Many of Brossa's plays and 'scenic poems' are collected in the six volumes of *Poesia escènica* (Barcelona: Edicions 62, 1973–83).

Joan Sales, *Incerta glòria*, 2 vols, *LMO* (Barcelona, 1982).

Mercè Rodoreda, *Obres completes: I* (Barcelona: Edicions 62, 1976). Contains *Aloma, Vint-i-dos contes* and *La Plaça del Diamant*.

—— *La Plaça del Diamant* (Barcelona: Club Editor, 1962).

—— *Mirall trencat, LMO* (Barcelona, 1982).

—— *La meva Cristina i altres contes, AC* (Barcelona, 1967).

—— *Semblava de seda i altres contes*, *AC* (Barcelona, 1978).
Pere Calders, *Unitats de xoc* (Barcelona: Edicions 62, 1983).
—— *Ronda naval sota la boira* (Barcelona: Edicions 62, 1981).
—— *Tots els contes (1936–1967)* (Barcelona: Llibres de Sinera, 1968; 2nd ed. Barcelona: J. Tremoleda, 1973).
—— *Invasió subtil i altres contes*, *AC* (Barcelona, 1978).
—— *Cròniques de la veritat oculta*, *LMO* (Barcelona, 1979).
—— *Tot s'aprofita* (Barcelona: Edicions 62, 1983).
Manuel de Pedrolo, *Contes i narracions*, 3 vols (Barcelona: Edicions 62, 1974–75).
—— *Novel.les curtes*, 4 vols (Barcelona: Edicions 62, 1976–82).
—— *Totes les bèsties de càrrega*, *LMO* (Barcelona, 1967).
—— *Homes i No* (Barcelona: Quaderns Teatre A.D.B., 1959).
Montserrat Roig, *Ramona, adéu* (Barcelona: Edicions 62, 1972).
—— *L'hora violeta* (Barcelona: Edicions 62, 1980).
—— *La veu melodiosa* (Barcelona: Edicions 62, 1987).

Chapter 5

Miquel Martí i Pol, *Obra poètica*, 2 vols (Barcelona: Edicions 62, 1989–91).
—— *Obra poètica*, 3 vols (Barcelona: Llibres del Mall, 1975–77).
—— *Crònica de demà* (Barcelona: Llibres del Mall, 1977).
—— *Estimada Marta* (Barcelona: Llibres del Mall, 1978).
Ramon Xirau, *Les platges* (Barcelona: Edicions 62, 1974).
—— *Graons* (Barcelona: Edicions 62, 1979).
—— *Dit i descrit* (Barcelona: Edicions 62, 1983).
Jordi Sarsanedas, *La Rambla de les Flors* (Barcelona: Ossa Menor, 1955).
—— *Postals d'Itàlia* (Barcelona: Roca, 1965).
—— *Contes (1947–69)*, *LMO* (Barcelona, 1994). Includes *Contra la nit d'Oboixangó* and *Mites*.
Francesc Vallverdú, *Poesia, 1956–1976* (Barcelona: Edicions 62, 1976).
—— *Regiment de la cosa pública* (Valencia: Tres i Quatre, 1983).
Pere Gimferrer, *Obra catalana completa: I (Poesia)* (Barcelona: Edicions 62, 1995).
—— *Mascarada* (Barcelona: Columna, 1996).
—— *El diamant dins l'aigua* (Barcelona: Columna, 2001).
—— *Fortuny* (Barcelona: Planeta, 1983).
Maria-Mercè Marçal, *Llengua abolida (1973–1988)* (Valencia: Tres i Quatre, 2000).
Narcís Comadira, *Desdesig* (Barcelona: Edicions 62, 1976). Includes 'Un passeig pels bulevards ardents'.
—— *Enigma* (Barcelona: Quaderns Crema, 2001). First published 1985.
—— *Àlbum de família* (Barcelona: Quaderns Crema, 2001). First published 1980.
—— *En quarantena* (Barcelona: Empúries, 1990).
—— *L'art de la fuga* (Barcelona: Quaderns Crema, 2002).
Francesc Parcerisas, *Trionf del present: Obra poètica 1965–1983* (Barcelona: Columna, 1991).

——— *Natura morta amb nens* (Barcelona: Quaderns Crema, 2000).

Joan Perucho, *Obres completes: I (Novel.la)* (Barcelona: Edicions 62, 1985).

——— *Obres completes: II–III (Narracions)* (Barcelona: Edicions 62, 1986–87).

——— *Històries apòcrifes* (Barcelona: Edicions 62, 1974).

——— *Llibre de cavalleries* (Barcelona: Edicions 62, 1985).

——— *Amb la tècnica de Lovecraft i altres contes,* ed. Julià Guillamon (Barcelona: Edicions 62, 1990).

Terenci Moix, *El dia que va morir Marilyn* (Barcelona: Edicions 62, 1969).

——— *Siro o la increada consciència de la raça* (Barcelona: Edicions 62, 1972).

——— *El sexe dels àngels* (Barcelona: Planeta, 1992).

Quim Monzó, *L'udol del griso al caire de les clavegueres* (Barcelona: Edicions 62, 1976).

——— *Benzina* (Barcelona: Quaderns Crema, 1983).

——— *Vuitanta-sis contes* (Barcelona: Quaderns Crema, 1999).

Biel Mesquida, *L'adolescent de sal* (Barcelona: Empúries, 1990). 2nd ed.

——— *Puta-Marès (ahí)* (Barcelona: Ucronia, 1978).

Jesús Moncada, *Camí de sirga* (Barcelona: Edicions de la Magrana, 1988).

——— *La galeria de les estàtues* (Barcelona: Edicions de la Magrana, 1992).

——— *Estremida memòria* (Barcelona: Edicions de la Magrana, 1997).

Baltasar Porcel, *Teatre* (Palma de Mallorca: Daedalus, 1965).

——— *Solnegre, AC* (Barcelona, 1973).

Jordi Teixidor, *El retaule del flautista* (Barcelona: Edicions 62, 1970).

——— *La jungla sentimental* (Barcelona: Edicions 62, 1975).

——— *Residuals* (Barcelona: Institut del Teatre, 1989).

Josep Maria Benet i Jornet, *Una vella, coneguda olor* (Barcelona: Occitània, 1963).

——— *La nau* (Barcelona: Edicions 62, 1983). 2nd ed.

——— *Berenàveu a les fosques* (Barcelona: Edicions 62, 1971).

——— *La desaparició de Wendy i altres obres* (Barcelona: Edicions 62, 1974).

——— *Descripció d'un paisatge i altres textos* (Barcelona: Edicions 62, 1979).

——— *Desig* (Valencia: Tres i Quatre, 1991).

Rodolf and Josep Lluís Sirera, *La pau (retorna a Atenes)* (Barcelona: Edicions 62, 1975).

——— *Homenatge a Florentí Montfort* (Barcelona: Edicions 62, 1972).

——— *L'assassinat del doctor Moraleda / El verí del teatre* (Barcelona: Edicions 62, 1978).

——— *Cavalls de mar* (Barcelona: Edicions 62, 1988).

Sergi Belbel, *Dins la seva memòria* (Barcelona: Edicions 62, 1988).

——— *En companyia d'abisme i altres obres* (Barcelona: Edicions 62, 1990).

——— *Caricies* (Barcelona: Edicions 62, 1992).

——— *Després de la pluja* (Barcelona: Centre Dramàtic de la Generalitat de Catalunya, 1995).

ENGLISH TRANSLATIONS

Ramon Llull, *The Book of the Lover and the Beloved*, tr. E. Allison Peers (London: SPCK, 1925) [rep. 1956].
———— *The Book of the Lover and the Beloved*, tr. Mark D. Johnston (Warminster: Aris & Phillips, 1995).
———— *The Art of Contemplation,* tr. E. Allison Peers (London: SPCK, 1925).
———— *Blanquerna*, tr. E. Allison Peers (London: Jarrolds, 1926) [many reprints].
———— *The Book of the Beasts*, tr. E. Allison Peers (London: Burns, Oates & Co., 1926).
———— *Selected Works*, tr. Anthony Bonner (Princeton: Princeton UP, 1985).
Ausias March, *Selected Poems*, tr. Arthur Terry (Edinburgh: Edinburgh UP, 1976). Literal prose translations.
———— *Selected Poems*, tr. Dominic Keown and others, 3 vols (Valencia: Shakespeare Foundation of Spain, 1986–93). Verse translations.
———— *A Key Anthology*, tr. Robert Archer (Sheffield: Anglo-Catalan Society, 1992). Literal prose translations.
Anon, *Curial and Güelfa,* tr. Pamela Waley (London: Allen & Unwin, 1982).
Joanot Martorell and Martí de Galba, *Tirant lo blanc*, tr. David Rosenthal (London and New York: Schocken, 1984; 2nd ed., Baltimore and London: Johns Hopkins UP, 1996).
———— *Tirant lo blanc*, tr. Raymond LaFontaine (Berne & New York: Peter Lang, 1993).
Arthur Terry, *Joan Maragall* (Sheffield: Anglo-Catalan Society, 2001). Contains literal prose translations of a number of poems.
Víctor Català, *Solitude*, tr. David Rosenthal (Columbia, LA: Readers International, 1992).
Josep Carner, *Poems*, tr. Pearse Hutchinson (Oxford: Dolphin, 1962).
———— *Nabí*, tr. J.L. Gili (London: Anvil, 2001).
Carles Riba, *Poems*, tr. J.L. Gili (Oxford: Dolphin, 1964) [rev. ed. 1970].
———— *Savage Heart*, tr. J.L. Gili (Oxford: Dolphin, 1993).
———— *Elegies of Bierville*, tr. J.L. Gili (Oxford: Dolphin, 1995).
Joan Salvat-Papasseit, *Selected Poems*, tr. Dominic Keown and Tom Owen (Sheffield: Anglo-Catalan Society, 1982).
J.V. Foix, *When I Sleep, Then I See Clearly. Selected Poems*, tr. David Rosenthal (New York: Persea Books, 1988).
———— *Readings of J.V. Foix: an Anthology*, ed. Arthur Terry (Sheffield: Anglo-Catalan Society, 1998). Contains literal prose translations by various hands.

Marià Manent, *The Shade of Mist*, tr. Sam Abrams (Barcelona: Instituto de Estudios Norteamericanos, 1992).

Homage to Joan Gili, ed. Arthur Terry (Sheffield: Anglo-Catalan Society, 1987). Contains literal prose translations of thirty-nine modern Catalan poets by various hands.

Joaquim Ruyra, *The Long Oar*, tr. Julie Flanagan (Warminster: Aris & Phillips, 1994).

Salvador Espriu, *Selected Poems*, tr. Magda Bogin (London and New York: Norton, 1989).

——— *Lord of the Shadow: Poems*, tr. Kenneth Lyons (Oxford: Dolphin, 1975).

——— *Selected Poems*, tr. Louis Rodrigues (Manchester: Carcanet, 1997).

——— *The Bull-Hide*, tr. Burton Raffel (Calcutta: Writers Workshop, 1977).

——— *The Story of Esther*, tr. Philip Polack (Sheffield: Anglo-Catalan Society, 1989).

Gabriel Ferrater, *A Small War and Other Poems*, tr. Arthur Terry (Belfast: Festival Publications, 1967). Also contains versions of poems by Pere Quart, Bauçà and Llompart.

——— *A Small War,* tr. Arthur Terry (Todmorden: Arc Publications, 2003).

Pere Calders, *The Virgin of the Railway and Other Stories*, tr. Amanda Bath (Warminster: Aris & Phillips, 1992).

Mercè Rodoreda, *The Time of the Doves*, tr. David Rosenthal (New York: Taplinger, 1980).

——— *My Cristina and Other Stories*, tr. David Rosenthal (Port Townsend, WA: Graywolf Press, 1984).

Narcís Comadira, *The English Experience* (Sheffield: Anglo-Catalan Society, 2000). Contains verse translations of a number of poems, including 'Un passeig pels bulevards ardents', by Sean Haldane and Arthur Terry.

Joan Perucho, *Natural History*, tr. David Rosenthal (New York: Knopf, 1988).

Quim Monzó, *O'Clock*, tr. Mary Ann Newman (New York and London: Ballantine Books, 1986).

Jesús Moncada, *The Towpath*, tr. Judith Willis (London: Harvill, 1994).

Sergi Belbel, *After the Rain*, tr. Xavier Rodríguez Rosell, David George and John London (London: Methuen, 1996).

Modern Catalan Plays, ed. John London and David George (London: Methuen, 2000). Contains Joan Brossa: *The Quarrelsome Party*, Rodolf Sirera: *The Audition*, Josep Maria Benet i Jornet: *Desire*, and Sergi Belbel: *Fourplay*.

INDEX

Printed and bound by CPI Group (UK) Ltd, Croydon, CR0 4YY

13/04/2025

14656523-0004